ERRATA

P. 2, col. 1. line 18, for Olaf read Olof.

39, col. 2, line 32, for Tyroconnell read Tyrconnell.

60, col. 2, line 24, for 13*th bp.* read 1*st bp.*

86, col. 1, line 8, for Garranes read Gurranes.

92, col. 2, line 29, for Lacghaire read Laeghaire.

96, col. 1, line 9, for (Urdee) read (Ardee).

ANGLO-SAXON
BIBLIOGRAPHY
INDICES

AN
ANGLO-SAXON
AND CELTIC
BIBLIOGRAPHY
(450–1087)

By WILFRID BONSER

INDICES

UNIVERSITY OF CALIFORNIA PRESS

BERKELEY AND LOS ANGELES

1957

PRINTED IN GREAT BRITAIN
BY A. T. BROOME AND SON, ST. CLEMENT'S, OXFORD
AND BOUND BY THE KEMP HALL BINDERY, OXFORD

PREFACE

These two indices have been placed in a separate volume in order to facilitate reference to the bibliography itself. The index volume may remain open at the subject being studied while the various references are being consulted.

The spelling of Anglo-Saxon proper names has been standardised in accordance with that adopted by Sir Frank Stenton.

I. AUTHOR INDEX

A. (A.), **10138–39**
Aafjes (Bertus), **6239**
Aaberg (Nils). *See* Åberg
Abbott (Jacob), **1194, 1483**
Abbott (Thomas Kingsmill), **11917–18**
Abbot (Wilbur Cortez), **1195, 4233**
Abeel (Neilson), **693**
Abegg (Daniel), **11**
Abercromby (*Hon.* John), **9525**
Åberg (Nils), **7727, 10036**
Abgrall (Jean Marie), **11739**
Abraham (Charles John), *bp. of Wellington*, **5678**
Abraham (Jeanne), **1431**
Abrahams (Phyllis), **13, 1520**
Acland (Charles Lawford), **8025**
Acland (John E.), **8713**
Acum (Thomas Ethelbert Aldred), **6498**
Adamnan, *St., 9th abbot of Hy*, **4884, 6204**
Adams (David Charles Octavius), **4124**
Adams (Eleanor Nathalie), **34**
Adams (George Burton), **1518, 3007**
Adams (Henry), **2356**
Adams (J.), **4033**
Adams (J. H.), **6013**
Adams (John), **5029**
Adamson (John), **9018**
Adamson (John William), **105**
Addis (John), **11458**
Addison (F.), **9471**
Addy (John), **8548**
Addy (Sidney Oldall), **2610, 7859, 7949, 10117, 10410**
Ade (Charles), **9193**
Ælfric, *abbot of Eynsham*, **5627–33**
Æthelwold, *St., bp. of Winchester*, **11924–25**
Aglen (Anthony Stocker), **11269**
Aird (R. Anderson), **10359–60**
Airy (Basil Reginald), **2825**
Airy (*Sir* George Biddell), **1400, 5955**
Airy (William), **2825**
Akerman (John Yonge), **3473, 3667, 7482, 7728–29, 8164, 8230, 8257–60, 8390–92, 8460–62, 8671–73, 8949–50, 9258, 11615**
Albanese (Clodomiro), **7098**
Alberdingk-Thijm (Petrus Paul Maria), **5514**

Albers (Bruno), **3743, 4885, 5469**
Alcuin, **5515, 5523, 7057–58**
Aldhelm, *St., bp. of Sherborne*, **3912, 7671**
Alexander (Henry), **6352, 6362–63, 6578**
Alexander (John James), **286, 862, 863, 1103, 1137, 1278–79, 1519, 1678–86, 2456, 2727, 2150–52, 3199, 3680, 3800, 3913, 4373, 5071, 5922, 5983, 6075–76, 6364–65, 6431, 6763–70, 9562**
Alexander (R. C.), **6047**
Alfred, *king*, **1196, 2457–58, 5658, 6146–47**
Alger (J. G.), **6395**
Allan (John), **8863, 8879, 8987, 9019, 9082**
Allan (William), **9259**
Allcroft (Arthur Hadrian), **2517, 3518, 7860**
Allen (Derek Fortrose), **8101, 8880–81, 9020, 9173, 9240**
Allen (F. J.), **10456**
Allen (Grant), **646**
Allen (John), **2330**
Allen (John Romilly), **4125, 8549, 9442, 9579, 9652, 9660, 9827, 9933, 9964–69, 9997, 10006–09, 10070–73, 10573–77, 10618, 10640, 10660–61, 10683, 10696, 10712–13, 10735, 10880–81, 10925–27, 10976, 10986, 11011, 11048, 11055, 11176, 11227–28, 11242, 11270–71, 11277, 11299, 11340–41, 11351, 11375–76, 11382–85, 11396, 11443, 11459–60, 11640, 11677, 11947–48**
Allen (W. Bird), **6924, 9923, 10578, 11352**
Allen (William Francis), **2757, 3259**
Allies (Jabez), **1813**
Allingham (Hugh), **8661**
Allison (R. A.), **1999**
Allison (Thomas), **3291, 3579, 6954**
Almack (A. C.), **3292**
Almond (T. Leo), **4126**
Amery (John Sparke), **1687**
Amery (P. F. S.), **2728**
Amira (Karl von), **2463**
Amyot (Thomas), **1166, 1432–33**
Anderson (Alan B.), **7831**

B

Anderson (Alan Orr), **220, 221, 223, 226, 756, 1039–41, 1601, 2581, 5839**
Anderson (Arthur), **11272**
Anderson (George Kumler), **7342**
Anderson (John), **6127**
Anderson (John Corbet), **2020, 2934**
Anderson (Joseph), **227, 3361, 3474, 7730, 8015, 8042, 8482–83, 8623, 9869, 11229, 11243, 11300–01, 11444, 11641, 11678–79, 11740–42, 11773, 11788–89**
Anderson (Marjorie), **2611**
Anderson (Marjorie Ogilvie), **223, 226, 758, 808**
Anderson, *afterwards* Cox (Mary Desirée) Mrs. *Trenchard Cox*, **12**
Anderson, *afterwards* Anderson-Arngart *afterwards* Arngart (Olaf Sigfrid), **549, 2612, 3153, 4154, 4213, 7662–63**
Anderson (R. C.), **8092c**
Anderson (Robert S. G.), **11285–88, 11302**
Anderson (Sven Axel), **694**
André (James Lewis), **10382**
Andrew (C. K. Croft), **11036–37**
Andrew (W. J.), **10662**
Andrew (Walter Jonathan), **8413, 8550–51, 8872, 8912–14, 9021, 9102, 9260–61**
Andrews (Charles McLean), **3260**
Andrews (Elizabeth), **4906**
Andrews (Francis Baugh), **3651, 3686**
Andrews (Herbert C.), **1814, 3293**
Andrews (James Petit), **9194**
Andrews (Robert T.), **287, 7923**
Andrews (William), **6504.**
Aneurin Gwawdrydd, **229**
Anglo-Saxon Chronicle, **76–82**
Angus (W. S.), **432, 433, 1280, 5984**
Angus (William), **288**
Anker (Joseph), **11743**
Anquetil (Eugène), **1434–35**
Anscombe (Alfred), **136, 289, 290, 434–36, 463, 502, 503, 522, 550, 551, 621, 864–67, 1008, 1042–44, 3053, 3085–87, 3154, 3560–61, 4454, 4766, 5956–57, 6014, 6077–78, 6341, 6366–67, 6395, 6396, 6432, 6505–06, 6561–62, 6579–80, 6683–87, 6699–6700, 8951, 9091, 9103, 9262–63, 11616**
Antiquary, An : *pseud.*, **6925**
Anwyl (*Sir* Edward), **230–32, 6926, 9950, 9970**

Appleby (E. J.), **10987**
Appleton (Edward), **1688**
Apuleius, *Barbarus*, **7407–08**
Arbois de Jubainville (Marie Henry d'), **42, 2524–42, 2678–79, 3362, 3475, 4688, 4767, 6998–99, 7483**
Archaeological Institute, **8076**
Archdall (Mervyn), **3744–45**
Archer (Thomas Andrew), **1401–02**
Architectural & Archaeological Society of Durham and Northumberland, **10328**
Ardill (John Roche), **4632, 4705–06**
Argles (Marsham), **10276**
Argyll (George Douglas Campbell), *8th duke*, **4907**
Arkell (William Joscelyn), **5866, 6729–30**
Armagh, *Book of*, **4567–68**
Armistead (C. J.), **11461**
Armitage (*Mrs.* Ella Sophia), **7861–63, 7880, 7950–52**
Armstrong (Aileen M.), **6651**
Armstrong (Albert Leslie), **7953**
Armstrong (Edmund Clarence Richard), **8490, 8520, 8552, 9752, 11108, 11642, 11680–82, 11790–92**
Armstrong (T. Percy), **116, 4382–83, 5072**
Arngart (Olof Sigfrid). *See* Anderson *afterwards* Anderson-Arngart, *afterwards* Arngart.
Arnold (A. A.), **43**
Arnold (Frederick H.), **1337–38**
Arnold (Thomas), **3764**
Arnold-Forster (Frances), **4081**
Arntz (Helmut), **9378–79, 9526–27**
Aronius (Julius), **253**
Ascoli (Graziadio Isaia), **5417**
Ashbridge (Arthur), **3261**
Ashdown (Charles Henry), **7864**
Ashdown (Margaret), **35, 83, 1281**
Ashley (*Sir* William James), **2729, 3262**
Ashpitel (Arthur), **10293**
Ashworth (Philip Arthur), **2464**
Asser (Joannes), *bp. of Sherborne*, **106–08**
Assmann (Bruno), **5634–36, 7059, 7484–85, 7643**
Astle (Thomas), **285, 291, 2458, 7291**
Astley (Hugh John Dukinfield), **3687, 4326, 10411–12, 11949**
Atkins (*Sir* Ivor), **84, 3801, 5759**
Atkinson (George), **10257**
Atkinson (George Mouncey), **9528, 9590, 9616, 9653, 11683**

Atkinson (John Christopher), **2988,
6079, 6369, 6399, 6425–26, 6620–21,
6731, 8804**
Atkinson (R. J. C.), **8250–51, 8393**
Atkinson (Robert), **2547**
Atkinson (Sarah), **4505**
Attenborough (Frederick Levi), **2400**
Attwell (Henry), **5516**
Auden (George Augustus), **1815, 8484–
85, 8515, 8553, 8624, 9022, 10721,
10928–30**
Auden (H. M.), **3936**
Auden (Thomas), **6080**
Aufhauser (Johann Baptist), **5225**
Auraicept, **9591**
Aurner (Nellie Slayton), **868**
Austin (Cedric R.), **6597**
Austin (Roland), **8674**
Austin (William), **2690, 8201–02**
Axon (William Edward Armitage), **7486**
Aylott (G.), **7924**

B., **7925, 9023**
B. (A.), **552, 7785**
B. (A. E.), **437**
B. (B. H.), **296**
B. (C.), **6732**
B. (C. C.), **5344**
B. (J.), **6771, 9218**
B. (J. J.), **6528**
B. (R. W.), **1816, 6015**
Babcock (William Henry), **869, 6227,
6254**
Baber (Harry), **3802**
Babington (Charles Cardale), **7775, 8111**
Backer (Joseph de), **4494**
Baddeley (Welbore St. Claire), **870,
6507–08, 6581–82, 10684**
Badger (A. B.), **10516**
Baelz (Martha), **6238**
Baesecke (Georg), **4362, 4364, 5560, 9380**
Baeumer (Suitbert), **5731**
Baggi (Giovanni Battista), **4707**
Bagnall-Oakeley (Mary Ellen), **10462,
10525, 10988**
Bagshawe (Thomas Wyatt), **8201, 8203**
Baildon (William Paley), **3263**
Bailey (A. C.), **4005**
Bailey (George), **10736**
Bailey (Kenneth C.), **11715**
Bailey-Kempling (W.), **10882**
Bain (George), **10074–75**
Baines (Thomas), **1928**
Bains (Doris), **7292**
Bairead (Fearghus), **4668**

Baker (A. T.), **1385, 4384**
Baker (Eric Paul), **4347–47a**
Baker (George Philip), **2020a**
Baker (H. Kendra), **116**
Baker (Harold), **7865**
Baker (Imogen), **2331**
Baker (Robert Sibley), **8237–39, 8554**
Baldricus, *abp. of Dol*, **1520**
Baldwin (A. H.), **9139**
Bale (J. E.), **10619**
Balfour (*Sir* James), **830a**
Balfour (John Alexander), **2201, 3363,
5001, 8486–87**
Balfour-Melville (E. W. M.), **292, 3097**
Ballard (Adolphus), **254, 2401, 2730–31,
2758, 3630**
Baltensberger (Hermann), **2465**
Banks (*Mrs*. Mary MacLeod), **4908,
11194**
Banks (R. W.), **2240**
Bannard (Henry E.), **871, 3476**
Bannenberg (G. P. J.), **5517**
Bannerman (William), **9852, 9864, 9870**
Bannister (Arthur Thomas), **1817, 4385,
6509**
Bannister (Henry Marriott), **5699, 5745–
46**
Barber (Edward), **4386–86a**
Barber (Henry), **2759, 5290, 6529–30**
Barber (J. L.), **8280**
Barbier (Paul), **504**
Barbour (James), **10765**
Barclay (T.), **9843**
Bardsley (Charles Wareing), **553, 554**
Barger (Evert), **2691**
Barham (C.), **9563**
Baring (*Hon*. Francis Henry), **117, 1339,
1403–04, 1521–23, 2001, 2021–22,
2760, 2821, 2862, 3018, 3054–56,
3098, 6081**
Baring-Gould (Sabin), **555, 1009, 1282–
83, 1689, 3746, 4082, 4387, 4446,
5030–31, 5073–77, 8065**
Barker (Eric E.), **44, 293**
Barker (Horace R.), **8555**
Barker (W. R.), **11684–85**
Barkly (*Sir* Henry), **1340, 2761**
Barnard (Etwell Augustine Bracher),
8286, 8296
Barnes (George Edward), **3233**
Barnes (Henry), **1010**
Barnes (W. Miles), **3803, 10140, 11012**
Barnes (William), **843, 2023–24, 3155,
3914**
Barnett (Thomas George), **8296**

Barns (Thomas), **872, 3867**
Barnwell (Edward Lowry), **10526, 11177, 11744**
Baron (J.), **3294**
Baron (John), **7731, 10427**
Barraclough (W. H.), **4439**
Barrett (Charles Robin), **5637**
Barrett (Lionel), **10277**
Barrett (M.), **4455**
Barrett (W. Bowles), **294**
Barron (James), **2202**
Barron (John), **10989**
Barrow (John), **4974**
Barry (Albert), **4599, 4633, 4689**
Barry (Edmund), **9617–20, 9706, 9728**
Barry (James Grene), **4669**
Barsanti (Ottavio), **4708**
Bartelot (R. G.), **1524, 2053**
Bartholomew (Maud H.), **4105**
Bartleet (Samuel Edwin), **1818–19**
Bartlett (J. Pemberton), **11462**
Bartrum (P. C.), **1157, 2241**
Bashe (Edwin J.), **6**
Bassenge (F. E.), **3937**
Bate (Charles Spence), **6772**
Bateman (Thomas), **8077, 8216–17, 9104, 9264, 10663, 11463**
Bates (Cadwallader John), **1104, 4280, 5923, 6082**
Bates (Edward Harbin), **2937–38, 3057**
Bateson (Mary), **2402, 2732, 3580, 5576–77, 7216**
Batson (Henrietta M.), **3804**
Batt (N. G.), **3652**
Batten (Edmund Chisholm), **10413**
Battiscombe (C. F.), **4281**
Battle of Brunanburh, **1284, 1302**
Battle of Maldon, **1285–87, 1302**
Batty (John), **10931**
Baudri, *de Bourgueil.* See Baldricus, *abp. of Dol*
Bauerreiss (P. Rumuald), **5226**
Baumont (Henri), **5446**
Bawdwen (William), **2818–19, 2838–39**
Baxter (James Houston), **1, 13**
Baxter (William), **2613**
Baye (Joseph de), *baron*, **7732, 11464**
Baylay (Atwell Mervyn Yates), **10722**
Bayley (Arthur R.), **1197, 1341, 5078, 9265**
Bayley (C. P.), **5942**
Baylis (Charles F.), **2910**
Baynes (Edward Neil), **8556, 11643**
Bazeley (William), **1820–21, 3688, 10237**
Beament (W. O.), **1524**

Beard (Charles R.), **11793**
Beaton (Donald), **3364, 4975, 11303**
Beaufort (L. C.), **10076**
Beaumont (William), **2822, 8521**
Beauséjours (E. de), **5447–48**
Beaven (Murray Lowthian Randolph) **438, 439, 1288**
Beazley (*Sir* Charles Raymond), **6205**
Becher (Christian Felix Richard), **5801**
Bechert (Rudolf), **2357–58, 5801**
Beck (F. G. M.), **873**
Beck (Horace Courthope), **11465**
Beck (James), **8675**
Beck (R. T.), **8165**
Becker (C. J.), **8625**
Becker (Gustavus), **7151**
Beckett (J. H.), **10383**
Beckley (F. J.), **10463**
Beddoe (John), **874, 2989, 8805–07, 10414**
Bede, *Venerable,* **4033a, 4155–65, 4183– 84, 4192–94, 4213, 4312**
Bede (Cuthbert), *pseud.* [= Edward Bradley], **10737**
Bedell (Alfred J.), **2951**
Beer (Rudolf), **7152**
Beeson (Charles H.), **4214**
Begley (John), **4670**
Beissel (Stephen), **11828**
Belaiew [= Byelyaev] (Nikolai Timo-thyeevich), **523, 1633, 8915–16**
Beldam (Joseph), **7776**
Bell (Alexander), **464, 1105–06, 1167, 1289**
Bell (Charles L.), **10238**
Bell (John), **11745**
Bellairs (G. C.), **8303**
Bellesheim (Alphons), **3365–66, 5499**
Bellingham (*Sir* Henry), *bart.*, **11686**
Belloc (Joseph Hilaire Pierre), **1438, 1484**
Bellot (Hugh Hale Leigh), **2440**
Bellows (John), **7786**
Beloe (Edward Milligen), **4034, 8557**
Beltz (G. F.), **1342**
Bémont (Charles), **1405**
Benedict, *St.,* **3580a, 5760**
Benedict (Robert Dewey), **6255**
Benham (W.), **2109**
Benham (*Sir* William Gurney), **1735**
Bening (H.), **875**
Bennet (E. K.), **295**
Bennett (George J.), **2025**
Bennett (J. A. W.), **9381**
Bennett (James Arthur), **1045, 1525, 7870**
Bennett (R. E.), **7609**

Bennett (Richard), 2692
Bense (Johan Frederick), 1633a
Benson (George), 1929, 8488, 9024, 9266–67
Benson (Gertrude R.), 7204
Bentham (James), 8745
Bentinck (Charles D.), 6846
Benton (Gerald Montague), 10620,11466
Benton (Sarah Henry), 1485
Benz (Richard), 6256
Benziger (Carl Josef), 5553
Berardis (Vincenzo), 7000
Berberich (Hugo), 7408
Berdoe (Edward), 7448
Beresford (W.), 5924
Berger (A.), 4348
Berger (Samuel), 5601, 5668, 7257
Bergin (Osborn), 7273
Bergne (John B.), 8962–63, 8988, 9174, 9219
Bersöe (S.), 8873
Bernard (A.), 3954
Bernard (J. H.), 5840, 7258
Bernaw (Charles A.), 1486
Berry (R. G.), 695, 7981, 7984
Bersu (Gerhard), 8066
Bertacchi (Daniele), 5458
Berwickshire Naturalists' Club, 10901
Besant (*Sir* Walter), 1198–99
Besser (Wilhelm Friedrich), 5470
Best (Richard Irvine), 191, 2543, 4498, 4732, 5840a, 7273
Best (W. Stuart), 3367
Betada náem n Érenn, 4488
Betha Colaim chille, 4892, 4896
Betha Colmáin Maic Lúacháin, 4833
Bethurum (Dorothy), 2359, 2403, 3543, 5802
Bett (Henry), 7099
Betten (Francis Sales), 5291, 5326
Betts (Reginald Robert), 876, 877
Beug (Kurt), 1290
Beumann (Helmut), 5363–65
Bevan (James Oliver), 8746
Beveridge (Erskine), 6847
Beveridge (Hugh), 1602
Beyerle (Konrad), 5227
Bible, *Heptateuch*, 5669
Bible, *Psalms*, 5699a–5704, 7205
Bible, *New Testament*, 7188
Bible, *Gospels*, 5679–80
Bibliographer, *pseud.*, 296
'Bibliothecar. Chetham.' *See* Jones (Thomas)
Bicknell (Alexander), 1200

Bidder (Harold F.), 8434–36
Bieler (Ludwig), 4541–42, 4556, 4562, 4569, 4600–03, 4658, 4709, 5418, 7259
Bigelmair (Andreas), 5228
Bigger (Francis Joseph), 4634, 4768, 10482, 11056, 11109–11, 11794
Bigsby (Robert), 1822
Bilderbeck (Alured Alcock Stokes), 1046
Bilson (John), 10141–42, 10258
Binchy (Daniel A.), 2544
Bing (Harold F.), 3938
Binnall (Peter Blannin Gibbons), 1823
Birch (Walter de Gray), 45, 46, 118–19, 255, 297–303, 696, 2762, 3477, 3581, 3668, 3689, 3741, 4336–37, 5578, 5790, 6283, 7206, 9362–63, 9971, 10634, 11829
Bird (H.), 6733
Bird (S. R.), 3106
Birette (Charles Louis), 1487
Birley (Robert), 5958
Birrell (Francis Frederick Locker), 1439
Birt (D. H. C.), 8092d
Bischoff (Bernhard), 5399, 7181
Bischoff (Dietrich), 4209
Bishop (Edmund), 4095, 4127, 5292, 5732, 7222
Bishop (Herbert Eustace), 4035, 4374
Bishop (Terence Alan Martyn), 1526
Bishop (W. C.), 5733, 5761
Bispham (Clarence Wyatt), 5471
Bittermann (Helen Robbins), 5152
Bjoerkman (Erik), 465, 556–63, 3200, 7375, 8808
Blaauw (William Henry), 304, 485, 4388
Blacam (Hugh de), 4710
Black (George F.), 9452, 11195–96
Black (George William), 6848
Black (W. H.), 233
Black (William George), 10579
Blackburn (F. A.), 3478
Blackett (W. R.), 9729
Blagg (Thomas Matthews), 7926
Blair (D. O. H.), 3366
Blair (David Hunter), 3747
Blair (Peter Hunter), 14, 47, 878, 1168, 1930–31, 5925–26, 6598
Blake (John), 1429
Blake (R. Marlay), 7449
Blane (Henry), 4282
Blanke (Fritz), 5554
Blasche (Herbert), 879
Blashill (Thomas), 2693
Blenner-Hassett (Roland), 1047

Blight (John Thomas), 11038
Bliss (Thomas), 8882
Bloch (Marc), 1387, 7450
Blomé (Bertil), 6773
Blomfield (Joan), 9382
Blount (Alma), 1048
Bloxam (Matthew Holbeche), 7733, 8287–89
Blum (Hans), 7189
Blume (Clemens), 5841
Blunt (Christopher E.), 8883, 8952–54, 9092, 9105
Blunt (J. H.), 1932
Boas (Marcus), 7060
Bobbio Missal, 5726
Bobbio, *monastery library*, 7153
Boddington (Edgar), 10361
Böe (Johs.), 11603, 11644
Boeckler (Albert), 11830–31
Boeddeker (K.), 466, 1049
Boehler (Maria), 564
Boehmer (Heinrich), 3295, 3457, 3978, 5293
Boeles (Pieter Catherinus Johannes Albertus), 844
Boenhoff (Leo), 3915
Boer (Richard Constant), 6148, 11423
Boger (Charlotte G.), *Mrs. E. Boger*, 1050, 1107, 1201–02, 2026
Boggis (Robert James Edmund), 3631
Boileau (*Sir* John P.), *bart.*, 8989
Boinet (Amédée), 11832
Boissannade (P.), 1634
Boivin-Champeaux (Louis), 1343
Boll (Franz), 5153
Bollandus (Joannes), 4083
Bolton (Charles A.), 4036, 4543–44, 4604–05
Bolton (William Thomas (Orde Powlett)), *4th baron*, 8714
Bonafede (G.), 7100
Bond (*Sir* Edward Augustus), 256, 7207
Bond (George), 1108
Bond (Thomas), 2027
Bonet-Maury (Gaston), 5449
Boniface, *St.*, *abp. of Mainz*, 5266–69, 5518
Bonnebakker (E.), 6257
Bonner (Arthur), 6353, 6610–11, 6701
Bonser (Wilfrid), 130, 2466, 3479, 4096, 4349, 7424, 7436–37, 7451–52, 7487–91
Bonwick (James), 3368
Boot (Alfred), 3582
Borchling (Conrad), 1634a

Borenius (Tancred), 10269
Borgstroem (Carl Hj.), 6848a
Borland (Robert), 9871
Borlase (William Copeland), 5032–33
Born (Lester K.), 7038
Bosanquet (Geoffrey), 1774
Boston (Cecilia), *Lady*, 2028
Boston (George Ives (Irby)), *4th baron*, 10010
Boswell (Charles Stuart), 7644
Bosworth (George Frederick), 1203
Bosworth (Joseph), 6146, 6149
Bothamley (C. H.), 7816
Bott (D. J.), 4389
Bouch (C. M. Lowther), 8339
Boult (Joseph), 697, 880, 2346, 3058, 4234, 6370
Boulter (H. E.), 8166
Boulton (*Sir* Harold Edwin), *bart.*, 8886
Bouniol (M. Bathild), 5317
Bourke (Cecil Frederick Joseph), 6583
Bourrienne (Valentin Victor Arthur), 2763
Boutemy (A.), 3632
Bouterwek (Carl Wilhelm), 3480
Boutflower (Douglas Samuel), 3585, 7190, 10362
Bowcock (Elijah Wood), 6505, 6510
Bowdon ( ), 1197
Bowen (Charles J.), 1395
Bowen (Emrys George), 5034–36a, 5867, 6218–21
Bower (R.), 10808
Bowker (Alfred), 1204–05
Bowker (George), 8167
Box (E. G.), 1175, 3633
Boyce (R. A. M.), 1527
Boyd (Halbert J.), 4283, 9872
Boyd (William C.), 9195
Boyer (Blanche B.), 7039
Boyle (John Roberts), 1344, 3690, 4390, 6186, 10278, 10329–30, 10902
Boyle (Patrick), 7113
Brackenbury (Henry), 305
Brade-Birks (S. Graham), 9383
Bradley (Henry), 6284–85, 6342, 6576, 7409, 7492, 7672, 9796
Bradshaw (Henry), 5602, 7425
Brady (John), 3852
Braendl (Matthaeus), 4350
Braeude (M. A.), 11926
Brailsford (J. W.), 8561
Brakspear (*Sir* Harold), 3669, 10384
Bramble (James R.), 9268

Brandl (Alois), 467, 1109–10, 7293, 7493, 10766

Branford (Victor Verasis), 4909–10

Brasch (Carl), 3134

Brash (James Cooper), 8747–48

Brash Richard Rolt), 2124, 9528–29, 9592, 9611, 9621–24, 9654, 9661–64, 9686, 9707–08, 9730–32, 9853, 9900–01, 9924, 9972–74, 10011–12, 10077, 10464, 10527–28, 10548–50, 11057.

Brassington (William Salt), 1824

Brate (Erik), 9797, 9873

Braude (Jakob), 2614

Brauer (H.), 48

Braun (Hugh), 1825, 3156, 7832, 7866, 7927–28

Bray (William), 2959

Breck (Edward), 5631

Breese (Charles E.), 8067, 9951–52

Bremer (Walther Erich Emanuel Friedrich), 758, 11112

Bremner (Robert Locke), 698, 2203

Brendan, *St., abbot of Clonfert*, 6239

Brenner (Eduard), 5700

Brent (Cecil), 8168

Brent (John), 8169–71, 11467

Brentnall (Harold Cresswell), 306–07, 2029, 3157, 6734, 7817, 10415, 10990

Brereton (R. P.), 10279, 10300

Bressie (Ramona), 7123

Brett (*Hon.* Maurice), 8715

Brett (Thomas), 3765

Brewis (Parker), 11468

Bridge (Arthur), 10385

Bridge (Joseph C.), 3235

Bridgeman (Charles George Orlando), 308, 468, 2459, 2467, 3059–62, 6016

Bridgett (Thomas Edward), 3296

Brie (Maria), 7494–95

Brierley (G. H.), 6688

Brigg (John J.), 10932

Briggs (John Joseph), 8218

Bright (James Wilson), 5703, 5705

Bright (William), 3297, 3544

Briscoe (John Potter), 11508

British Archaeological Association, 7919, 10301

British Museum, 120, 256, 7123a–c, 7734, 8093, 8864–66, 9364–65, 11419, 11469–70, 11617–18, 11833

Broadmead (W. B.), 5985

Brock (Edgar Philip Loftus), 2285–86, 3369, 3691, 8437, 10037, 10178, 10204, 10259, 10863, 10991

Brocklebank (C. Gerald), 5977

Brodeur (Arthur G.), 1051, 9384

Broegger (Anton Wilhelm), 699, 700, 2287, 9196

Broensted (Johannes), 11950

Bromberg (Erik I.), 3201

Bromehead (Cyril Edward Nowill), 1797, 8558

Bromwich (J. I'A.), 5706

Brooke (C. N. L.), 3979

Brooke (F. A.), 3088

Brooke (George Cyril), 8857, 8865, 8884, 8955, 8964, 8990, 9025, 9083, 9106–07, 9140, 9197, 9220, 9269–71

Brooke (John Charles), 9472–73

Brooke (Zachary Nugent), 3545–46

Brooks (W. M.), 1291

Brooksbank (J. H.), 1826

Brophy (Patrick J.), 4671

Brotanek (Rudolf), 4215, 5638

Brou (Alexandre), 3939

Brou (Louis), 5707

Broughton (Richard), 3583

Brown (Arthur Charles Lewis), 1052, 1663, 3481

Brown (C. E.), 10664

Brown (Carleton Fairchild), 4391, 7645, 7673

Brown (Gerard Baldwin), 9453, 10037a, 10038–39, 10143–45, 10738, 10767–68, 10864–65, 11471, 11816

Brown (J. Wood), 5406

Brown (Philip William French), 4391a

Brown (Robert), 1827, 3236, 4235, 6563–64

Brown (Stephen J.), 10580

Brown (William), 4284, 7848

Brownbill (John), 1828, 2030, 2845, 3063–64, 3086, 3089–90, 4128

Browne (A. L.), 1528

Browne (E. O.), 4025a

Browne (George Forrest), *bp. of Bristol*, 881, 1206, 1386, 2306–07, 2615, 3298–3300, 3519–20, 3916, 3940–41, 4236, 5294, 7061, 9443–44, 9474–75, 9530, 9874, 9925, 10573, 10581–84, 10621, 10641–42, 10665–67, 10723–24, 10739, 10769–70, 10883, 10933, 10992–95, 11013, 11595

Browne (Walter Raleigh), 6286, 6849

Browning (A. Giraud), 2031

Brownlow (William Robert Bernard) *bp. of Clifton*, 2616, 3202, 3805, 5229–30, 5295–97, 5315, 10996

Bruce (J. Douglas), 1669

Bruce (J. Ronald), 8522, 8795
Bruce (James Douglas), 1053, 5708–09
Bruce (John), 309, 8026
Bruce (John Collingwood), 1440
Bruce-Mitford (Rupert Leo Scott), 1736, 7318a, 8093–96, 8103, 8112, 8559–60, 8655, 11472–77
Bruckner (Albert), 7173
Brueckl (J.), 6217
Bruening (Gertrud), 4887
Brunner (Heinrich), 257, 2441, 2468
Brunner (Karl), 565
Brushfield (Thomas Nadauld), 1690, 4392, 6531–32, 6774
Brut y Tywysogyon, 234, 235
Bruun (Johan Adolf), 11834
Bruyne (Donatien de), 4769
Bryan (Benjamin), 6017
Bryan (William Frank), 258
Bryant (Arthur), 647, 882, 1207, 1345, 1529
Bryant (Sophie), 759, 2545
Bryce (Thomas H.), 524, 8788–91, 10506
Bryce (William Moir), 4967
Brynmôr-Jones (Sir David), 2586–87, 2680
Buchanan (Keith McPherson), 5942a
Buchannan (George), 4393
Buck (A. G. Randle), 10997
Buck (Carl Darling), 9424
Buck (Katherine Margaret), 4561
Buckler (Charles Alban), 4911
Buckler (F. W.), 1635
Buckler (John Chessell), 4911, 10239
Buckley (James), 9625, 10551
Buckley (W. E.), 15, 469, 566
Buckman (James), 8231, 8626–27, 11478–79
Buckstaff (F. G.), 2469
Buckton (T. J.), 6397
Buddicom (R. A.), 310
Budgen (W.), 3099, 6059
Bugge (Alexander), 701–03, 1292, 1295, 5893, 6955, 8809
Bugge (Sophus), 704, 11424
Buhle (Edward), 7319
Buick (George Raphael), 8628, 8662, 9606–08, 11113
Buléon (Jérome), 4500, 5163
Bull (Edvard), 4084
Bull (Frederick William), 8240, 11619
Bull (Thomas), 10866
Bulleid (Arthur), 11480
Bulleid (C.), 5986
Bulst (Walther), 4210

Bunt (Cyril George Edward), 10977
Bunting (Edward), 7320
Burbidge (Frederick Bliss), 1829
Burchell (J. P. T.), 8438, 8561
Burder (Alfred William Newsom), 10416–16a
Burgess (Joseph Tom), 1830, 7735, 7929, 8290–91, 11481
Burkitt (A. H.), 10179
Burkitt (Francis Crawford), 5202, 5670, 5727, 11927
Burlington Fine Arts Club, 11835
Burnard (Robert), 3019
Burne (Alfred H.), 1168a, 5959, 6083, 7818
Burne (Sambrooke Arthur Higgins), 6018
Burrell (H. J. E.), 10622
Burrow (Edward J.), 7822
Burrows (John William), 1346, 5978, 8113
Burrows (Montagu), 311, 1208
Burton (Frank E.), 9175, 9272
Burton (John), 3584
Burton (Philip), 4912
Burton (Sir Richard Francis), 9531
Burtt (Joseph), 121
Bury (John Bagnell), 4570–72, 4594, 4606, 4672
Busch (Fritz Otto), 705
Bushell (William Dene), 4037, 5203, 6927, 9975
Bushnell (George Herbert), 1587
Buss (Franz Joseph von), 5298
Bute (John Patrick (Crichton-Stuart)), 3rd marquis, 6258
Butler (Dugald), 4285
Butler (Elenor), 6805
Butler (George Grey), 1933
Butler (Hubert), 7453–54
Butterwick (T.), 10180
Butterworth (George), 3868, 10118, 10240–46
Buxton (Etheldreda Mary Wilmot), 7062
Buxton (Leonard Halford Dudley), 8394, 8810
Buzzi (Guilio), 7155
Byles ( ), of Boxmoor, 11482–83
Byrhtferth, 7361
Byrne (Mary E.), 2518, 5776
Byrne (Matthew J.), 6806

C. (B. M.), 4770
C. (H. D.), 7321
C. (J.), 3562

Cabrol (Fernand), 3301, 5776a, 7063
Caedmon, 11928
Cahen (Maurice), 9385
Cahill (E.), 760, 5129, 7001
Caine (Caesar), 9026
Cainneach [Canice], *St., of Kilkenny*, 4771
Calberg (Marguerite), 11816a
Caldecott (J. B.), 9198
Calder (Charles S. T.), 8043, 8523, 9875, 11273, 11304
Callander (J. Graham), 11305
Callary (Philip), 3853
Callwell (Joseph), 9753
Calthrop (M. M.), 3806
Calverley (William Slater), 10771, 10798–10802, 10809–24, 10860
Cam (Helen Maud), 648, 2347–49, 2733, 3158–60, 6019
Cambiaso (Domenico), 5459
Cambrian Archaeological Association, 7819, 9798
Cameron ( ), *Dr., of Brodick*, 6850
Cameron (A. H. F.), 6433
Cameron (C. Lovett), 2032
Cameron (John), 2519, 7281
Campbell (Alistair), 1284, 1293, 1351, 2460, 4003, 4012, 7216a
Campbell (Duncan), 2264
Campbell (J. J.), 4166
Campbell (Niall D.), 5002
Campbell-Hyslop (C. W.), 7930
Campenhausen (Hans von), *Baron*, 5130
Cane (Robert), 9241
Canham (A. S.), 312, 1831, 3644
Canice, *St. See* Cainneach
Canterbury Benedictional, 5762
Canterbury, *Cathedral Library*, 313
Canty (M.), 2125
Capelle (Bernard), 4237
Capper (Douglas Parodé), 706
Cappuyns (Maïeul), 7101
Caraher (Patrick), 9199
Caraman (P. G.), 3302
Carbonell (Barbara M. H.), 1691, 6398
Cardew (G. Arthur), 1832
Carey (Francis Patrick), 4506
Carlyle (E. I.), 1833
Carlyon-Britton (Philip William Poole), 8885, 8917–18, 8965–66, 8991–92, 9084, 9141, 9176, 9221–22, 9242, 9273–78
Carlyon-Britton (Raymond C.), 9223
Carmichael (Alexander), 6851
Carmody (W. P.), 9609

Carne (John), 3807, 6020
Carnoy (Albert Joseph), 3330a
Caro (G.), 5579
Carpenter (L. W.), 8676
Carpenter (R. Herbert), 10280
Carr (Ralph), 6652, 8562, 9844–45, 9854, 9865, 11951
Carr (Sidney S.), 10903
Carr-Ellison (Ralph), 6653–54. *See also under* Ellison
Carrie (John), 314
Carrington (Samuel), 11445
Carroll (Frederick M.), 3766
Carroll (Mary Thomas Aquinas), 4238
Carruthers (James), 8886, 9243
Carson (R. A. G.), 9279
Carter (George Edward Lovelace), 2734–35, 3161, 6075, 7553, 11014
Carter (H. G.), 8139
Carter (Thomas), 6533
Carter (William Fowler), 330, 2971–72, 6021
Carthew (George Alfred), 8114
Cash (J. O.), 3869
Cashmore (Herbert Maurice), 1209
Cassan (Stephen Hyde), 4038
Casson (Stanley), 8524, 10585–87
Casson (T. E.), 1294
Catcheside (F. L.), 4286
Cater (W. A.), 3870
Cathcart (William), 3370
Caulfield (Richard), 4528, 9626, 10552
Cavalier (H. O.), 10302
Cave (Alexander James Edward), 8749–51
Cave (Walter), 10428–29
Cave-Browne (J.), 2451, 3871
Cave-Browne (J.), 2451, 3871
Cellach, *St., bp. of Killala*, 4772
Cellachan, *king of Cashel*, 1295
Census. *See* Great Britain, *census. See* Ireland, *census*
Ceolfrid, *abbot of Wearmouth and Jarrow*, 3585
Cerne, *Book of*, 5777
Certani (Giacomo), 4507, 4607
Chadwick (H.), 4106
Chadwick (Hector Munro), 761, 883, 1150, 2265, 9476
Chadwick (Nora Kershaw), 16, 649, 1011, 1603, 4976
Chafy (William Kyle Westwood), 10303, 10740
Chalmers (P. Macgregor), 4977
Chalmers (Peter), 4968
Chamberlain (George Ashton), 4608

Chambers (B. M.), **1441**
Chambers (*Sir* Edmund Kerchever), **1054, 1664**
Chambers (John David), **3303, 10588**
Chambers (Raymond Wilson), **49, 470, 471, 650, 866, 2617–18, 4239, 6956, 7219, 7553a, 7628–29**
Champneys (Arthur Charles), **4351, 10465**
Chancellor (E. C.), **5960, 6702**
Chanter (John Frederick), **1692–94, 3304, 4129, 5080, 6775**
Chanter (John Roberts), **3808**
Chapman (John), **5681, 7191–92**
Chappell (William), **7322**
Charles (Bertie George), **707, 6928–30**
Charleson (C. Forbes), **11251–52**
Charleson (John), **5733a**
Charleston (Malcolm Mackenzie), **8489**
Charlesworth (F.), **1934**
Charlton (Edward), **8629, 9454, 9477, 10904, 11259**
Charlton (John), **10998**
Charlton (William L.), **9478**
Charma (Antoine), **3980**
Charnock (Richard S.), **6473**
Chart (David Alfred), *ed.*, **11058**
Chase (Frank Herbert), **5671**
Chatwin (Philip Boughton), **8716, 11484**
Cheetham (F. H.), **4287**
Chefneux (Helène), **1442**
Cherry (Richard Robert), **2360**
Chevalier (Jacques), **1012, 3371–72**
Chevalier (Ulysse), **2–3**
Chew (Helena Mary), **3458**
Child (F. J.), **2424**
Childe (Vere Gordon), **8044, 10119**
Chinnock (E. J.), **6655**
Chippindall (W. H.), **6022**
Chisholm (Colin), **4913**
Chope (Richard Pearse), **1210, 1694a, 1695, 2694, 3692–92a, 5081, 6371, 6776, 6792**
Chrétien (Douglas), **7251**
Chrimes (Stanley Bertram), **2332**
Christiansen (Reidar Thoralf), **708**
Christie (A. Grace I.), *Mrs. Archibald H. Christie*, **11816–17**
Christie (Alexander), **1443**
Christie ( ), *Mrs. Archibald*, **2872**
Christison (David), **6852, 8002–05**
Christison (*Sir* Robert), **3482**
Christmas (Henry), **8887, 8956, 8967, 9108**
Christy (Miller), **5979, 6060, 6434**

Church (Alfred John), **651**
Church (Richard William), **4026**
Churchill (William S.), **8888**
Churton (Edward), **3305**
Chute (Desmond), **5460**
Cinthio (Erik), **11952**
Cipolla (Carlo), *count*, **5461, 7154–55**
Civil (G.), **315**
Clapham (*Sir* Alfred William), **10146–48, 10181–82, 10229, 10260–61, 10275, 10450, 10589–90, 10714, 10867, 10934, 10998, 11253**
Clapham (*Sir* John Harold), **2288, 2990**
Clare (Osbert de), **1387**
Clark (C. R.), **10978**
Clark (Eleanor Grace), **11425**
Clark (George Thomas), **1834, 1935, 7867–69, 7890, 7931–33, 7954–56, 8068–69**
Clark (Ivo M.), **11306**
Clark (James Midgley), **7040**
Clark (Jane), **10553**
Clark (Joseph), **5082**
Clark (Mary Kitson), **11483–86**
Clarke (Camden), **8219**
Clarke (*Mrs.* Daisy Emily Martin), **3483, 3872, 6777**. *See also under* Martin-Clarke
Clarke (David K.), **3162**
Clarke (Esther Dinah), **7630**
Clarke (F.), **884**
Clarke (Hyde), **122, 809, 2764**
Clarke (John Randall), **1055**
Clarke (Kate M.), **3693, 11015–17**
Clarke (Roy Rainbird), **1737–38, 8563**
Clarke (Samuel), **1488**
Clarke (W.), **2609**
Clarke (W. Nelson), **1169**
Clarke (William George), **1739, 7891**
Classen (Ernest), **76, 7631**
Classen (Karl Moritz), **7362**
Claussen (Bruno), **6259**
Clay (Richard Challoner Cobbe), **8463–64**
Clay (Rotha Mary), **4097**
Clay-Finch (*Mrs.*), **1347**
Clayton (P. B.), **10270–71**
Clemen (Paul), **10040**
Clemoes (Peter), **7124**
Clerc ( ), **3373**
Clibborn (Edward), **11697**
Clifford (*Mrs.* Brookes), **10685**
Clifford (H.), **3873**
Clifford (William Joseph Hugh), *bp. of Clifton*, **1211, 6048**

Clift (J. G. Neilson), 1296, 2033, 2546, 10363

Clinch (George), 7833, 8439

Clinnick (Anthony Allen), 3904

Clouston (Joseph Storer), 1158, 2204

Clutterbuck (James C.), 8395–96, 8677

Clutterbuck, (R. H.), 3694

Cobb (F. W.), 10623

Cobbett (Louis), 10304, 10624

Cobbold (Edgar Sterling), 7787, 7930

Cochrane (Robert), 2170, 3904a, 7260, 9593, 9610, 9627, 9747, 9754–55, 10466, 10554–55, 11114, 11645–47, 11687

Cockayne (Oswald), 1111, 3586, 5659, 7410, 7554

Cockburn (John Henry), 5987

Cocks (Alfred Heneage), 8304

Coffey (George), 8490, 11648

Coffey (Peter), 4914

Coghlan (Daniel), 3243

Cogswell (Thomas Smith), 10625

Colbeck (Alfred), 1936

Cole (Edward Maule), 567, 6061, 6622–23, 7834, 8340

Cole (Robert Eden George), 1835, 3809

Cole (T. H.), 2002

Cole (T. W.), 525

Coleman (James), 180, 4773–74, 9628, 10556–57, 11115, 11746

Coleman (William L.), 6534

Coles (Frederick R.), 6853, 8006, 8491

Coles (Rupert), 3020

Colfi (B.), 1056

Colgan (John), 4456

Colgrave (Bertram), 4008, 4216–17, 4240, 4288–91, 7193, 7282, 7674

Colgrave (Hilda), 4292

Collen (George William), 17

Colles (J. A. Purefoy), 9647

Collier ( ), Mrs., 5083

Collier (Mrs. B. F.), 1836

Collingwood (Robin George), 652, 9835, 10772

Collingwood (William Gershom), 316, 710, 1297–99, 1937–39, 2205, 3306, 3374, 4133, 5961, 6511, 6656, 6834, 7555, 7580, 7849, 7957, 8717, 9836, 10041–42, 10591–94, 10626, 10668, 10758–59, 10773–76, 10803, 10807, 10825–42, 10884–89, 10905, 10935–41, 10979, 11244, 11254, 11289–90, 11487

Collins (A. E. P.), 8718

Collins (James T.), 4039

Collins (Morley B.), 10517

Collins (Victor), 5136

Collins (William Edward), 3942, 4120

Collisson (S. O.), 10417

Collura (Paolo), 7156

Colquhoun (F. Mary), 5003

Colum (Padraic), 4915

Combe (Boyce Harvey), 9177

Combe (Taylor), 8341, 9085

Comerford (Michael), co-adjutor bp. of Kildare, 2126

Comey (Martin), 3767

Commissioners for publishing the ancient laws and institutes of Ireland, 2547

Compton (C. H.), 2588, 3375, 3695

Comte (Jules), 1444

Comyn (David), 776

Concannon (Helena), 4609, 4659, 5441, 5472–74

Conchubranus, 4775

Condamine (Albert), 4241

Conder (Edward), 10686–87

Congreve (Anthony L.), 8342

Connellan (M. J.), 4673, 4711, 4776–78

Connellan (Owen), 6435

Conran (Michael), 7323

Consitt (Edward), 4293

Constable (J. Goulton), 6565

Conway (Sir William Martin), 10777, 11795

Conybeare (Fred C.), 3563

Conybeare (John William Edward), 1212, 1300, 1740

Conyngham (Lord Albert D.), 8172, 9280

Cook (Albert Stanburrough), 50, 106, 317, 568, 2361, 2404, 3917–19, 4040–41, 4242–43, 4394–95, 5763, 6206, 6957–59, 7370–71, 7376, 9386, 9425, 9455–56, 10778–81, 11836

Cook (Arthur Bernard), 3484

Cooke (Edward), 1530

Cooke (Edward Alexander), 3854, 4916

Cooke (T. Etherington), 11307

Cooke (Thomas Lalor), 7581, 9756, 11747

Cooke (William), 1741

Cooksey (Charles Frederick), 1057, 6084

Cooper (A. J. Campbell), 10430

Cooper (A. N.), 1112

Cooper (Ernest Read), 1761

Cooper (James), 3943, 5004

Cooper (Thomas Parsons), 7958

Cooper (William Cooper), 8204

Cooper (William Durrant), 6689

Coornaert (Émile), 3045

Coote (C. M.), 8305
Coote (Henry Charles), 569, 885, 2362, 2911, 5868
Copley (Gordon J.), 885a, 6187, 8810a–b
Corbett (E. C.), 886
Corbett (John Stuart), 2242–43
Corbett (William John), 653–55, 1531, 3091, 3264
Corcoran (Timothy), 7002
Cordasco (Francesco), 7371a
Cordner (W. S.), 3485
Cordoliani (A.), 4185
Cornelius (Heinrich), 6372
Corner (George Richard), 318, 3203
Corney (Bolton), 1445–46
Cornford (Margaret E.), 3696
Cornish (J. B.), 1058, 7965
Corrie (John M.), 11649
Corssen (P.), 3564
Cortelyou (John van Zandt), 7377
Coryn (Marjorie Stella), 1489
Cossons (Arthur), 6023
Costello (Dudley), 11397
Costello (John A.), 2548
Cotton (Arthur R.), 8440
Cotton (Charles), 3810
Cotton (Henry), 3855
Cottrill (Frank), 1837, 7892, 10595, 10741, 10999, 11446
Couch (Jonathan), 2850
Couch (Thomas Quiller), 3244
Couffon (R.), 5164
Coughtrey (Millen), 8630
Coulson (William), 6085
Coulton (John James), 6474–75
Courtois (R.), 4635
Coventry, Minster, 319
Cowell (George Young), 4508
Cowen (John David), 8492–93, 8564, 8678, 8719–21, 11604
Cowin (W. S.), 736
Cowper (Henry Swainson), 320, 887, 2363, 7745, 7959, 9027
Cox (E. W.), 10643
Cox (Ernest W.), 4396
Cox (Sir George William), bart., 5299
Cox (James Stevens), 9281–82
Cox (John Charles), 3459–60, 3811–12, 3944, 6535–36, 7556, 7934, 8220, 8272, 8631, 9479, 10294–95, 10305
Cox (Liam F.), 4779
Cox (Mrs. Trenchard). See Anderson, afterwards Cox (Mary Desirée)
Cracknell (F. K.), 1838
Cragg (William A.), 6062

Craigie (Sir William Alexander), 709, 6150–51, 8811, 9799, 9855, 11426
Crake (A. D.), 3521
Craster (Sir Herbert Henry Edmund), 3814, 4294–95, 7217
Cravens (Mary Joseph), 3307
Craw (James Hewat), 7850, 8343
Crawford (Henry Saxton), 9748, 9757–58, 10558–61, 11059–60, 11080–82, 11116–27, 11796, 11910, 11953
Crawford (Osbert Guy Stanhope), 888, 889, 1059–60, 1151, 1406, 2034–36, 2695, 3616, 3697, 4288, 4917–18, 5869, 5903, 5988, 6063, 6086, 6222, 6287, 6795, 7736, 7820, 8078, 8889, 11230, 11605, 11634
Crawford (Samuel John), 18, 2619, 4042, 5630, 5669, 5813, 7294, 7361, 7632
Crawford (W. C.), 11245
Crawfurd (John), 8812
Crawley (M.), 10715
Creasy (Sir Edward Shepherd), 1407
Creeke (Anthony Buck), 9028–32, 9200
Creighton (   ), canon, 1940
Creighton (Charles), 7438, 7455
Creighton (Mandell), bp. of London, 656
Cremin (Cornelius), 1301
Crépin (Joseph), 5500–01
Cresy (Edward), 10431
Crippen (T. G.), 3970
Crofton (Henry Thomas), 3100
Crofts (C. B.), 322, 1696
Croke (William J. D.), 4690
Croker (Thomas Crofton), 8494
Cronne (Henry Alfred), 1839
Crosley (A. S.), 8097
Cross (Samuel H.), 6152
Cross (William), 1408
Crossley (Frederick Herbert), 10149
Crossman (Sir William), 1941
Croston (James), 10644–45
Crow, pseud., 1532
Crow (Charles Langley), 1302
Crowe (John O'Beirne), 7582
Crowfoot (Mrs. Grace Mary), 11818–21
Crowther (G. F.), 9224, 9283–85
Crowther-Beynon (Vernon Bryan), 8273–78, 10742, 11488–89
Crozals (Jacques Marie Ferdinand Joseph de), 3981
Crozier (Isabel), 11128
Cruden (Stewart), 8027
Cubbon (William), 2190, 7003, 8522, 8525
Cudworth (W.), 10364

Cuff (James Dodsley), 9033, 9037
Cuillandre (J.), 6931
Culhane (Robert), 4712, 5764
Cullen (John B.), 4780–94, 5502
Cumberland (A.), 8173–74, 11490
Cuming (Henry Syer), 1742, 4043–44, 4130, 4397–98, 8679, 9426, 11491–93
Cumming (Joseph George), 2191, 6835, 9800–03, 11178, 11198–99
Cummings (C. L.), 6657
Cummins (J. I.), 4296
Cunningham (James), 9876
Cunningham (William), 3135
Cunnington (Cecil Willett), 3000
Cunnington (Mrs. Maud Edith), 7737, 8465–71, 11494
Cunnington (Phillis), 3000
Cunnington (S.), 711
Cunnington (William), 8472
Curle (Alexander Ormiston), 8007, 8045–46, 8722, 10120–23
Curle (Cecil L.), 10078, 11231
Curle (James), 8047, 8495, 11650
Curlew, pseud., 5005
Curling ( ), Captain, 1776
Currey (Francis Edmund), 10483
Currey (Percy H.), 10305
Currie (R.), 6854
Cursiter (James), 8028
Cursiter (James Walls), 8016, 9158, 11260, 11688
Curtayne (Alice), 4457, 4509, 4713, 4919
Curtin (R.), 3461
Curti-Pasini (G. B.), 5462
Curtis (Henry), 2696
Curtler (William Henry Ricketts), 3101
Curtois (Huntley), 3522
Curtoys (William Francis Denny), 4352
Curwen (Eliot), 8371, 8565, 8752
Curwen (Eliot Cecil), 5962, 7920, 8371–72, 8565, 8752, 10635
Curwen (John F.), 1527, 10843
Cust (Anna Maria Elizabeth), 11420
Cusack (Mary Frances), 4458, 4610
Cuthbert, St., 4297
Cutts (Edward Lewes), 3945, 8680
Cuvillier (Alfred), 5154
Czarnowski (Stefan Zygmunt), 4714

D. (A.), 5058
D. (F.), 8968, 8993, 9034, 9109
D. (M. M.), 6566
Dagg (George A. de M. Edwin), 3905
Dahl (Louis Harald), 5215

Dahl (Sehr Torsten Frantz Granzow), 84a
Dale (Edmund), 6960
Dale (Joseph), 10386
Dale (Thomas Lawrence), 10743
Dale (William), 8414–15, 8957, 9225, 9286
Dalgairns (J. B.), 3526
Dallow (Wilfrid), 9445
D'Alton (E. A.), 4611
Dalton (J.), 4399
D'Alton (John), 762
Dalton (John P.), 3486
Dalton (Ormonde Maddock), 8566, 11419, 11427, 11447–49, 11495–96
Daniel (A. T.), 2948
Daniell (Francis Henry Blackburne), 1533
Danks (William), 3643
Dann (M. E.), 4006
Darby (Henry Clifford), 1743–44, 2837, 3021–25, 5870–72, 5927, 5943–45
Darby (Stephen), 2037
D'Ardenne (S. T. R. O.), 9427
Dare (M. Paul), 6024
Dareste (Rudolphe), 2520
Darlington (Reginald Ralph), 1348, 2736, 3308, 3653, 4032
Dasent (Sir George Webb), 712
Dauncey (Kenneth Douglas Masson), 890, 11954
Davey (Henry), 7324
David (Charles Wendell), 1534
David (H. E.), 11703
David (Pierre), 7261
Davidson (Hilda Roderick), née Ellis. See Ellis
Davidson (J.), 4978
Davidson (James Bridge), 323, 324, 891, 1697–99, 3874, 5928–29
Davidson (James Milne), 11308
Davidson (Septimus), 8115
Davies (Arthur Morley), 1840, 3065, 3163–64a
Davies (D. Alexander), 8753
Davies (D. Griffith), 11061
Davies (D. H.), 9976
Davies (D. S.), 10697–10702
Davies (Ellis W.), 2244, 8567, 10013, 11369–70
Davies (J. Conway), 5037
Davies (J. H.), 7610
Davies (James), 1841, 5038, 6087
Davies (John), 8813–14
Davies (Oliver), 7738, 10467–68, 10484, 11129–30, 11717

Davies (Reginald Trevor), 2765
Davies (Robert), 9287, 11450
Davila (Thomas), 5216
Davis (C. E.), 10418
Davis (Charles Rexford), 5639
Davis (*Sir* Edmund), 8632
Davis (Eliza Jeffries), 2350
Davis (Frederick), 6537
Davis (Henry William Carless), 19, 259, 325, 1535, 1942, 2364
Davis (Jessie C.), 2035
Davis (Joseph Barnard), 526, 8754–55
Davis (Ruby), 4244
Davis (Thomas), 10529
Davis-Winstone (W. E.), 6512
Davoud-Oghlou (Garabed-Artin), 2365
Dawkins (*Sir* William Boyd), 892, 1113, 1636, 8796, 11955
Dawson (Abraham), 4674
Dawson (Charles), 1447–48
Dawson (M. L.), 2245, 5059
Dawson (William), 3376
Day (Robert), 8723, 11689
Day (Victor), 5326
Deanesly (Margaret), 893, 1637, 2266, 3309–10, 3634, 3815
Deck (Isaiah), 8116
Dedieu (L.), 5475
Deedes (Cecil), 1745, 4400
Delap (M. J.), 9665
Delisle (Léopold Victor), 2766, 7182
Dell'Acqua (Carlo), 3982
Delmar (E.), 11956
Demarest (E. B.), 1943, 2620–22
De Montmorency (James Edward Geoffrey), 1061, 2366, 6612–13
De Montmorency-Morris (Hervey), 10530
Dempe (A.), 1062
Denne (Samuel), 2767, 10205
Derham (Walter), 1777
Derolez (R.), 9532–33
Desch (Cecil H.), 524
D'Evelyn (Charlotte), 4211
Devenish (W. H.), 3204
Devonshire Association, 2863
De Wald (Ernest Theodore), 7208
Dexter (Thomas Francis George), 3906, 6932, 11039
Diack (Francis C.), 6855–56, 9534, 9856–57, 9877–78
Diamond (Lucy), 2367, 4715
Dickens (A. G.), 3816
Dicker (Charles William Hamilton), 1536, 11018

Dicker (Michel) *et* Ricard (E.), 3337
Dickins (Bruce), 36, 85, 440, 1114, 1349, 1604, 3487, 3875, 4401, 8633, 9400, 9412, 9457a, 9458–59, 9480
Dickinson (Francis Henry), 326, 4636, 5930, 5989, 6738, 11000
Dickinson (L. J.), 1063
Dickinson (W. Binley), 9142–43
Dickinson (William Croft), 222, 226
Dickinson (William Howship), 1064
Dickson (William), 10906
Dictionary of National Biography, 20
Diefenbach (Lorenz), 505
Dietrich (Eduard F.), 5640
Dietrich (Franz Eduard Christoph), 7496–97, 7675, 9446, 9457
Dietrichson (Lorentz Henrik Segelcke), 11261
Digot (Auguste), 5450
Dillon (John), 4612
Dillon (Myles), 1159, 7583
Dinan (W.), 763
Dinneen (P. S.), 776
Dinwiddie (J. L.), 10782, 10782a
Dirks (Jacob), 8919
Ditchfield (Peter Hampson), 1170, 2038, 2623, 3617, 8397, 10646, 10889a, 11019
Diverrès (Paul René Yves Marie), 7417
Dixon (William Henry), 4045
Dobbie (Elliott van Kirk), 4218
Dobbs (Margaret E.), [Maíghréad ní C. Dobs], 506–09, 810, 1013–14, 1160, 2127–30, 4716, 6807, 6857, 7584
Doble (Gilbert Hunter), 1638, 3946, 4131, 4375, 5039–43, 5084–93, 5165, 5165a, 5765
Dobson (Dina Portway), 5963, 7739, 8426, 10043, 10596, 10688, 11001, 11020
Dodds (George), 3876, 7740, 10703, 11200–01
Dodds (Madeleine Hope), 2737, 4298
Dodwell (Barbara), 3008, 3205–06, 3245
Dodwell (C. R.), 11836a
Doerries (Hermann), 5231, 7102
Doherty (William), 3768, 11131, 11748
Dolan (Gilbert), 3547
Dolan (John Gilbert) 3920
Dold (P. Alban), 7262
Dolley (R. H.), 8958, 9110, 9152
Dolmetsch (Arnold), 7325
Domenici (G.), 5419, 5476
Domesday Book. *See in* Subject Index

Domesday Monachorum, **3635**
Donahue (Charles), **3488, 7633**
Donaldson (Gordon), **222, 2231**
Donatus (*Sister* Mary), **4459**
Donovan (Helen E.), **8232**
Doran (Joseph M.), **11822, 11929**
Doré (Alice), **10206**
Dottin (Georges), **4545, 7585, 11749**
Douce (Francis), **1461, 9366, 9413, 10942**
Douglas (David Charles), **37, 51, 327, 328, 1350, 1537–40, 2452, 2768, 3009, 3618, 3624, 3635**
Douglas (James), **8078a**
Douse (T. Le Marchant), **6703**
Dowden (John), *bp. of Edinburgh*, **3377–78, 7263, 9837**
Dowdeswell (L. R.), **329, 3698**
Dowding (William), **6049**
Dowker (George), **3877, 3947, 10636**
Downes (George), **5894**
Downman (Edward A.), **7893, 7935, 7938**
Downs (R. S.), **1842, 7936**
Doxey (John S.), **9288–89**
Draak (Maartje), **6239**
Draeseke (Johannes), **7103**
Drake (H. H.), **1449**
Drake (O. S. T.), **3489**
Draper (F. W. M.), **415**
Draper (Warwick Herbert), **1213–14, 6961, 8117**
Dream of the Rood, **9457a**
Drew (Charles D.), **3265, 5938, 6735**
Drew (Thomas), **10485**
Drinkwater (C. H.), **6025**
Drinkwater (H.), **7788**
Droegereit (Richard), **1639, 2267**
Dronke (E. F. J.), **5366–67**
Drummond (James), **4920, 11246**
Dryden (*Sir* Henry), *bart.*, **8029, 8241–42, 10281**
Dublin, *National Museum of Science and Art*, **10079–80**
Du Bois (Arthur E.), **3490**
Dubois (Marguerite Marie), **5641**
Du Boys (Albert), **3983**
Du Chaillu (Paul Belloni), **713, 5895**
Duchesne (Louis), **154–56, 5166**
Duckett (Eleanor Shipley), **3747a, 4132, 7064**
Duckett (*Sir* George Floyd), *bart.*, **486–89, 1409, 6690**
Duckworth (Wynfrid Laurence Henry), **8756–61**
Duclos (   ), **11823**
Dudden (Homes), **3948**

Duemmler (Ernst), **3280, 7065–66**
Duesbury (Henry), **10150**
Duft (Johannes), **11900, 11900a**
Dugdale (*Sir* William), **3587**
Duignan (Michael), **2697, 8526, 8799, 11797, 11911**
Duignan (William Henry), **330, 409, 6513–17**
Duine (François), *pseud.* [Henri de Kerbeuzec], **5167–69, 5204–08**
Duke (*Sir* Henry E.), **1700**
Duke (John Alexander), **3379–80**
Duke (William), **11309–10**
Du Méril (Édélstand), **1450**
Dunbar (Agnes B. C.), **4085**
Duncan (Dalrymple), **8048**
Duncan (Henry), **10783**
Duncan (James), **6808**
Dunglas (Charles Alexander), *lord, afterwards 12th earl of Home*, **11690**
Dunn (J. W.), **10365**
Dunn (John Joseph), **5131**
Dunn (Joseph), **6260**
Dunning (Gerald Clough), **1746, 1780, 8232, 8306, 8441, 8567a, 8568, 8585a, 10044, 10124**
Du Noyer (George Victor), **10469, 10531, 11100**
Dunraven (Edwin Richard Wyndham), *3rd earl of*, **10470, 11691–92**
Duns (John), **11798**
Dupont (Étienne), **1541–42**
Dupuy (Achille), **7067**
Durham, *cathedral library*, **10868**
Durham, *monastery*, **5766, 7218**
Durrieu (Paul), **7209**
Dyke (*Sir* Percyvall Hart), *bart.*, **8569**
Dymond (Charles W.), **6088**

E. (F. A.), **6704**
Earle (John), **260, 1204, 1215, 2039–41, 3266, 3998, 5964, 6399–6400, 6518, 6584–85, 6736, 7388, 7789, 7870, 11596**
Earwaker (John Parsons), **10647**
Eassie (W.), **10532**
Eastwood (J. W.), **6962**
Ebersolt (Jean), **11837, 11901**
Ebert (Adolf), **3311, 7372, 7676**
Ebrard (Johann Heinrich August), **3381, 5132, 5300**
Eckenstein (Lina), **3588**
Eddius, *Stephanus*, **4007–09**
Edleston (J.), **8890**
Edmond (J. P.), **8527**

Edmonds ( ), *Canon of Exeter*, 7125
Edmonds (Columba), **3382**
Edmonds (F. S.), **1843**
Edmondston (Thomas), **6858**
Edmunds (Flavell), **6288**
Edward, the *Confessor*, *king*, **1388–90**
Edwards (Arthur J. H.), **8496–98, 11693**
Edwards (J. H.), **8292–93**
Edwards (John Goronwy), **2589**
Edwards (W.), **5170**
Edwards (William), **1944**
Edzardi (Anton), **4353**
Eeles (Francis Carolus), **11311–12, 11750, 11799**
Egbert, *St.*, *abp. of York*, **5580**
Egerton (Ethel), **10648**
Egli (Emil), **5561**
Ehwald (Rudolf), **3912, 3921, 7677**
Ekblom (Einar), **6153, 6737**
Ekblom (R.), **6154–57**
Ekwall (Eilert), **331, 570, 2698, 5896, 6289–94, 6343–44, 6354, 6373, 6401–03, 6436–37, 6519, 6614, 6658–59, 6705, 7835, 8815**
Elcock (Charles), **9759**
Elder (J. P.), **4195**
Elgee (Frank *and* Harriet Wragg), **7741**
Elger (Thomas Gwyn Empty), **8205, 8634**
Eliason (Norman E.), **7678–79**
Ellacombe (Henry N.), **7389**
Ellett (G. G.), **7456**
Ellice (Edward Charles), **6859**
Elliot (Margaret Mary Victoria), **2627**
Elliot (Nenion), **2582**
Ellis (Alfred Shelley), **472, 1543–44, 2878, 2992, 3066, 3267, 6006**
Ellis (Dorothy M. B.), **3699**
Ellis (G. E.), **11040**
Ellis (George), **8816**
Ellis (*Sir* Henry), **2470, 2769, 9035, 9367–70, 11930**
Ellis, *afterwards* Davidson (Hilda Roderick), **7742, 10597–99, 11202**
Ellis (Thomas Peter), **2590–94, 3102**
Ellison (Ralph Carr), **6345, 9481, 9858.** *See also under* Carr-Ellison
Elliston-Erwood (Frank Charles), **2042, 10207–08**
Ellwood (T.), **1945**
Elrington (H.), **10387**
Elstob (Elizabeth), **5629, 5642**
Elston (Charles Sidney), **1015**
Elton (Charles), **811, 3207, 3246**
Elton (Charles Isaac), **894, 3247**

Elton (John), **2692**
Elwes (G R.), **571**
Elworthy (F. T.), **6738**
Ely (Talfourd), **8681**
Elyard (S. John.), **2043**
Embleton (Dennis), **6660**
Emerson (Oliver Farrar), **6158, 7557**
Emerton (Ephraim), **5269**
Emery (William), **3700**
Eminson (Thomas Benjamin Franklin), **5897, 6295, 6438–45, 6567–73**
Emmerich (Franz), **5401**
Emmison (F. G.), **6064**
Encomium Emmae, **1351**
Enda, *pseud.* *See* Lawless (Nicholas)
Endres (J. A.), **3984**
Engel (Arthur), **8858**
Englebert (Omer), **4086**
Engling (Johann), **5519**
English (Henry Scale), **86, 3645, 3672**
Engstroem (Charles Robert Lloyd), **1216**
Erdmann (Axel), **845**
Erdmann (Christian Friedrich David), **5301**
Erhardt-Siebold (Erika von), **7343, 7457, 7680–88**
Erwood (Frank Charles Elliston). *See* Elliston-Erwood
Escritt (L. B.), **8442**
Esdaile (George), **2738, 2823, 2847, 7836**
Esposito (Mario), **4, 4546, 4573, 4775, 4785, 5133, 5778, 7004–07, 7012, 7041–43, 7157, 7174, 7252–53, 7264, 7400–01**
Essen (Léon van der), **5503, 5520**
Estrich (Robert M.), **2308**
Etten (F. J. P. van), **5521**
Ettlinger (*Mrs.* Ellen), **11101**
Ettmueller (L.), **4363**
Eudemare (François d'), **1490**
Evans (*Sir* Arthur), **8920, 11497**
Evans (B. E.), **11620**
Evans (E. D. Priestley), **6404, 6446**
Evans (E. Estyn), **5873**
Evans (Herbert Arthur), **7871**
Evans (J. Wilson), **5931**
Evans (Joan), **7344, 11498, 11861**
Evans (*Sir* John), **7743, 8682, 8724, 8891–93, 8969, 8994, 9036, 9093, 9111–12, 9144, 9178, 9201, 9290–92, 11499**
Evans (John Gwenogvryn), **236**
Evans (John H.), **895**
Evans (Sebastian), **130**

Evelyn-White (Charles Harold), **2838,** **3268**

Evelyn-White (Hugh Gerard), **2838–39**

Evison (V. I.), **11500**

Ewen (Cecil Henry L'Estrange), **572,** **8817**

Ewing (Alexander), *bp. of Argyll*, **4911,** **4921**

Exeter Book, **7219, 7689**

Eyre (Charles), *abp. of Glasgow*, **4299–** **4300**

Eyre-Todd (George), **1065**

Eyton (Robert William), **332, 1352,** **2770–71, 2939, 2950, 3701**

F., **3026, 6447, 6661**

F. (E.), *of Youghal*, **10533**

F. (H. L.), **4301**

F. (P. A.), **4302**

F.R.S.A.I., **11062**

Faber (Frederick William), **4010**

Fabricius (Rudolphus Antonius), **5302**

Fabrovitch (E.), **4354**

Faegersten (Anton), **6739**

Fahey (J. A.), **3565, 3748, 3769, 4786,** **5603, 11838**

Fahey (Jerome), **2131–3**

Fair (Mary C.), **10844**

Fairbank (F. R.), **3817**

Fairholt (Frederick William), **11501,** **11559, 11694**

Fairhurst (Horace), **8008**

Fairless (Joseph), **9037–38**

Falconer (J. P. E.), **2044**

Falk (Franz), **5232, 7183**

Fane (William Dashwood), **10306**

Fanshawe (G. C.), **10432**

Fanucchi (Giuseppe), **5407**

Faral (Edmond), **1066**

Farmer (Henry George), **7326**

Farnell (E. N.), **6706**

Farquhar (James Vaux Cornell), **10349**

Farrant (Reginald D.), **2192, 3103**

Farrer (James), **9846, 9850**

Farrer (William), **261, 1747, 2824, 2901–** **02, 2993, 3165**

Faulke-Watling (C.), **1410, 6599**

Faulkner (Charles), **8995**

Faussett (Bryan), **8175**

Fawtier (Robert), **5209–10**

Fawtier-Jones (Ethel C.), **5196**

Fazakerley (Mary Eleanor), **7411**

Feachem (R. W.), **8523**

Featherstonhaugh (Walker), **9039, 10907**

Feddersen (Arthur), **7744**

Federer (Charles Antoine), **573, 1946**

Fee (Thomas), **2133, 3383**

Fehr (Bernhard), **3136, 5632, 5643, 5767,** **7412**

Feiler (Emil), **5760**

Feilitzen (Olof von), **574, 575**

Felix, *hermit of Crowland*, **4343**

Fell (T. K.), **1947**

Fellows (G. E.), **2739**

Fenger (Helene), **1640**

Fennell (William J.), **9040, 11110–11**

Fenning (W. D.), **5932**

Fenton (John), **2874**

Ferguson (A. B. Ochiltree), **4922**

Ferguson (James), **812, 1016, 8818–19**

Ferguson (Mary Catherine), *Lady*, **1606**

Ferguson (Richard Saul), **7745, 7960,** **10784**

Ferguson (Robert), **1948, 9414**

Ferguson (*Sir* Samuel), **2549, 4547,** **9535–36, 9594–95, 9612, 9623, 9709,** **9723, 9760–61, 9902, 9934, 9977,** **10471**

Fergusson (Charles), **2206**

Fergusson (James), **8017–18**

Fernquist (Carl-Henric), **87**

Ferrey (Benjamin), **10151**

Fest (Sāndor), **1353,4969**

Fetherston (John), **8294**

Ffoulkes (W. Wynne), **8528**

Ffrench (James F. M.), **2134, 11203**

Fickermann (Norbert), **5270**

Fiecc, *St.*, **4574, 4625**

Field (A. M.), *jr.*, **11912**

Field (John Edward), **88, 333, 2045,** **2831, 3619–20, 4046, 7966**

Field (Louise Frances), *Mrs. E. M. Field*, **6963**

Fierville (Charles), **5747**

Files (George Taylor), **10125**

Finberg (Herbert Patrick Reginald), **334,** **1701–02, 2046, 2699, 3199, 3681–84,** **5933–34, 6026, 7967**

Findlay (*Sir* John Ritchie), *bart.*, **527**

Finn (Reginald Arthur Welldon), **123,** **2981**

Finny (W. E. St. Lawrence), **2047, 2309,** **3878, 8443, 10433**

Finsterwalder (Paul Willem), **5155, 5581**

Fischer (August), **7558**

Fischer (J.), **5233**

Fischer (Otto), **5303**

Fischer (D. J. V.), **3312, 3589, 4047**

Fischer (J.), **6933, 9978**

Fisher (J. L.), **1354**

C

Fisher (John), **5031, 5044–45, 11751**
Fisher (John Hurt), **7295**
Fisher (Joseph), **3104**
Fishwick (H.), **3879**
Fiske (Christobel Forsyth), **7559, 8820**
Fitch (E. W.), **9293**
Fitch (S. Edward), **8206**
Fitzgerald (Edward), **9629, 9733, 10486**
Fitzgerald (W.), **11132**
Fitzgerald (*Lord* Walter), **2135–36, 4510, 5904, 9687, 9702–03, 10562–63, 11133**
FitzGerald (William), **9688–89**
Flasdieck (Hermann M.), **5660**
Flaskamp (Franz), **5234–37, 5304–11, 5368**
Flecker (William Herman), **3384**
Fleetwood (John), **7458**
Fleetwood (William), *bp. of St. Asaph, Ely*, **5094**
Fleischhacker (Robert von), **7345**
Fleischmann (Aloys), **7327**
Fleming (D. Hay), **11278–81**
Fleming (Lindsay), **2700**
Fleming (William), **4613**
Fletcher (A. W.), **1844, 10296**
Fletcher (Eric George Molyneux), **896, 10152, 10156**
Fletcher (James Michael John), **1171, 4402–04**
Fletcher (Joseph Smith), **4011**
Fletcher (Robert Huntington), **1067**
Fletcher (W. G. D.), **9294**
Flohrscheutz (Armin), **89**
Flom (George Tobias), **6662, 7068, 7220**
Flood (Joseph Mary), **3385**
Flood (William Henry Grattan), **2137–38, 3856, 4787, 7008, 7228–29**
Flower (John Wickham), **6448, 6707, 8444–45**
Flower (Robin Ernest William), **81, 181, 3067, 3386, 4027, 7009, 7219**
Floyer (John K.), **52, 7126, 8446**
Foerste (W.), **845a**
Foerster (Max), **53, 157, 576, 577, 622, 3208, 4107, 4212, 5644–46, 5682, 5710–11, 5795–96, 5814–16, 5823–26, 6346, 6449–50, 6860, 7219, 7221, 7346, 7498–7502, 9482**
Foerster (W.), **1068**
Foggon (J.), **4245**
Folkard (Arthur), **578**
Fonahn (A.), **9159**
Fonsagrives (J.), **5171**
Foord (Edward), **1799**

Foot (Arthur Wynne), **8797**
Footprints, **4460**
Forbes (Alexander Penrose), *bp. of Brechin*, **4872, 7265, 11752**
Forbes (Alexander Robert), **6861**
Forbes (Frances Alice Monica), **4923**
Forbes (George Hay), **5748**
Forbes (M. D.), **9458–59**
Forbes-Leith (William), **11935**
Fordyce (C. J.), **4186**
Forester (T.), **1196**
Foreville (Raymonde), **1515**
Forsberg (Rune), **335, 6296**
Forsey (George Frank) **7363**
Forssander (J. E.), **11957**
Forssner (Thorvald), **579**
Forster (R. H.), **3880**
Forstmann (Hans), **4338–39**
Fortescue (Hugh Fortescue), *4th earl*, **6778**
Forsbroke (Thomas Dudley), **3590**
Foster (Charles Wilmer), **2908, 8307**
Foster (J. T.), **1115**
Foster (John Reinhold), **6163**
Foster (*Sir* Thomas Gregory), *bart.*, **7689**
Foster (Walter K.), **8118**
Foster (*Sir* William Edward), **1588**
Foulis (*Sir* James), *bart.*, **1641**
Foulon (C.), **7611**
Fournier (Paul), **5582, 5604–06**
Fowke (Frank Rede), **1451, 1451a**
Fowler (C. Hodgson), **10262**
Fowler (George Herbert), **336, 1355, 2826–27, 6065**
Fowler (Gordon), **8119**
Fowler (James), **528, 10943**
Fowler (Joseph), **2048, 3922, 11021**
Fowler (Joseph Thomas), **3881, 4303–06, 4405, 4884, 7194, 9483–84, 10263, 10704–06, 11621**
Fowler (William Warde), **1845**
Fox (Aileen Mary), *Lady Fox*, **2681, 8529, 9935**
Fox, *afterwards* Pitt-Rivers (Augustus Henry Lane), **8683**
Fox (C. Frederick), **2289**
Fox (*Sir* Cyril), **2681, 5935, 7009a, 7777, 7779a, 7790–95, 8120–21, 8147a, 8570, 8635, 10014, 10627–28, 11451**
Fox (G. J. B.), **10388**
Fox (Levi), **1545, 1846**
Francis (E. B.), **7894**
Francis (George Grant), **9979**
Francis (Grant R.), **9295**
Francis (Henry James), **1356**

Francis (R. S.), **9145-46**
Francis (René), **1491**
Franklin (T. Bedford), **2772**
Franks (*Sir* Augustus Wollaston), **8554,
8571, 9371, 9415, 11452, 11502,
11622, 11753**
Fraser (Henry Malcolm), **2949**
Fraser (J. E.), **11313**
Fraser (John), **813, 814, 6862, 7266,8030**
Fraser (William), **8219, 8221-22, 10307,
11695**
Frazer (Wiiliam), **8530-31, 8821, 10081,
11696, 11774**
Freeman (A. Martin), **182**
Freeman (Edward Augustus), **490, 657,
658, 1116, 1303, 1357-58, 1411,
1492, 1546-47, 1703, 1748, 1847,
1949, 2003, 2268-69, 3657, 3702,
10308**
Freeman (George H.), **10434**
Freer (A. S. B.), **6347**
French (Gilbert), **1452, 10600**
French (John), **1217, 2701**
French (Richard Valpy), **2624**
French (W. H.), **7330**
Frere (Sheppard Sunderland), **8373,
8438, 8447**
Frey (Joseph), **7069**
Friart (Norbert), **5217**
Friedberg (Emil), **2471**
Friedel (Victor H.), **897, 5779**
Friesen (Otto von), **9387**
Fripp (   ), *Mrs. Edward Fripp*, **2049**
Frithigodus, **4012**
Frost (Marian), **2004, 8374**
Frost (Reuben Caesar), **2773**
Fry, *Miss*, **1548**
Fry (*Sir* Edward), **3166**
Fry (H. A.), **491**
Fryer (A.), **4307**
Fryer (Alfred Cooper), **4048, 4308, 7010,
10944**
Fuchs (Gertrud), **4365**
Fuhrmann (Joseph Paul), **5134**
Fulda, *abbey*, **5369**
Fullbrook-Leggatt (L. E. W. O.), **5874**
Funk (Franz Xaver von), **3387**
Furley (Abraham), **2814**
Furley (Robert), **1778**
Fursey, *St.*, *abbot of Lagny*, **5218-19**
Furst (Clyde), **3923**

G. (M. P.), **580**
G. (R. M.), **5875**
G. (W. S.), **4108**

Gabbema (Simon Abbes), **5504**
Gabrielsson (Ruben), **11958**
Gadde (Fredrik), **7634**
Gaffard (Paul), **6228**
Gaffney (James), **3388**
Gaffney (John), **4614**
Gage (John), **3313, 9485, 11931-32**
Gaidoz (Henri), **4575, 7503, 7586, 9596,
10534**
Gairdner (James), **54**
Galbraith (James John), **10082, 11232,
11314**
Galbraith (Vivian Hunter), **262, 337,
338, 2774-75, 2864, 2886, 3625,
6964, 7560**
Gale (Samuel), **3237**
Gall, *St.*, **5562**
Galloway (Alexander), **2207**
Galloway (William), **4979, 6863, 11274,
11315-16, 11641**
Galpin (Francis William), **7330a, 11134**
Galton (Theodore H.), **3654**
Gamer (Helena Margaret), **5612**
Gammack (James), **4861, 4873, 5006**
Ganly (William), **4788-89**
Gannon (Patrick Joseph), **4717**
Gans (Eduard), **2472**
Ganshof (François Louis), **7070**
Gardiner (E. R.), **1170**
Gardner (Arthur), **10601-02**
Gardner (Delphis), **4555**
Gardner (Eric), **8448**
Gardner (Iltyd), **11386**
Gardner (John Edmund Garratt), **1069**
Gardner (Samuel), **10389**
Gardner (Willoughby), **8070, 9296**
Garfitt (G. A.), **7872**
Gargan (Denis), **4615**
Garmonsway (George Norman), **78, 5627**
Garnett (Richard), **815**
Garnier (Russell Montague), **3105**
Garrett (Robert Max), **11503**
Garrood (Jesse Robert), **8572**
Garstang (John), **8344**
Garstin (John Ribton), **9716, 11775**
Gaskoin (Charles Jacinth Bellairs), **7071**
Gasquet (Francis Aidan), *cardinal*, **3949-
51, 7222**
Gaupp (Ernst Theodor), **898**
Gaut (Robert Charles), **5945a**
Gayre (George Robert), **7459**
Gaythorpe (Harper), **8725**
Gebhardt (Oscar von), **7158**
Gee (Henry), **3314, 3591**
Gegenbauer (J.), **5370**

Gehle (Henrik), 4246
Geidel (Heinrich), 6159
Geldner (Johann), 7426
Gelling (Margaret), 263, 339, 6297, 6586
Gem (Samuel Harvey), 5647
Gentry (Thomas G.), 581
Geoffrey, *of Monmouth*, 128–30
George (T. J.), 899, 8243–44
George (Thomas), 11606
Gerard (Ethel), 8388
Gering (Hugo), 1608, 11428
Gerke (Friedrich), 10083, 11959
Gerould (Gordon Hall), 1304, 1665, 3999, 4340, 6499
Gertz (M. Cl.), 1359
Gerville (de), 6223–24
Getty (Edmund), 2139, 10564
Gevenich (Olga), 6298
Geyer (Bernhard), 6965
Geyer (Paul), 4879
Gianelli (Antonio Maria), *bp. of Bobbio*, 5477
Gibb (Robert), 11776
Gibbon (Robert W.), 10507
Gibbs (E. M.), 9160
Gibbs (Marion), 3010
Gibson (A. Craig), 9428
Gibson (J. Pattison), 10908
Gibson (W. J.), 11661
Gibson (William Sidney), 2473
Gibson-Craig (James T.), 11255
Giffin (Mary E.), 1666
Gilbert (E. C.), 10247
Gilbert (Edward), 10331, 10366–67
Gilbert (*Sir* John Thomas), 7283–84
Gilchrist (Anne G.), 10945
Gildas, 5780
Giles (John Allen), 659, 1218, 7296
Gill (Henry Septimus), 9179, 9297
Gill (W. Walter), 6836, 7587
Gill (William), 4355
Gillespie (Patrick), 11083
Gillett (Henry Martin), 4247
Gillies (Hugh Cameron), 6864, 7427
Gilson (Julius Parnell), 7223
Ginnell (Laurence), 2550
Girvan (Ritchie), 6966
Given (Maxwell), 11135
Gladysz (Bronislas), 4248
Glanusk (Joseph Russell Bailey), *1st baron*, 8071
Glennie (John Stuart Stuart), 5965
Gloucestrensis, *pseud.*, 10126
Glover (J. E.), 6934
Glover (Richard), 2290

Glover (Stephen), 1848
Glunz (Hans Hermann), 5672–73
Gmuer (Theo), 5563
Gocelin, 4000, 4406
Goddard (A. R.), 1305, 7937
Goddard (E. H.), 8466, 8470, 8473–74, 11002–03
Godfrey (Walter Hindes), 10181–82, 10390–94
Godfrey-Faussett (E. G.), 6695
Godfrey-Faussett (Thomas Godfrey), 1779, 8176
Godsal (Philip Thomas), 899–904, 1070, 7837
Godwin (H.), 8105b
Godwin (Henry), 2050–52, 3818
Godwin-Austen (Robert A. C.), 6708, 7968
Goebel (Julius), *jr.*, 2474
Goedheer (A. J.), 1607
Geoje (Michiel Johannes de), 6261
Goepfert (Fritz Adam), 5402
Goetting (Hans), 5371
Goetzinger (Nikolaus), 5522
Gógan (Liam S.), 4637, 9762, 10084
Gogarty (Oliver St. John), 4675
Gogarty (Thomas), 3857, 4718, 4790–91
Goldney (Francis Bennett), 11504
Goldrick (P. J.), 4660
Goldschmidt (Adolph), 7210, 10045, 11421, 11839–40
Gollancz (*Sir* Israel), 11928
Gomme (Bernard), 4a
Gomme (E. E. C.), 77
Gomme (*Sir* George Laurence), 4a, 55, 1798, 2475, 2625, 3166a, 3269–72, 6355
Gonser (Paul), 4341
Goodall (Armitage), 6624–25
Goodchild (W.), 340, 5312
Goode (Frank B.), 3626
Goodier (Alban), 4249
Goodrich-Freer (Ada M.), *Mrs. H. H. Spoer*, 2208–09
Gordon (Eric Valentine), 582, 1286, 1306–07, 6451, 6626
Gordon (H. D.), 9147
Gordon (James Frederick Skinner), 7267
Gordon (Margaret), 4970
Goscelin, *monk of Canterbury*, 4000, 4406
Gosney (J. R. B.), 724
Gotch (John Alfred), 8245
Gottlieb (Theodor), 7159
Goudie (Gilbert), 227, 2210, 8031, 9879–81, 11262, 11651

Gougaud (Louis), **183, 3389–90, 4098–4102, 4461–62, 4719–20, 5135–38, 5172–74, 5451, 5607, 5749, 5781, 5842–44, 6207, 7011–12, 7127–28, 7285, 7331, 10085–87, 11800**

Gough (Alfred Bradley), **7561**

Gough (Richard), **9161, 10785**

Gould (Isaac Chalkley), **2890, 4327, 7873, 7895–7901, 7938–40, 7961, 7969**

Gourlay (W. R.), **1017, 1071, 2211**

Gover (John Eric Bruce), **6520, 6538–39, 6600, 6615–16, 6709, 6740, 6779, 6935**

Gowland (Tom S.), **6027, 6627**

Goyau (Georges), **3592, 5139**

Gradwell (Robert), *bp. of Lydda*, **4616**

Graeme (A. Sutherland), **8032**

Graf (Leopold), **2702**

Grafton (E. M.), **10890**

Graham (Angus), **764, 8019–20**

Graham (Hugh), **7013–14, 8049**

Graham (Robert C.), **11233, 11247**

Graham (Rose), **3703, 6967, 10057**

Graham (T. H. B), **1950, 3248–49, 4133**

Graham-Smith (G. S.), **8663**

Gramm (Willi), **7460**

Grantley (John Richard Brinsley), *5th baron*, **8959, 8970, 8996, 9041–44**

Grattan (John), **8798**

Grattan (John Henry Grafton), **7413, 7504**

Graves (Charles), *bp. of Limerick*, **184, 4576, 7268, 9537–42, 9613, 9630, 9655–56, 9666–73, 9734, 9882, 11063**

Graves (James), **7505, 9749, 9763, 9859, 9926, 10487, 11084, 11697, 11801**

Graves (Philip P.), **6089**

Graville (C. R.), **9543**

Gray (Andrew Edward Phillimore), **2903, 3391, 3523**

Gray (Arthur), **905, 1360, 1749, 4407, 8822**

Gray (E. N. O.), **1951**

Gray (Harold St. George), **714, 2107, 7746, 8427**

Gray (Howard Levi), **2702a**

Gray (James), **2212, 6865**

Gray (John), **816**

Gray (Louis H.), **6741, 6837**

Gray (M.), **11022**

Gray (Nicolete), **11960**

Great Britain, *Census*, **3167**

Greaves (C. S.), **341**

Green (Adwin Wigfall), **2457**

Green (Alice Stopford), **765, 766, 7114**

Green (Arthur Robert), **529, 530, 10435–36**

Green (Charles), **8573, 10891, 11505**

Green (Emanuel), **1219, 1849**

Green (Everard), **1220**

Green (Francis), **10516**

Green (J. R.), **3658, 4049**

Green (John Richard), **660, 661, 1850**

Green (Phyllis Mary), **10436**

Green (W. C.), **1750**

Greenaway (George William), **51**

Greene (Parnell), **1851**

Greene (W. H.), **5936**

Greenwell (William), **1952, 2310, 3315, 10332, 10869–70, 11652**

Greenwood (A. D.), **2053**

Greg (Robert Hyde), **10535**

Gregory (John V.), **6663–64**

Gregory (*Sir* Richard), **7347**

Grein (Christian Wilhelm Michael), **7690**

Greith (Carl Johann), *bp. of St. Gall*, **3548, 5564–65**

Grendon (Felix), **7506**

Gresham (Colin A.), **237, 531**

Greswell (William Henry Parr), **342, 906, 1221–22, 1549, 1704, 3659, 6028, 6742–43**

Grey (Gerald), **2054**

Grienberger (Theodor von), **9388, 9401–03, 9429, 9447, 11429–30**

Grierson (Elizabeth Wilson), **4134, 4874**

Grierson (Philip), **1361, 1642, 6968, 7129, 8894–95**

Grieve (Alexander), **5523**

Grieve (Symington), **2213, 8499**

Griffinhoofe (H. G.), **4971**

Griffith (A. F.), **2005, 8375–77**

Griffith (Edward), **2914**

Griffith (Francis Llewellyn), **8449**

Griffith (Guyon), **9180**

Griffiths (R. G.), **1852**

Grimes (Charles Hugh Duffy), **1550**

Grimes (W. F.), **11398**

Grinsell (Leslie Valentine), **343–45, 6090**

Grisar (Hartmann), **5734**

Griscom (Acton), **129, 238**

Groen (Fredrik), **7461**

Gropp (Ernst), **7664**

Grose (J. Donald), **346**

Grose (S.), **2055**

Grosjean (Paul), **185, 3566, 4135, 4376, 4463–67, 4529, 4536, 4577, 4617, 4676, 4691, 4721–22, 4792–97, 4888–91, 5095–98, 5505, 6240**

Gross (Charles), **5, 3046**

Gross (Max), 56
Grossmann (Dieter), 5363
Grotefend ( ), 6262
Grove (L. R. A.), 8636, 8726, 10946, 11653
Grube (F. W.), 2703, 7462
Grubitz (Ernst), 90
Grueber (Herbert Appold), 8864, 8866, 8896, 9094, 9113–14, 9148–49
Gruetzmacher ( ), *Prof., Heidelberg*, 5220
Gruffydd (W. J.), 239, 7588
Grundy (George Beardoe), 264, 347–55, 532, 907, 3027–28, 6188–94, 6374, 6710, 6744
Gruyer (Paul), 5175
Gudenius (Henricus Philippus), 5302
Guénin (G.), 5176
Guest (Edith M.), 10744, 11064, 11085, 11102
Guest (Edwin), 907a, 908–10, 5937, 6299, 7796
Guillaume, *de Jumièges, de Poitiers. See* William
Guillemard (Julien), 1493
Guizot (Francis Pierre Guillaume), 1494
Gummere (Francis Barton), 911
Gundersen (Borghild), 7015
Gundlach (Wilhelm), 5420
Gunn (Adam), 2214, 6866
Gunn (Æneas), 767
Gunn (John), 4924, 10183–84, 11913
Gunning (John), 4523
Gunston (Thomas), 9160
Gurney (Frederick G.), 6091
Gurney (Hudson), 1453, 9372
Guthlac, *St.*, 4342
Gwynn (Aubrey), 1643, 3549–51, 3770, 3858, 3985, 5478
Gwynn (Denis Rolleston), 4925
Gwynn (Edward John), 3771, 4468, 4567, 5623
Gwynn (John), 4568
Gwynn (Lucius), 4109, 11802

H., 6452
H. (B. B.), 1454
H. (C.), 4408
H. (D. R. S.), 6375
H. (H. de B.), 4409
Hablitzel (Johann), 4196
Hackenberg (Erna), 473
Haddan (Arthur West), 3316–17
Haff (Karl), 1644
Hahn (Heinrich), 4167, 5271, 5313, 6208

Haigh (Daniel Henry), 57, 474, 533, 912, 1172, 2476, 3704–06, 8874, 8921–22, 8971–75, 8997, 9045–46, 9095, 9298, 9486–91, 9516, 9544, 9615, 01248, 10786, 10946a
Haigh (Gordon), 3707
Hailstone (E.), 1308
Haines (J.), 10552
Haines (Reginald), 8279
Hald (Kristian), 913
Hales (John W.), 356, 1223
Haliday (Charles), 715
Hall (A.), 492, 817, 1408
Hall (G. Rome), 10909
Hall (Hamilton), 493, 494, 1362, 4050
Hall (Henry), 6601
Hall (Hubert), 124, 3106
Hall (J. G.), 8345
Hall (John), 10333
Hall (T. G.), 8762
Hallam (H. E.), 1852a
Hallam (Henry), 2333–34
Hallam (W. H.), 8684
Haller (Albrecht von), *baron*, 1224
Hallett (Shackleton), 5966
Hallett (T. G. P.), 914
Halliday (George Eley), 10518, 11377–79, 11387
Halliwell (James Orchard), 3708
Halpin (James), 7269
Hamel (Anton Gerard van), 58, 131, 159, 165, 186–87, 915, 1072, 1608, 7589, 7612
Hamelin (F.), 7072
Hamilton (Adam), 3709
Hamilton (Gustavus E.), 2140
Hamilton (John R. C.), 716, 2215
Hamilton (Marie Padgett), 3318
Hamilton (Nicholas Esterhazy Stephen Armytage), 2840
Hamilton (Zachary Macaulay), 11263
Hammer (Jacob), 128, 1117, 7613
Hamper (William), 357, 8998, 9416–17, 9492
Hampson (Charles Phillips), 5990, 6665
Hampson (R. T.), 265, 6160
Hanbury (W. H.), 10669
Hancock (F.), 6745
Hancock (William Neilson), 2547
Handschin (J.), 7332
Hanna (J. W.), 4677, 6128
Hannah (Ian Campbell), 1455, 11234
Hansen (Auguste), 3001
Hanson (William George), 7016
Harbin (E. H. Bates), 2940

Harbottle (T. B.), 7732
Hardcastle (C. D.), 6628
Harcourt (Charles George Vernon), 3952
Harcourt-Smith (*Sir* Cecil), 8097a
Harden (Donald Benjamin), 8398, 8573a, 8574
Harder (Hermann), 7402, 7635, 9418–20, 9430
Harding (   ), *Lt.-Col.*, 9299
Hardman (F. W.), 1780
Hardman (J. W.), 4136
Hardwick (Charles), 1073, 1118–19
Hardy (*Sir* Thomas Duffus), 59, 7211–12
Hardy (William John), 3314
Hardy (William Masters), 10437
Hare (N.), 11041–42
Harkness (William), 10552
Harley (Laurence S.), 10185
Harmer (Florence Elizabeth), 60, 76, 266, 2477–78, 3137, 9373
Harold II, *King*, 1363
Harper (J. W.), 5007
Harper (W. J.), 10649
Harris (Dorothy C.), 4798
Harris (Emily), 2962
Harris (George), 2626
Harris (Harold Augustus), 1751, 6092, 6105
Harris (John), 10980
Harris (Mary Dormer), 1853
Harris (S. G.), 1705
Harrison (Frederic), 1225
Harrison (Frederick), 1204, 6969
Harrison (Henry), 5314, 6666
Harrison (James Park), 4219, 8763, 10153, 10186, 10209, 10309–12, 10437, 11933, 11961
Harrison (P. Walton), 1120
Harrison (S. N.), 6838
Harrod (Henry), 3819
Harrsen (Meta), 7130
Hart (Cyril E.), 3029
Hart (James Morgan), 4250
Hartland (Edwin Sidney), 4410
Hartland (Ernest), 11405
Hartley (Dorothy R.), 2627
Hartley (W. N.), 11914
Hartmann (Jacob Wittmer), 738
Hartmann (K. A. Martin), 5661
Hartmann (Ludo Moritz), 5463
Hartnett (P. J.), 7988
Hartshorne (Albert), 7902
Hartshorne (Charles Henry), 1364, 2935, 8246, 10154
Harward (Thomas Netherton), 1589

Haseloff (Günther), 11506
Haskins (Charles Homer), 358, 1551, 2270
Haskins (George Lee), 359
Haslam (Victor A.), 10670
Haslam (William), 10519
Hassé (Leonard), 11698
Hastings (Frank), 10910
Haswell (George W.), 10313
Hatch (Edwin), 3319
Hau (J.), 5524
Hauck (Albert), 5238
Haughton (Samuel), 1609
Haupt (Moriz), 4356
Hauréau (Jean Barthélemy), 7043a
Hausknecht (Emil), 3924
Haverfield (Francis John), 4638, 6300–01, 7131
Haviland (Alfred), 9804
Hawkes (Arthur John), 9300
Hawkes (Charles Francis Christopher), 1854, 7751, 8308, 8685, 11636
Hawkins (Edward), 8859, 8875, 8897, 8999, 9034, 9047–48, 9202, 9226, 9301–04, 11507
Hay (Malcolm Vivian), 3567, 5421
Hayes (J. P.), 7017
Hayman (Samuel), 2141, 9631
Hayward (Frank Herbert), 1226
Hayward (*Sir* John), 1495
Hazeltine (Harold Dexter), 2368, 2479
Head (Barclay Vincent), 8923, 9181
Head (J. Merrick), 2056
Head (John Frederick), 1855, 8309, 8637, 11607
Headlam (*Sir* Cuthbert), *bart.*, 8823
Healy (Francis J.), 2551
Healy (John), *abp. of Tuam*, 188–89, 717, 2142, 2552, 3392, 3772–73, 3820, 4309, 4548, 4639, 4678, 4723, 4799–4801, 4880, 5315, 5479, 5506, 5735, 7018–19, 7044–45, 7104, 7118, 11065
Healy (W.), 1309
Heanley (R. M.), 7562
Hearnshaw (Fossy John Cobb), 662, 1227
Heather (Percy J.), 4411
Heaton (Harriet A.), 11508
Heber (   ), 5239
Hedley (Anthony), 6667
Hedley (John Cuthbert), *bp. of Newport*, 3953
Heer (Gottfried), 5555
Hegel (Karl), 3047
Hegge (Robert), 4310

Heiermeier (A.), **6453–54**
Heinrich (J. B.), **5316**
Heinsch (Joseph), **1121**
Heinzel (Otto), **5712**
Helbœck (Hans), **2706a, 7390**
Heller (Dominikus), **5372**
Hellmann (Siegmund), **5373–74, 7115**
Hellwig (H.), **583**
Hemingus, **360**
Hemingway ( ) *Dr.*, **9493**
Hemmeon (Morley de Wolf), **3250–51**
Hemp (Wilfrid J.), **11342, 11388**
Hemphill (Samuel), **11934**
Hempl (George), **4168, 6455, 9389,
9404–06, 9494, 9517, 11431**
Hems (Harry), **4110**
Hencken (Hugh), **8532**
Hencken (Hugh O'Neill), **7747, 8638,
9564, 10603, 11204**
Henderson (Andrew), **1496**
Henderson (Ernest Flagg), **2369**
Henderson (F. B.), *Mrs.*, **4028**
Henderson (George), **718**
Henderson (James), **11654**
Henderson-Howat (Agatha Mary Doro-
thea), **4972**
Henebry (Richard), **4892, 9632, 9735**
Henel (Heinrich), **61, 4187, 5628, 7348,
7364–65, 7403, 7507**
Henfrey (Henry William), **9162–63,
9305–06**
Heningham (Eleanor K.), **1391**
Hennessy (William Maunsell), **2553, 7270**
Hennig (John), **4469–70, 4724, 4802,
5140–41, 5221, 5403, 5480, 5845,
6263**
Henniker (John Major (Henniker-
Major)), *5th baron*, **8686**
Henning (R.), **3209**
Hennon (C.), **3954**
Henry (Françoise), **3774, 7020, 8533,
8575, 9764, 10078, 10088–90, 10127–
29, 10472, 11066–67, 11136–39**
Henschenius (Godefridus), **4083**
Henshall (Samuel), **2820**
Hepple (Richard B.), **1552, 4051, 7132–33**
Herben (Stephen J.), **62, 8687**
Herbert (*Hon.* Algernon), **4511**
Herbert (John Alexander), **11841**
Herbst (C. F.), **9163–64**
Herdman (*Sir* William Abbott), **2193**
Hereford (Philip), **4159–60**
Hermann (Franz Wilhelm Emil), **2480,
3210**
Hermann (Hermann Julius), **11842**

Heron (James), **3393**
Heron (John), **8223**
Herringham (Christiana J.), **11962**
Herrmann (Léon), **1456, 4725**
Hertel (G.), **5422, 5481**
Hertford (Francis Hugh George (Sey-
mour)), *5th marquis of*, **8295,
11509**
Hervey (*Lord* Francis), **3627**
Hervey (John William Nicholas), *baron
Hervey*, **2952–53**
Herzfeld (Georg), **4412, 7691**
Hesleden (William), **5991**
Hess (Heinrich Maria von), **5317**
Heuser (Wilhelm), **6617**
Heusgen (Paul), **5525**
Heusinkveld (Arthur Helenus), **6**
Hewat (Kirkwood), **11256**
Hewins (William Albert Samuel), **4087**
Hewison (James King), **2216, 3394,
9459a, 10787–88, 11317**
Hewitt (John), **4111, 8688**
Hewlett (J. H.), **7797**
Hewson (Edward F.), **9710**
Heygate (W. E.), **5980**
Heywood (Nathan), **8898, 9000–01,
9049–54, 10650**
Heywood (Samuel), **3211**
Hibbert (Samuel), **2583**
Hibbert-Ware (S.), **11235**
Hicketier (F.), **7692**
Hicks (F. W. Potto), **2057**
Hickson (Mary Agnes), **6809–10**
Hieber (Hermann), **11843**
Hief (F. R. G.), **8247**
Higgs (Frederick), **8689**
Hilbelink (Aaltje Johanna Geertruida),
7407, 7414
Hildebrand (Bror Emil), **8867**
Hildyard (E. J. W.), **8346**
Hill (A. Du Boulay), **2058, 10314–15,
10438, 10745–46**
Hill (Arthur), **10488**
Hill (Elspeth), **4251**
Hill (Geoffrey), **916**
Hill (Geoffry), **1553**
Hill (*Sir* George), **8098**
Hill (George Francis), **9150**
Hill (H. Copinger), **10629–30**
Hill (James William Francis), **1856–57**
Hill (John Samuel), **6746**
Hill (N. Gray), **8416**
Hill (Philip V.), **8924–27, 8976**
Hillier (George), **8417**
Hillman (S.), **2246**

Hills (Gordon M.), 3628, 10316, 10395, 10489, 10727
Hills (William), 9096
Hind (G. E.), 3710
Hinde (John Hodgson), 1953–55
Hipkins (Frederick Charles), 1858–59, 6540, 10297
Hirst (J.), 3593
Hirst (Tom Oakes), 6682
Historicus, *pseud.*, 1860
Hitchcock (Francis Ryan Montgomery), 3524, 4549–50, 4726, 11140
Hitchcock (Richard), 10565
Hjaltalín (Jón Andrésson), 227
Hoare (Christobel M.), *Mrs. Ivo Hood*, 2917
Hoare (Edward), 8960, 9182, 9244, 11699
Hoare (*Sir* Richard Colt), *bart.*, 361
Hobhouse (Edmund), *bp. of Nelson*, N.Z., 2941–43
Hodge (E. Humfrey V.), 8764
Hodgen (Margaret T.), 2704
Hodges (Charles Clement), 10334, 10350, 10368–69, 10871, 10911–15, 10947
Hodges (John C.), 2682
Hodgetts (James Frederick), 2628, 7748, 8824
Hodgkin (John), 1228
Hodgkin (Robert Howard), 441, 663
Hodgkin (Thomas), 475, 664, 1956
Hodgson (J. Crawford), 4357
Hodgson (J. F.), 3882, 10335, 10845–46, 10872
Hodgson (John), 1957, 9055
Hoefler (Constantin), *Ritter von*, 5318
Hoenncher (Erwin), 5674–75
Hoerle (G. N.), 5408
Hoffman-Hirtz (Marie), 90a
Hofmann (J.), 5399
Hofmann (Konrad), 11432
Hofmann (Matthias), 2776
Hogan (Edmund Ignatius), 4471, 4578, 4587, 4727, 6796
Hogan (J. F.), 4803, 5240–44, 5404, 5409–10, 5507–08, 5556–58, 11902
Hogan (James), 2143, 2554
Hogan (John), 3395, 4472, 4804
Hogarth (Frederick Whewell), 5992
Hogg (Alexander Hubert Arthur), 6129, 7838–39, 7962
Hogg (G.), 7798
Hogg (John), 1365
Hogg (Robert), 10847–48
Holden (Richard), 10948
Holder (Alfred), 6797, 7184

Holderness (Thomas), 1122, 5993, 6629
Holdsworth (*Sir* William Searle), 2370
Hole (Charles), 3320
Holgate (Mary Scarlett), 6691
Holland (Thomas), 4252
Hollander (Lee M.), 1310, 1958
Hollings (Marjory), 3068
Hollingworth (Edith Joan), *Mrs. E. Savery*, 8122
Hollingsworth (A. G.), 7463
Holly (D.), 5946
Holm (Sigurd), 8868
Holmboe (C. A.), 8928, 9151
Holmes (Richard), 10949
Holmes (Thomas Scott), 3525, 3821, 5452
Holmes (Thomas Vincent), 7903, 7921
Holmes (Urban T.), 8929
Holmqvist (Wilhelm), 10046
Holt (P.), 4088
Holtby (J. R. D.), 8801
Holthausen (Ferdinand), 1497, 4169, 5782–83, 5797, 5827, 7508–13, 7693–95, 9407, 9431, 11433
Holyrood, *Chronicle of*, 223
Holzmann (Walther), 3552
Homan (W. MacLean), 2006
Homberger (Otto), 11844
Home (Gordon), 1799, 4253
Home (Robert), 5994
Honeyman (Herbert Lewis), 7874, 10370
Hood (Robert), 6668
Hook (C.), 1196
Hook (Walter Farquhar), *dean of Chichester*, 4029, 4052–53
Hooley (*Mrs.* R. W.), 11634
Hooppell (R. E.), 10336, 10371
Hoops (Johannes), 7224, 7391–93
Hooton (E. A.), 8403, 8765
Hope (*Mrs.* Anne), 3526, 5319
Hope (Henry G.), 1667
Hope (Robert Charles), 6302
Hope (*Sir* William Henry St. John), 3883, 7875, 7904, 10210–18, 10372
Hope-Taylor (Brian), 7970, 8449a, 8576
Hopkin-James (Lemuel John), 5683
Hopkins (Annette Brown), 1074
Hopkins (W. J.), 10317
Hopwood (David), 6711
Hordijk (C. Pijnacker), 5526
Hore (Herbert Francis), 2144
Hore (S. Coode), 1752
Horn (Wilhelm), 7514

Horne (Ethelbert), *abbot of Downside*, 1229, 3920, 4679, 7515, 8428–30, 10450, 11004, 11700

Hornsby (William), 2994, 3069, 8347

Horsley (John William), 6500

Horst (Karl), 91–93

Horstmann (Carl), 4089, 6241

Horton-Smith (R. J.), 8766

Horwood (A. R.), 1861

Hoskier (Herman Charles), 5684, 7225

Hoskins (William George), 1706–07, 1862, 6029, 6541, 6780–81

Houghton (Frederick Tyrie Sidney), 6195

Houghton (John F.), 534

Housman (D.), 8123

Housman (Henry), 4013

Hovey (Walter Read), 11845

Howard (Eliot), 1230–31, 1753

Howard (F. T.), 1075

Howard (George Elliott), 2629

Howard (Henry), 1232, 9495

Howarth (E.), 10950

Howel, *the Good. See* Hywel Dda, *king of Dyfed*

Howell (Emrys Jones), 5946a

Howell (Wilbur Samuel), 7058

Howells (W. W.), 8799

Howlett (J. A.), 4805

Howlett (Richard), 3822

Howorth (*Sir* Henry Hoyle), 94–96, 109, 158, 917, 918, 1311, 1411, 1554–57, 1645–46, 2967, 3321, 3396, 3526a, 3749, 3955, 4680, 7195, 8825, 8977, 9086–87, 10760

Howse (William Henry), 2247, 2930

Hoyt (Robert Stuart), 2271, 2271a

Hruschka (Alois), 6356

Hubert (Alfons), 5245

Huber (P. Michael), 4004

Hubert (Henri), 768, 1018

Hudd (Alfred Edmund), 8021, 10249, 10689

Hudleston (Ferdinand), 10373

Hudson (William), 2007–08, 2630, 2740, 3168, 3212, 3273–74

Huebener (Gustav), 664a, 6161–62, 7516–17

Huebner (Emil), 9408

Huet (G. Busken), 6264

Hugh, *Candidus, abbot of Peterborough*, 3673–74

Hughes (Henry Harold), 535, 8800, 11353–56, 11362–65, 11371–72, 11399, 11406–09

Hughes (Hubert David), 7134

Hughes (J. C.), 362

Hughes (Jonothan), 5966

Hughes (Michael W.), 919

Hughes (R. G.), 1753a

Hughes (Reginald), 10047

Hughes (Thomas), 1233, 9115

Hughes (Thomas McKenny), 3960, 7778, 8124–25

Hughes (William), 3397

Hugo (Thomas), 3711, 4054, 8876

Hulburd (Percy), 6376

Hull (Eleanor), 719, 769, 770, 3491–92, 7021, 7518–19

Hull (Vernam Edward), 1018a, 2272, 2555–56, 4197, 4473, 4537, 7022

Hulme (William H.), 5685

Hume (Abraham), 10651

Humphreys (Arthur Lee), 2059

Humphreys (Henry Noel), 7297, 11846

Humphreys (John), 8296–97

Hunt (Alfred), 5995, 6093–94, 7349, 10707

Hunt (John), 11088, 11141

Hunt (William), 3322, 3712

Huntbach (A.), 3275

Hunter (D. M.), 8050

Hunter (Joseph), 1558

Huntingford (George Wynn Brereton), 3493, 6095, 6712–13

Hurd (Howard) 8177

Hurley (Timothy), 4728

Hurnard (Naomi D.), 2481

Hussey (Arthur), 2777, 6096

Hutcheson (Alexander), 4311, 11275, 11282

Hutchinson (P.), 2705

Hutchinson (P. O.), 1708

Hutchinson (W.), 1959

Hutson (Arthur E.), 584, 7590

Hutton (William Holden), 4014, 4137

Huysche (Wentworth), 1863

Hyde (Douglas), 771

Hyett (F. A.), 1864

Hynes (John), 4806

Hynes (S. B. E.), 4807

Hywel Dda, *king of Dyfed*, 2595, 2595a

Iago (William), 9565–75, 11043–44

I'anson (J.), 4015

Ignatius, *pseud.*, 4016

Imelmann (Rudolf Hans Robert), 1594, 4138

Inderwick (Frederick Andrew), 2371

Ingledew (Walter A.), 10419

Ingram (James), **6163**
Inguanez (Mauro), **4220**
Inisfallen, *Annals of*, **190–91**
Inman (Alfred H.), **2778–79**
Innes (Cosmo), **772**
Innes (Thomas), **773, 774**
Innocent (Charles Frederick), **10155, 10604, 10951**
International Congress of prehistoric and protohistoric sciences, **920**
Iona, *pseud.*, **4926**
Ireland, *Census*, **7439**
Ireland, *Commissioners of Public Works*, **11086**
Irvine (Christopher), **4511**
Irvine (James Thomas), **10219–20, 10282–84, 10298–99, 10439, 10692, 10716, 10952, 11005**
Irvine (William Fergusson), **2848, 6521**
Irving (George Vere), **1960–61, 5876, 7850a, 7971**
Irwin (Raymond), **6969a**
Italy, *Ministero della Pubblica Istruzione*, **11846a**

J. (C. D.), **7135**
J. (E.), **2060**
J. (H. T.), **1234**
J. (J.), **9227**
Jaager (Werner), **2291, 4165, 4312**
Jabet (George), **8826**
Jackson (Charles Edwyn), **6669**
Jackson (Edward Dudley Colquhoun), **10152, 10156**
Jackson (J. N.), **5876a**
Jackson (John Edward), **2061, 3670, 8475**
Jackson (Kenneth), **200, 240, 1076, 1962, 5967, 6456, 6630, 7591–94, 9903**
Jacobs (Harry), **10130**
Jacobsthal (Paul), **10091**
Jakobsen (Jakob), **6867–68**
James (*Sir* Henry), **2816**
James (John), **1963, 5099**
James (Montague Rhodes), **1388, 4221, 4413, 5713, 5846–47, 6970–71, 7136–39, 7563–64**
James (R. R.), **7415, 7464**
James (T. D.), **10015**
Jameson (Anna Brownell), **4139**
Jamieson (   ), *Rev. Dr.*, **818**
Jamieson (John), **4927**
Jane (Lionel Cecil), **107**
Jankuhn (H.), **846–48**
Janssens (Hubert), **5527**

Jansson (Valter), **6163a**
Jarvis (Edwin), **11655**
Jastrow (Ignaz), **2482**
Jeavons (Sidney A.), **10725**
Jeffcock (John Thomas), **363**
Jeffcott (John M.), **6839**
Jeffrey (F. B.), **1235**
Jenkins (Claude), **4254, 6209**
Jenkins (J. Travis), **2706**
Jenkins (Robert Charles), **1781, 3884–86, 8178, 10221–22, 10235**
Jenks (Edward), **2372, 2372a, 3169**
Jenner (Henry), **1077, 1709, 3213, 5686, 5750, 6936–37, 9576, 11829**
Jennings (J. R. B.), **9245**
Jenny (Wilhelm Albert von), **10047a, 11434**
Jenson (O.), **3553**
Jerman (H. Noel), **7851–52**
Jerram (Charles Stanger), **585**
Jerrold (Douglas), **665**
Jervise (A.), **10566**
Jessen (Knud), **2706a**
Jessep (Henry Lethbridge), **10396, 10440**
Jessup (Frank W.), **6691a**
Jessup (Ronald Frederick), **364, 7749, 8179, 10223, 11510–11**
Jeudwine (John Wynne), **63, 775, 2373**
Jewett (Sarah Orne), **1559**
Jewitt (Llewellynn), **2857, 8079, 8224, 8310, 10849, 11179, 11205, 11264, 11512, 11597**
Joass (J. Maxwell), **8051,**
Joce (T. J.), **6066, 11023**
Johnman (W. A. P.), **8033**
Johnson (Charles), **2, 13, 2631, 2918**
Johnson (R. J.), **10337**
Johnson (W. Branch), **2891**
Johnson-Ferguson (*Sir* Edward Alexander James), *2nd bart.*, **6869**
Johnston (Alfred Wintle), **224, 1610, 2217–18, 2584, 5008, 6870–71, 8827**
Johnston (James), **3956**
Johnston (James Brown), **6303, 6670, 6872–74**
Johnston (K. J.), **6574**
Johnston (Philip Mainwaring), **1412, 6692, 10187, 10397–10403, 10441–45, 10637–38, 10981**
Johnstone (P. K.), **921, 922, 1078–81, 5100, 5968–70**
Jolliffe (John Edward Austin), **1782, 2273–74, 2632, 3070–71, 3107–08, 3170, 6377**
Jonas, *abbas Elnonensis*, **5442–43**

Jonas (Alfred Charles), **1783, 10048**
Jones (Arthur), **1611**
Jones (Bertram), **8348**
Jones (Charles Williams), **4183–84, 4188–89, 4222–23, 4253, 4343, 7350, 7366**
Jones (Edward), **7333**
Jones (*Sir* Evan D.), *bart.*, **6130**
Jones (Griffith Hartwell), **4447, 5142, 6210**
Jones (Gwilym Peredur), **510, 623, 720, 2248**
Jones (Harry Longueville), **7799, 8072, 9577–78, 9936, 10016, 11343, 11389**
Jones (James P.), **6522**
Jones (M. H.), **6938**
Jones (Morris Charles), **1366, 11754**
Jones (Owen), **2596**
Jones (Putnam Fennell), **4170, 6972**
Jones (T. Gwynn), **2683, 7023**
Jones (Thomas), **234, 235, 6939**
Jones (Thomas) ['Bibliothecar-Chetham.'], **4256, 7073**
Jones (Tom), **6940**
Jones (W. A.), **1668**
Jones (W. Basil), **8828–29**
Jones (W. Lewis), **132**
Jones (Walter H.), **2311**
Jones (William), **2312**
Jones (William Henry), **365, 366, 2062–66, 2982, 3887, 7840**
Jones (William Henry Rich), **2979, 3823–24, 3925, 6747–48, 10420–21**
Jones (William Lewis), **1082**
Jones (Winslow), **11024**
Jope (Edward Martyn), **8560, 8577–78**
Jordan (R.), **848a**
Jordan (Richard), **7378**
Jost (Karl Theodor), **97, 5648, 5803–04**
Joyce (James Wayland), **3323**
Joyce (Patrick Weston), **192, 2684, 6228a, 6811–14, 9648**
Joynt (Maud), **3390, 4881, 5572**
Jubinal (Achille), **6265**
Judd (J. M.), **8052**
Judge (Cyril Bathurst), **367, 7646**
Juhasz (Koloman), **5246**
'Juliana', **2936**
Jung (J.), **6211**
Jung-Diefenbach (Josef), **5509**
Just (John), **586, 1964, 9496**

K., **10717**
K., **6405**
Kaerre (Karl), **7394**
Kaines-Thomas (E. G.), **10445a**

Kantorowicz (Ernst Hartwig), **11847**
Karaus (Arthur), **2442**
Karlstroem (Sigurd), **6348, 6378, 6782**
Karslake (J. B.), **2707**
Kattenbusch (Ferdinand), **3398**
Kay (J. Taylor), **6671**
Kaye (Walter Jenkinson), **8500, 9497**
Keane (Marcus), **10473**
Keary (Charles Francis), **721, 8864, 8930–31, 9002, 9056, 9116, 9228**
Keating (Geoffrey), **776**
Keays-Young (Julia), **368**
Keegan (James), **4928**
Keeney (George Stockdale), **8349–50**
Keep (Herbert W.), **6693**
Keepe (Henry), **11579**
Keiller (Alexander), **7750**
Keim (H. W.), **3594**
Keith (*Sir* Arthur), **8767–68**
Keith (Duncan), **777**
Keitz (A. von), **5320**
Kelham (Robert), **2405, 2780**
Kell (Edmund), **8418, 8425, 9003**
Keller (Ferdinand), **7298, 11903**
Keller (May Lansfield), **8690**
Keller (Wolfgang), **98, 7299–7300, 9409, 9545**
Kells, *Book of*, **11915–18**
Kelly (Francis), **10507**
Kelly (James J.), **4474, 4729, 4808, 4929–30**
Kelly (M. T.), **4809–10**
Kelly (Matthew), **4475**
Kelly (Matthew J.), **3775**
Kelly (Paul Vincent), **7963**
Kelly (Richard J.), **4811, 10567**
Kemble (John Mitchell), **267, 268, 369, 476, 587, 588, 666, 3825, 6379, 8080, 9410, 9460, 9498**
Kemp (R. S.), **7271**
Kendall (Hugh Percy), **2996, 3030**
Kendrick (*Sir* Thomas Downing), **722, 5898, 7751, 8081, 8099–8101, 8108, 8311–12, 8501, 8579–82, 8639–42, 10049–53, 10272, 10605, 10652, 10747, 10761, 11006, 11142, 11453–54, 11513–17, 11635–37, 11656–57, 11777, 11803, 11963–65**
Kennedy (Charles William), **7696**
Kennedy (Evory Hamilton), **2708**
Kennedy (John W.), **7853**
Kennedy (W. N.), **7854**
Kenney (James Francis), **7, 4893, 6266**
Kent (Charles William), **2633**
Kent (Ernest A.), **10188**

Kenward (J.), 8261
Kenworthy (Joseph), 10953
Kenyon (*Sir* Frederic George), 7226, 7286
Kenyon (Joseph), 8877, 8978, 9004, 9097
Kenyon (R. Lloyd), 3276, 9307
Keogh (Thomas M.), 1612
Ker (Neil Ripley), 64, 4224, 7140, 7301
Kermack (W. R.), 923, 3859
Kermode (Philip Moore Callow), 1019, 2193, 3494, 8502, 8534-35, 9805-11, 10520-21, 11180-83, 11207-19, 11658, 11701, 11804
Kermode (R. D.), 11184, 11220
Kern (J. H.), 1123, 5662, 7697
Kerr (   ), *Mrs. Francis Kerr*, 4313
Kerr (John Edward), *jr.*, 1083
Kerr (William Shaw), 3554
Kerry (Charles), 4414
Kershaw (Samuel Wayland), 9308
Kerslake (Thomas), 778, 924, 1124-25, 1710, 1865, 2067-69, 5905, 6097, 6380
Keyser (Charles Edward), 10726
Keyser (Jacob Rudolph), 723, 3324
Keyworth (Samuel), 4931
Kid ner Tarw, 4415
Kilbride-Jones (Howard Edward), 8583, 11518
Killen (William Dool), 3399
Kinahan (George Henry), 8664, 10490
Kinard (James Pinckney), 5805
King (Henry Hall), 4225
King (Horace Herbert), 9309
King (John Edward), 4156
King (Richard John), 925, 1711, 4140, 9390, 11025
King (Robert), 3400
Kingsford (Hugh Sadler), 9374
Kinnebrook (William), 9812
Kinvig (Robert Henry), 2194, 5947
Kirbiriou (L.), 5165a
Kirk (George Edward), 10954
Kirk (Joan R.), 11598
Kirk (John Lamplugh), 11659
Kirk (R. E. G.), 2031
Kirke (Edith M.), 2897
Kirke (Henry), 6542
Kirker (Samuel Kerr), 7982, 10568
Kirkland (Walter), 6457, 6543, 6553a
Kirwan (W. H.), 4932, 5222, 5482
Kissan (B. W.), 3986
Kitchin (George William), 4314
Kitzinger (Ernst), 4315, 8101, 11517, 11519, 11966

Klaeber (Frederick), 3325, 4171, 5663, 7665
Kleinclausz (Arthur), 7074
Kletler (Paul), 3138, 7105
Klindt-Jensen (Ole), 724
Kluge (Friedrich), 7141, 7367
Klump (Wilhelm), 3139
Knappert (Laurentius), 5568
Kneale (William), 9813
Kneen (John Joseph), 624, 2195, 6840-43, 8534
Kneuer (K.), 7666
Knight (George Alexander Franks), 3401, 4448, 10506
Knoch (August), 6458
Knocker (G. M.), 1753a, 8126
Knott (Eleanor), 5848
Knowles (E. H.), 10850-52
Knowles (James S.), 9448
Knowles (James T.), *jr.*, 10748
Knowles (Joseph A.), 4512
Knowles (Michael David), 3595-97, 3636, 3987, 6973
Knowles (W. H.), 10250, 10318, 10873, 10916
Knowles (William James), 7334, 11702
Knox (Archibald), 11185
Knox (Hubert Thomas), 1161, 4812, 6131, 7983, 9724
Knox (R. B.), 3750
Knox (Robert), 8769
Kobell (Luise von), 11848
Koch (H.), 3568, 5321
Koeberlin (K.), 5687
Koebner (Richard), 2709
Koehler (Johann Jakob), 7379
Keohler (Theodor), 4172
Koehler (Walther), 5322-23
Koehler (Wilhelm Reinhold Walter), 11848a.
Koekeritz (Helge), 6303a, 6714-15, 6739
Koebling (Eugen), 5828
Koemstedt (Rudolf), 11849
Koepke (Johannes), 589
Koerting (Gustav), 1498
Kolderup-Rosenvinge (Jens Laurids Andreas), 2406
Kolsrud (Oluf), 3860
Konrath (M.), 7647
Koutaissoff (Elisabeth), 6164
Kovalevsky (Maxime), 3252
Kowalski-Fahrun (Herta), 7075
Kraag (C. M.), 8770
Krabbo (Hermann), 7119
Krapp (George Philip), 1236, 5704

Krappe (Alexander Haggerty), **1647**, **4730**, **7565**, **7614–17**
Krebs (H.), **23**, **566**
Krier (J. Bernhard), **5528**
Krogmann (Willy), **7636–38**, **7648**
Krom (Nicolaus Johannes), **849**
Kross (Theodor), **2634**
Krusch (Bruno), **3569–70**, **5423**, **5443–44**
Kube (Emil), **99**
Kuhliche (F. W.), **1866**
Kuhlmann (Bernhard), **5324**
Kuhn (Sherman M.), **7227**
Kunstmann (Friedrich), **5583**
Kupfersmidt (Max), **100**
Kurth (Betty), **10874**
Kurth (Godefroid Joseph François), **5325–26**
Kurtz (Benjamin P.), **4344**
Kurze (Friedrich), **5373**, **5375**
Kuypers (Arthur Benedict), **5777**
Kuznetsov (S. K.), **6165**
Kylie (Edward J.), **5268**, **5327**

L. (C. W.), **8932**, **9057**, **9229**
L. (H. W.), **9953**
Laborde (Edward Dalrymple), **1312–13**, **6098**, **6166**, **7639**
La Borderie (Louis Arthur Le Moyne de), **137**, **4933**, **5177–80**, **8830**
Labowsky (Lotte), **7106**
Lacaille (Armand D.), **11318–19**
Lach-Szyrma (Wladyslaw Somerville), **779**, **3527**, **5877**, **7024**
La Dangie de Renchi (Matthieu de), **1499**
Ladds (Sidney Inskip), **2741**, **7941**
Laenen (J.), **5529**
Laffetay (Jacques), *abbé*, **1457**
Laforêt (Jean Baptiste), **7076–77**
Lahaye (Léon), **5510**
Laheen (Kevin), **4731**
Laidlaw (Walter), **10917**
Laing (Alexander), **11276**
Laing (G. E.), **10188a**
Laing (Henry), **11320**
Laing (Samuel), **8022**
Laistner (Max Ludwig Wolfram), **4193**, **4225–26**, **4257**, **6974**, **7046**, **7142**
Lamb (Helen A.), **10092**
Lamb (John William), **4030**
Lambarde (William), **2407**
Lambert (Catherine), **7428**
Lambert (Édouard), **1458**
Lambert (Henry), **8450**
Lambert (Joseph Malet), **3048**

Lamborn (Edmund Arnold Greening), **2928**, **4416**, **10982–83**
Lamont (Augusta), **10093**
Lampen (Willibrord), **5328**, **5530–33**
Lamplough (Edward), **1964a**
Landon (L.), **3171**
Landsberger (Franz), **11904**
Lanfranc, *abp. of Canterbury*, **3987**
Langan (Thomas), **3776**
Langdon (Arthur Gregory), **9579–84**, **11045–53**
Lange (Joost de), **1590**
Langenfelt (Gösta), **850**, **6304**, **7649**
Langford (John Alfred), **1867**, **2974**
Langhorne (Daniel), **667**, **819**
Langrishe (Richard), **9711**
Lanigan (John), **3402**
Lanore (M.), **1459**
Lantfred, *monk of Winchester*, **4001**
Lantier (Raymond), **1152**
La Piana (George), **5269**, **5272**
Lappenberg (Johann Martin), **668**
Lapsley (Gaillard Thomas), **2275**, **3109**
Largillière (René), **5181–83**
Larking (Lambert Blackwell), **370**, **2896**
Larson (Laurence Marcellus), **1367–68**, **2335**
La Rue (Gervais de), *abbé*, **1460–61**
Lascelles (*Hon.* Gerald W.), **3037**
Latchmore (Frank), **9005**
Latham (Robert Gordon), **1648**, **8831**
Latouche (Robert), **5184**
Latourette (Kenneth Scott), **3326**
Lau (Hermann), **5247**
Lauer (Philippe), **1560**
Laughlin (J. Laurence), **2483**
Launey (H. Fr. de), **1462**
Laur (W.), **851**
Laurie (Arthur Pillans), **11850–52**
Laux (Johann Joseph), **5329–30**, **5424**, **5483–84**, **7120**
La Varende (Jean de), **1500**
Laver (Henry), **1237**, **7905–06**, **10189–92**
Laver (P. G.), **7907–08**
Law (Alice), **5996**
Lawford (Edward), **8207–08**
Lawless (Nicholas) [Enda, *pseud.*], **2145–46**, **4813–14**, **6132**
Lawlor (Henry Cairnes), **2147**, **3777**, **4579**, **4815**, **5906**, **10094**, **11068**, **11143**
Lawlor (Hugh Jackson), **4498**, **4732**, **4894**, **5445**, **5688–90**, **7254**, **7440**, **11853**

Lawrence (L. A.), **8933, 9088, 9098, 9230, 9310–12**

Lawrence (William Witherle), **7698**

Lawrie (*Sir* Archibald Campbell), **371**

Laws (Edward), **8073, 8832, 9980**

Lawton (W. P.), **1868**

Layard (Doris), **8747, 8771**

Layard (Nina Frances), **8127–31**

Lea (Harry), **10789**

Leabhar Bretnach, **159**

Leabhar Gabhála, **193**

Leabhar na Huidre, **7272–73**

Leach (Arthur Francis), **110, 269, 3712a, 6975**

Leadman (Alexander D. H.), **1126, 1369, 1965, 4417**

Lear (Floyd Seyward), **2484**

Leask (H.), **8053**

Leask (Harold G.), **10131, 10474, 10491–92, 11144**

Leatham (Diana), **3403, 5060**

Le Bachelet (X.), **4258**

Le Bras (Gabriel), **5582**

Léchaudé d'Anisy (Amédée Louis), **2781**

Ledwich (Edward), **7335, 10536, 11069**

Lee (Philip G.), **9633, 10095–96**

Lee (Timothy), **1314, 7025**

Lee-Warner (J.), **341**

Leeds (Edward Thurlow), **725, 926–28, 3140, 7752, 7756, 8132, 8248–51, 8262–65, 8280, 8398–99, 8476, 8584, 8643, 8691, 10054, 11520–29, 11660, 11967**

Leeney (O. H.), **10404**

Lees (Beatrice Adelaide), **1238, 2954**

Lees (Thomas), **1315, 4316, 4418, 5009, 10892**

Lefebvre de Noëttes ( ), *commandant*, **1463–64**

Lefroy (J. H.), **8934, 9717**

Lega-Weekes (Ethel), **590, 1712, 3110, 3462, 4373, 7228**

Le Gentilhomme (P.), **8899**

Legg (John Wickham), **2313**

Legg (Leopold George Wickham), **2314, 2319**

Leggatt (T. G.), **3031**

Le Grand (Albert), **5185**

Lehmacher (Gustav), **442, 1020**

Lehmann (Karl), **2374**

Lehmann (Paul), **4198–99, 7047, 7175, 7186**

Leicester, *Museum and Art Gallery*, **1837**

Leicester (*Sir* Peter), *bart.*, **2849**

Leicht (Alfred), **5664–65**

Leigh (*Hon.* James Wentworth), *dean of Hereford*, **372**

Leigh (Stephen de), **4640**

Leith (William Forbes), *see* Forbes-Leith (William)

Leitritz (Johannes), **6976**

Leitschuh (Franz Friedrich), **11854**

Lejard (André), **1464a**

Lejay (Paul), **7160**

Lemoine (J. G.), **11855**

Lenihan (M.), **8727**

Lennard (Reginald), **929, 2710, 2944, 3032, 3072, 3214, 6977**

Leo (Heinrich), **3277, 6305**

Leofric Collectar, **5768**

Leofric Missal, **5751, 5784**

Leonard (George Hare), **4328**

Leonhardi (Günther), **5785**

Le Patourel (John Herbert), **1370, 2453–54**

Leprieur (Paul), **11856**

Lerner (L. D.), **7351**

Leroquais (Victor), **5752**

Le Schonix (Roach), **125, 5411**

Le Strange (Hamon), **11530**

Lethaby (William Richard), **1465, 1800, 4377, 7972, 10132, 10273, 10767, 10790–91**

Lethbridge (Roper), **3404**

Lethbridge (Thomas Charles), **1754, 2635, 6099, 6229, 7520, 7779–80, 8102, 8133–42, 8503, 8585–87, 8644, 10133, 11531, 11703**

Lethieullier (Smart), **1466–67**

Letienne (A.), **1431**

Letronne (Jean Antoine), **7048**

Lett (H. W.), **7984, 11145**

Levé (A. M.), **1468–70**

Levêque (Louis), **3957**

Leveson-Gower (Granville), **6716**

Levi (T. A.), **2597**

Levien (Edward), **1595, 3327, 3713–14, 10727**

Levison (Wilhelm), **1127, 2455, 4009, 4173, 4259, 4419, 4980, 5156, 5281, 5288, 5515, 5534–37, 9499**

Lewes Museum, **11608**

Lewin (Thomas), **8833**

Lewis (E. A.), **3141**

Lewis (Hubert), **2598**

Lewis (Lionel Smithett), **3660**

Lewis (Timothy), **1669, 2599–2601**

Lidbetter (Robert M.), **10853**

Liddall (William John Norbray), **6875–76**

Liebermann (Felix), **38, 65–67, 96, 160, 373, 374, 669, 1316, 1561, 2292, 2315, 2336, 2375, 2408–23, 2443–49, 2485–89, 2636, 3049–50, 3215–16, 3598, 3988, 4138, 4141, 5538, 5584–86, 6631, 6717, 7078, 7465–66, 9058, 9375**

Liebrecht (Felix), **7566**

Lietzmann (Hans), **7079**

Lightfoot (Joseph Barber), *bp. of Durham*, **3328**

Lincoln and Nottingham (Lincs.) Architectural Society, **8313–14**

Lincoln County Museum, **8315**

Lindeboom (Johannes), **5539**

Lindeloef (Uno), **5714–16, 5829**

Lindkvist (Harald), **1966**

Lindley (E. S.), **4420**

Lindquist (Ivar), **7521**

Lindqvist (Harald), **3217**

Lindqvist (Sune), **1153, 1153a, 7753, 8103**

Lindsay (A. W.), **9765**

Lindsay (Jack), **1649**

Lindsay (John), **8860, 8869, 8900–01, 8979, 9059–63, 9117, 9183, 9203, 9246**

Lindsay (Thomas Martin), **7026**

Lindsay (Wallace Martin), **7185–86, 7255, 7302–07**

Lines (H. H.), **7800**

Lingard (John), **3329**

Linklater (Eric), **1613**

Linton (D. L.), **5891**

Lionárd (Padraig), **9634**

Lipson (Ephraim), **3278**

Lismore, *Book of*, **4476, 4496**

Lithgow (Robert Alexander Douglas), **5907**

Little (Andrew George), **3218**

Little (E.), **7841**

Little (George Aloysius), **6267, 6815**

Little (K. L.), **8792**

Littledale (Henry), **8209, 11532**

Liverpool, *Public Museums*, **11186**

Livett (Grevile Mairis), **3826, 10224–27, 10265**

Livingstone (Colin), **6877**

Llallawg, *pseud.*, **6133, 9981**

Llewellin (George T.), **6406–07, 6783**

Llewellin (William), **8074**

Lloyd ( ), *chevalier*, **2249**

Lloyd (Howel William), **1317, 1614, 5061, 5101, 11410**

Lloyd (*Sir* John Edward), **241, 625, 780, 930, 1084, 1318, 1615, 2250–51, 2602, 6941**

Lloyd (John Maurice Edward), **7801**

Lloyd (Joseph H.), **6134**

Lloyd (Richard Duppa), **3463**

Lloyd (William Valentine), **5102**

Llwyd (Angharad), **7618**

Lobel (Mary Doreen), **4741a**

Lobineau (Gui Alexis), **5186–87**

Locke (John), **8425**

Lockett (Richard Cyril), **8902, 9006**

Lockhart (William), **1616**

Lodge (H. Cabot), **2490**

Loeffler (Josias Friedrich Christian), **5331**

Loeffler (Karl), **7176, 7187**

Loehe (Hans), **4192**

Loew (Heinz), **7121**

Loewenberg (J.), **6268**

Loeweneck (Max), **7418**

Loftie (William John), **1204, 1801**

Logeman (Henri), **2376, 3926, 5830, 6167, 9411, 9432**

Logerman (Willem S.), **3599**

Loisel ( ), *abbé*, **5753**

Lomier (Eugène), **1501**

London, *Guildhall Museum*, **7754**

London Museum, **1802–03**

Lonergan (P.), **4681**

Long (Edward T.), **4142, 5786**

Long (Omera F.), **7080**

Long (R. H.), **3861**

Longhurst (Margaret Helen), **10955, 11422**

Longley (Thomas), **2908**

Longpérier (Adrien de), **8878, 8935, 9007–08**

Longstaff (John Cleasbey), **6749**

Longstaffe (William Hylton Dyer), **1967–68, 3827, 4317, 9009, 9313, 10338, 10351, 10374, 10918**

Longuemare (Élie), **3989**

Loofs (Friedrich), **3405, 5273**

Loomis (Charles Grant), **4143, 7467–68**

Loomis (Grant), **1173–74, 4144, 4329**

Loomis (Laura Hibbard), **4112–13**

Loomis (Roger Sherman), **626, 1085–87, 1471, 1670**

Lopez (Robert Sabatino), **1650**

Lord (T. E.), **10339**

Lorentz (Friedrich), **7081**

Lot (Ferdinand), **138–39, 161, 670, 931–34, 4580, 5188, 5971 6225**

Loth (Joseph), 162–64, 242, 443, 511, 536, 627, 820, 1088–90, 1651–52, 1671, 2219, 2521, 2557, 2603, 2711, 3495, 3751, 4114, 4816, 5046, 5103–05, 5189–90, 5211, 5972, 6135, 6798

Louis (René), 4682

Lovegrove (E. W.), 10157

Low (Charles William), 11533

Low (John Low), 3585, 3715, 4318, 7196–97

Lowe (Elias Avery), 4174, 5726, 7213, 7287, 7308–09

Lower (Mark Antony), 1413–14, 3716, 8645, 8772

Lowerison (Bellerby), 8143

Lowndes (Charles), 8316–17

Lowry (David E.), 726

Lowry-Corry (*Lady* Dorothy), 10134, 11103–04, 11128, 11146–48

Lowson (George), 11236

Lowther (Anthony William George), 8451–52, 8588

Loyd (L. C.), 1562

Loyn (H. R.), 3219

Luasa (Máire ní), 4817

Lucas (A. T.), 2712, 11089

Lucas (Charles), 7779a

Lucas (John Clay), 9010, 9184

Lucas (John F.), 8225

Lucchini (L.), 4358

Luce (A. A.), 5691

Luce (*Sir* Richard Harman), 3671

Ludwig (Gottfried), 4934

Luebeck (Konrad), 5332, 5376–85

Luedeke (H.), 935

Luff (S. G. A.), 4981

Lugnano (Placido), 5485, 5608, 7161

Lukis (William Collings), 1968a, 8351

Lukman (N.), 671

Lumb (George Denison), 9118

Lumby (J. H.), 2904

Lumby (Joseph Rawson), 6978

Lunham (T. A.), 4530

Lunt (William Edward), 3555

Lynam (Charles), 10193, 10340, 10375, 10671, 10728–30, 11400

Lynch (J. Fetherston), 2148, 4818

Lynch (Maud), 4513

Lynch (Patrick J.), 4618, 4935, 9674–76, 10475, 10493

Lynn (William Thynne), 23, 140, 3958

Lyons (Jessie M.), 6306

Lyttelton (Charles), *bp. of Carlisle*, 9500, 10854

D

M. (G. W.), 5106

M. (J.), 1617

M. (J. J.), 10476

MacAdam (Robert), 9247

Macalister (Robert Alexander Stewart), 193, 194, 781, 782, 2149, 2170, 3778, 4476, 4661, 4819–21, 7229, 7404, 8801, 9518, 9546–52, 9597–98, 9635–40, 9649–50, 9677–81, 9690–92, 9712–13, 9718–19, 9736–37, 9750, 9769–74, 9779, 9828, 9838, 9883, 9904–05, 9937–38, 10018, 10097, 10492, 10494–95, 11087, 11090–95, 11105, 11149–50, 11248, 11344–45, 11357, 11390, 11401, 11411

Mac an Bháird (E. R.), 11704

MacAndrew ( ), *provost*, 821, 3406

Macandrew (*Sir* Henry Cockburn), 783

MacArthur (William), 9814, 11187

MacArthur (*Sir* William Porter), 7441–45, 7468a, 7469

Macauliffe (M. J.), 2558

Macbain (Alexander), 628, 629, 3752, 6878–80, 7274, 7522

McBryde (J. M.), *jr.*, 7523

MacCabe (William Bernard), 3330, 4822

MacCaffrey (James), 4477, 4692

McCall (Hardy Bertram), 8646, 8728, 9314, 10956–57

MacCarthy (Bartholomew), 195, 444, 3407–08, 4581, 5486, 5736–37, 5754

MacCarthy (Charles J. F.), 2559, 3779, 4478, 4531–32

McCarthy (E. J.), 5487

McCarthy (S. T.), 2150

McCaul (John), 9421

McClelland (John), *jr.*, 11755

McClintock (Henry Foster), 3002–03, 11824–25

McClure (Edmund), 591, 630, 631, 6307, 9519

McConchie ( ), *bailie*, 8054

MacCorry (John Stewart), 4936

Macrae (Donald), 9866

McCrie (George M.), 8504

Macculloch (J. A.), 822

McCulloch (W. T.), 8536

MacDermott (Anthony), 6269

MacDermott (Máire), 8729, 11151

Macdonald (A.), 6168

MacDonald (Alasdair), 823

Macdonald (Allan John Macdonald), 3990–92

Macdonald (Angus), 6881

Macdonald (Archibald), **4886, 6882**
Macdonald (*Sir* George), **9884**
Macdonald (James), **3907, 6883–84, 8055**
MacDonnell (Charles P.), **196, 5143**
MacEchern (Dugald), **6885**
MacEclaire ( ), **5609**
MacErlean (John), **4662, 4823–24**
Macfadyen (Dugald), **1239**
Macfarlan (James), **10792**
MacFirbisigh (Duald), **727**
MacGibbon (A. L.), **10422**
MacGibbon (David), **10508**
McGovern (J. B.), **1869, 3092, 4680, 5997, 11756**
MacGregor (Cecilia), **1392**
MacGregor (D.), **4937**
MacGregor (D. Mackintosh), **4641**
McGregor (Duncan), **3409, 5849**
MacInery (M. H.), **4825**
McInroy (William), **11757**
McIntire (W. T.), **1969, 5899**
MacIntosh ( ), *Rev.*, **8730**
McIntosh (Angus), **5806**
MacIntyre (Donald) **4315**
Mack (R. P.) **8980**
Mackay (Aeneas James George), **3253**
Mackay (Donald), **7275**
Mackay (James), **8056**
Mackay (John), **6886**
Mackay (William), **5010**
McKeehan (Irene Pettit), **4330**
MacKenna (James Edward), **4826, 10098, 11104, 11805**
Mackenzie (Donald A.), **784, 7027, 8023, 8057, 11237**
Mackenzie (Henry), *bp. of Nottingham*, **1128**
MacKenzie (Kenneth), **6887**
Mackenzie (W. M.), **2201**
MacKenzie (W. Mackay), **11265**
MacKenzie (William), **7524**
MacKenzie (William Cook), **6888–90, 8834**
McKerlie (Peter Handyside), **2220**
McKerral (Andrew), **3111**
McKerrow (M. H.), **10793**
McKie (J.), **6891**
Mackie (J. D.), **4982**
Mackilliam (Annie E.), **1240**
Mackinlay (J. Boniface), **4331**
Mackinlay (James Murray), **1129, 4359, 4449, 4875, 5011–15, 6892**
Mackinnell (W. A.), **5908**
Mackinnon (James), **3410, 4983**

Mackintosh (D.), **8835**
McKnight (George Harley), **1241**
McLachlan (*Dame* Laurentia), **5807**
Maclagan (C.), *Miss*, **11238, 11249–50, 11283, 11321–22**
Maclagan (Christian), **11239**
Maclagan (*Sir* Eric Robert Dalrymple), **1472**
Maclagan (Michael), **4161**
Maclagan (Robert Craig), **4876**
McLauchlan (Thomas), **6893**
Maclean (Arthur John), *bp. of Moray and Ross*, **5016**
MacLean (George Edwin), **5649**
Maclean (Hector), **824, 6894–94**
Maclean (*Sir* John), **7802**
Maclean (Roderick), **6896**
Maclear (George Frederick), **3600**
Maclennan (Duncan M.), **7256**
McLennan (John Ferguson), **2637**
Macleod (D. J.), **11661**
Macleod (Donald), **11710**
McLeod (John N.), **6136**
Macleod (Norman), **11705**
Macleod (R. C.), **2221**
Maclise (Daniel), *R.A.*, **1563**
MacMichael (James Holden), **3238, 10958**
McMillan (W.), **5017**
Macnab (Duncan), **4642**
Macnamara (George W.), **11152–53**
Macnaught (John Campbell), **3556, 3753, 7650**
McNeill (Florence Marian), **4938**
MacNeill (Eoin, John), **191, 193, 197–99, 445, 446, 512, 632, 728, 785, 786, 825, 2151–52, 2560–62, 3330a, 3410a-b, 4582–85, 4643, 4663, 4693, 4733–35, 6816, 6822, 7028, 9553, 9599, 9775**
MacNeill (John Thomas), **5610–13**
McNeill (Malcolm), **8505–06**
MacNeill (Patrick), **4664**
Macnish (Neil), **826**
Macphail (James Calder), **4939**
Macpherson (J. R.), **6204**
Macpherson (John), **826a**
Macpherson (Norman), **8731**
Macray (J.), **11599**
MacRitchie (David), **537, 827–29, 2222, 7755, 8836**
MacSuibhne (Padraic), **200**
MacSweeney (Michael T.), **4644, 4736**
Madden (Frederic William), **8981**
Madden (*Sir* Frederick), **375**

Madge (Sidney Joseph), **1870**

Magnusen (Finn), **9422, 9461**

Magnússon (Eiríkr), **1945, 6834, 7352, 7525**

Magoun (Francis Peabody), *jr.*, **101, 101a-b, 477, 1130, 1242, 1564, 3496–97, 3828, 6212, 6308, 6979–80, 7526–28**

Maguire (Edward), **4827, 4882–83**

Maguire (R.), **3557**

Mahler (Margaret), **7803**

Mahr (Adolf), **10099–10100, 11706–08**

Maine (*Sir* Henry James Sumner), **2276, 3279**

Maitland (Frederic William), **2277, 2377–79, 2389, 2604, 2742, 2782, 3112**

Maitland (George), **376, 2009**

Major (Albany Featherstonehaugh), **936–38, 998, 2035, 5878, 6050, 7821–24**

Malcomson (Robert), **9119**

Malden (Henry Elliot), **939, 2070, 2957–58, 6030**

Malnory (A.), **5453**

Malone ( ), **4828**

Malone (Kemp), **21, 940, 941, 1091–92, 6169–75, 6349, 6718, 8837**

Malone (Michael), **10496**

Malone (Sylvester), **201, 4619–21, 4645–48, 4694–97, 4737–38, 4829, 5738**

Mander (Gerald P.), **1871, 3062**

Mandy (William H.), **2042**

Manitius (Maximilian), **3927, 6981**

Mann (A. H.), **2638, 3498**

Mann (Ludovic MacLellan), **11257**

Manning (Charles Robertson), **6100, 7909, 9315, 11534**

Manning (Owen), **2458, 2959**

Manning (Percy), **7756, 8266**

Mansel-Pleydell (J. C.), **6350**

Manser (Anselm), **4260**

Manton (J. O.), **9316–17**

Manx Museum, **2293, 8537**

Manzoni (G.), **4360**

Marble Arch, *pseud.*, **6719**

March (F. A.), **2424**

March (Henry Colley), **6381, 7757, 10055, 10101, 10606–07, 11026**

Marcus (G. J.), **6230–31**

Marcus (Hans), **6357**

Margaret, *St., queen of Scotland*, **11935**

Margary (Ivan D.), **6196, 8378, 9185**

Marignan (Albert), **1473**

Markham (Christopher A.), **2922, 8252–53, 10718–19**

Markham (*Sir* Clements), **1204**

Markland (James), **7973**

Marks (Arthur W.), **5938**

Marquardsen (Heinrich), **2491**

Marquis (James T.), **5998–99**

Marsh (Thomas Coxhead Chisenhale), **2873**

Marsh (W. J.), **10855**

Marsh (William E.), **9099**

Marshall (David William Hunter), **2223**

Marshall (Edward), **1131, 3172, 4055**

Marshall (Edward H.), **830, 1415**

Marshall (George), **1565, 3959, 7842**

Marstrander (Carl Johan Sverstrup), **729, 1175, 2196, 3411–12, 3499, 6459, 6844, 9391, 9693, 9776, 9815–16**

Martin (Alan R.), **3717, 8453**

Martin (Cecil Percy), **8802**

Martin (J. W.), **6897**

Martin (John May), **942, 6101**

Martin (Léon Eugène), **5464, 5488**

Martin (P. Harney), **3754**

Martin (R. R.), **10749**

Martin-Clarke (*Mrs.* Daisy Elizabeth), **6982, 8104, 10638a.** *See also under* Clarke

Martinus, *Hiberniensis*, **7049**

Marwick (Hugh), **2224–27, 2294–95, 6898–6900, 8507, 9885, 11266**

Marx (Jean), **68, 1502, 1514**

Maryon (Herbert), **8692–94, 8732**

Marzuttini (G. D.), **4361**

Masai (F.), **11857**

Maseres (Francis), **2337**

Maskelyne (Nevil Story), **6750**

Maskelyne (T. S.), **2071, 6102–03**

Mason (Arthur James), **3960**

Mason (J. R.), **10856**

Mason (J. Redfern), **3528**

Mason (T. H.), **11070**

Mason (W. H.), **10750**

Massé (Henri Jean Louis Joseph), **10251**

Massey (William), **8226**

Massingberd (W. O.), **3220**

Masterson (M. J.), **4830**

Matcham (George), **1243**

Mateu y Llopis (F.), **9152**

Matheson (Colin), **11968**

Matheson (Donald), **6901**

Mathews ( ), *Canon of Lincoln*, **1132, 10857**

Matthews (H. J.), **1416**

Mattingley (Harold), **8903**

Matzerath (Joseph), **3142–43**

Matzke (John Ernst), **2425**

Maude (J. H.), **3331**

Maughan (John), **9462, 9501**
Maule (Henry), **830a**
Maurer (Georg Ludwig von), **2492**
Maurer (Karl), **5386**
Maurer (Konrad von), **2380, 2493, 2639–40, 3173**
Maurer (Wilhelm), **2494**
Mawer (*Sir* Allen), **730–33, 1176–77, 1319, 1970, 5900, 6104, 6309–15, 6358–59, 6408, 6427, 6460, 6523, 6587, 6602, 6632, 6672–75, 6694, 6697, 6751, 6784**
Maxwell (*Sir* Herbert Eustace), *7th bart.*, **225, 4983a, 6902–03a, 11292–94, 11709**
Maxwell (I. S.), **5947a**
Maxwell (*Sir* John Stirling), **10509**
Maxwell (William Delbert), **4984**
May (A. McL.), **8729**
May (Akerman), **7758**
May (George Lacey), **1244**
May (Thomas), **10893**
Maycock (A. L.), **4261**
Mayer (Anton), **5144**
Mayer (Joseph), **10319**
Mayhew (Anthony Lawson), **6603**
Mayhew (Samuel Martin), **11188**
Maynard (Guy), **8144**
Maynard (J. G.), **4560**
Mayo (Charles Herbert), **6461, 9318**
Mayo (Dermot Robert Wyndham Bourke), *7th earl*, **734**
Mazzoni (D.), **3928**
Mead (E. D.), **1245**
Mead (William E.), **7353**
Meade (R. J.), **3929**
Meade-King (Richard Liddon), **2072**
Medland (Henry), **10320**
Medland (Thomas), **2010**
Meehan (Joseph B.), **9778, 11758**
Megaw (Basil R. S.), **735, 3003, 3780, 7759, 8508, 8647, 8733, 11202, 11221–22, 11662**
Megaw (Eleanor M.), **735, 736**
Meier (Gabriel), **7050**
Meigh (Alfred), *photographer*, **10959**
Meikle (James), **6904**
Meiklejohn (M. J. C.), **6618**
Meissner (John Ludwig Gough), **3413, 4586, 4665**
Mellish (Charles), **2337**
Mellor (J. E. M.), **2641**
Mellor (John), **1246**
Mellows (William Thomas), **3673–75**
Melrose, *Chronicle of*, **226**

Melton Mowbray, *Museum*, **11535**
Menzies (Lucy), **4940, 4973**
Menzies (William Gladstone), **11806**
Meraude (Noel de), **4514**
Mercati (Angelo), **7198**
Mercati (Giovanni), *cardinal*, **5412, 7162**
Mercier (Jerome), **1872**
Mériot ( ), **5454**
Meritt (Herbert), **2642**
Merivale (Charles), *dean of Ely*, **3600, 5333**
Meroney (Howard), **7529–30**
Merriman (P. J.), **787**
Merton (Adolf), **11905–06**
Mescal (Daniel), **4831**
Messenger (Ernest C.), **6996**
Mestorf (J.), **11972**
Metcalfe ( ), **3414**
Metcalfe (Frederick), **39**
Metcalfe (W. M.), **4877, 4986**
Methold (Thomas Tindal), **3264**
Metlake (George), *pseud. See* Laux (Johann Joseph)
Meyer (A.), **3456**
Meyer (Kuno), **202, 513, 633, 634, 2153–54, 2563, 4175, 4538, 4832–34, 4895, 5047, 5787, 6226, 6242, 7029, 7531, 7595, 7651**
Meyer (Paul), **1393**
Meyer (Peter), **11900, 11900a**
Meyer (Wilhelm), **141, 4200, 5788–89, 5850, 6243**
Meyer (Willi), **943**
Meyer von Knonau (Gerold), **5559**
Meyrick (O.), **8477**
Meyrick (Thomas), **5107, 6213**
Mezger (Fritz), **2495–96, 2643–44, 6316, 7532**
Micheli (Geneviève Louise), **11858, 11907**
Michie (J. G.), **9886**
Micklethwaite (John Thomas), **4115, 10158–59, 10194, 10352, 11536**
Middendorff (Heinrich), **6428**
Middlemiss (J. T.), **7199**
Middleton (John Henry), **3280, 3888, 8145, 10252–53, 11859**
Mildenberger (Kenneth), **10056**
Miles (George), **3829**
Miles (Louise Wardlaw), **1247**
Millar (Eric George), **11860, 11936**
Miller (E.), **1744**
Miller (Edward), **1566, 2497, 2645**
Miller (Hugh), **11323, 11710**
Miller (Isobel A.), **222**
Miller (Peter), **6137**

Miller (Samuel Henry), **1320, 1371, 1596, 1755–56, 3646, 3676, 4116, 6476–77**
Miller (Thomas), **671a, 1618, 4227**
Milles (Jeremiah), **9520, 11537**
Milligan (Seaton Forrest), **4941, 8509, 9777, 11663, 11759**
Mills (Joseph Travis), **1133**
Milman (Henry Salusbury), **5909, 7804**
Milne (Frank A.), **7619**
Milne (George), **6462, 11324**
Milne (J. Grafton), **8904, 9319**
Milne (John), **6905–06**
Milne-Home (Grace), **5851**
Milner (George), **10960**
Milner (John), **7230**
Milton (John), **672**
Mincoff (Marco Konstantinos), **5692, 7533**
Minns (G. W.), **10446**
Mitchell (Anthony), *bp. of Aberdeen*, **3415**
Mitchell (Arthur), **3416, 8010, 9839**
Mitchell (George Bennet), **11325**
Mitchell (Gerard), **5425, 5614**
Mitchell (Gordon), **4016a**
Mitchell (H. P.), **10057, 11538**
Mitchell (Henry), **2011**
Mitchell (John M.), **9847**
Mitchell (T. Carter), **4421**
Mitterer (P. Sigisbert), **5334–35**
Ml. (J.), **10341**
Moar (Peter), **11267**
Moberley (George H.), **6588**
Mockler (J.), **2338**
Moé (Émile A. van), **11861**
Moeller (H.), **851a**
Moens (W. J. C.), **3033**
Moffat (Alexander G.), **1321, 6942**
Mohr (W.), **5879**
Moir (J. Reid), **8104a**
Moiraghi (Pietro), **3993**
Moling, *St.*, **4539**
Moloney (Michael F.), **7470**
Moltzer (Henri Ernest), **6244**
Molyneux (William), **1873**
Mommsen (Theodor), **4262**
Monahan (John), **3781, 4835**
Mone (Franz Joseph), **5587**
Money (Walter), **6051–52, 8400**
Monkhouse (William), **7942**
Monnier (Francis), **7082**
Monro (Robert), **8538**
Montagu (H.), **9064, 9089, 9120, 9231, 9320–21**
Montalembert (Charles Forbes René de), *count*, **3601**

Montgomerie (D. H.), **7974**
Montmorency. *See* De Montmorency
Moodie (J. M.), **8454**
Moody (Henry), **2883, 2983**
Moonen (Honorius), **4007**
Mooney (John), **1619**
Moor (C.), **3830**
Moore (Arthur William), **635–37, 1653, 2197, 2228**
Moore (Courtenay), **4836, 10102**
Moore (Edwin), **4345**
Moore (George), **9860**
Moore (Grace Edna), **1394**
Moore (H. Cecil), **7805–06, 10254**
Moore (Margaret F.), **2783**
Moore (S. H.), **2921**
Moore (Samuel), **5676**
Moore (Stuart), **2784**
Moore (Wilfred J.), **6214**
Moorhouse (Frederick), **10653**
Moorman (Charles), **1133a**
Moorman (Frederick William), **6317, 6633**
Moran (Patrick Francis), *cardinal abp. of Sydney*, **1654, 3417, 3744, 4479, 4622, 4837–38, 5157, 5336, 6245, 7030**
Morant (Alfred W.), **3629**
Morant (Geoffrey McKay), **8773, 8784**
Moreau (Édouard de), **5511**
Morgan (C. Octavius S.), **2296**
Morgan (F. W.), **3034–35, 5948–51**
Morgan (James F.), **2785**
Morgan (T. O.), **2252**
Morgan (Thomas), **377, 788, 1757, 1874–75, 2073, 3500, 6943–45**
Morice de Beaubois (Pierre Hyacinthe), **5191–92**
Morin (Germain), **4201–02, 4228, 4263, 5248, 5426–27, 5693, 5728, 5769, 5852, 7083–84**
Morin (Jean), **5588**
Morley (Claude), **1372, 1758–61, 3889, 6105, 10195–96, 10631**
Morris (A. J.), **7910**
Morris (Ernest), **11760**
Morris (G. E.), **6544**
Morris (Henry), **1021–22, 2155, 4480, 4739–40, 5910–11, 6138, 6197, 6817, 7985, 8803, 8838, 9720, 11096, 11711, 11761, 11807**
Morris (James A.), **11326**
Morris (John E.), **7877**
Morris (Joseph E.), **3890**
Morris (Lewis), **9907**

Morris (Marmaduke C. F.), 6634
Morris (William Alfred), 2339, 2498, 3174–76
Morris (William Bullen), 4623, 4683, 4741–42
Morrison (George Herbert), 4942
Morrison (Hew), 11327
Morrison (Walter), 6106
Morshead (J. Y. A.), 1713–14
Mortimer (John Robert), 6067, 8352–53, 8774–75
Mortimer (William Williams), 1876
Morton (John), 2923
Mossé (F.), 638
Mostyn (John), 2786
Mottay (J. Gaultier du), 5193
Mottram (Ralph Hale), 4742a
Moule (H. J.), 2871, 3718, 10160
Mowat (John Lancaster Gough), 2929
Mowbray (Cecil), 11284
Muegge (Helmut), 5387
Muellendorff (Julius), 5540–41
Mueller (Eduard), 7699
Mueller (Johan Peter), 5337
Mueller (K.), 4743
Mueller (Karl Otto), 5282
Mueller (Lucian), 3930, 7700
Mueller (Rudolph), 592
Muenter (A. Heinrich), 8776
Muentz (Eugène), 11862
Muir (P. McAdam), 9463
Muir (William), 4943
Muirchu Maccumachtheni, 4587
Mulcahy (C.), 4744, 5853
Mulcahy (David B.), 4839
Mulchrone (Kathleen), 2156, 4588–93, 4698, 4772
Muller (M. R. Maitland), 8418a, 8419
Mullinger (James Bass), 7085
Munch (Peter Andreas), 737, 5912, 9817–18, 9887
Munding (Emmanuel), 5569
Munford (George), 495, 2381, 2919, 6478
Munro (Robert), 8648, 8665–67
Munroe (Robert), 3501
Muratori (Lodovico Antonio), 7163
Murch (Jerom), 1178
Murphy (Denis), 2157, 3782, 4515, 11808–09
Murphy (Gerard), 4699, 4745
Murphy (J.), 3418
Murphy (Michael), 4533, 6818
Murphy (N.), 4840–41
Murray (Alexander), 831

Murray (Alexander D.), 6139
Murray (Desmond P.), 4842
Murray (Sir James Augustus Henry), 1134, 4319
Murray (Katharine Maud Elisabeth), 2278
Murray (Laurence P.), 2158–60, 3783, 4666, 4684, 4843, 4944, 5913
Murray (Margaret Alice), 593, 7567, 10608, 11007
Murray (R. W.), 8649
Murrin (D.), 4985
Mutschmann (Heinrich), 6545
Mutton (Alice F. A.), 944
Muuss (Rudolph), 1634a
Myddfai, 7416–17
Mynors (Roger Aubrey Baskerville), 7231
Myres (John Nowell Linton), 652, 945–47, 1804, 5880, 7760, 7975, 8082, 8318, 8589–97

N. (J. G.), 538
Nanson (William), 9464
Napier (Alexander), 11328
Napier (Arthur Sampson), 270, 478, 3931, 4056, 5589–90, 5694, 5808, 5811, 5817, 7232, 7534, 7568, 7652, 9322, 11435–36
Napper (H. F.), 948, 2963, 6000, 6107
Nash (D. W.), 9600
Nash (Treadway Russell), 2985
Nash-Williams (Victor Erle), 9906, 9921, 9939, 9982–83, 10019, 10033, 11346–49, 11412
National Museum of Scotland, 11329
Naylor (George), 8180
Neckel (Gustav), 9392
Nedeles (Louis), 5048
Neilson (George), 1417, 2229, 6001, 7878, 8058
Neilson (H.), 3036
Neilson (Nellie), 2898–99
Neish (James), 11330
Nelson (Philip), 9065–72, 9121–23, 9232–33, 9323–25, 11623–24
Nennius, abbot of Bangor, 165–66
Nerman (Birger), 1154
Nerney (D. S.), 4551, 5854
Nesbitt (Alexander), 9433, 11712
Neuendorff (B.), 1322
Neuss (Wilhelm), 5249
Neville (Ralph), 949
Neville (Richard Cornwallis), 4th Baron Braybrooke, 8146–47

Nevinson (Charles), 1877
New Paleographical Society, 7288
Newell (R. S.), 11008
Newell (Charles S.), 10375a
Newell (Ebenezer Josiah), 3419–20, 3861a, 4624, 5049, 5062
Newell (William Wells), 167, 1093, 3661
Newstead (Robert), 9124
Newton (E. F.), 8319
Newton (William Waring Hay), 9423
Nichols (Francis Morgan), 3011, 7911
Nichols (John Gough), 950
Nichols (Robert Cradock), 447
Nicholson (Edward Williams Byron), 142, 514, 832, 951–54, 1023, 1094–95, 5615, 9829
Nicholson (J. Holme), 10894
Nicholson (John), 6068, 6635
Nicholson (R. Steele), 4746
Nicklin (Phyllis Amelia), 5952, 6695
Nicol (John), 8059–60
Nicolson (John), 6318
Nicolson (William), 9465, 9502
Nightingale (J. E.), 3719
Nigra (Costantino), count, 7177, 7276
Nilsson (Nils Martin Persson), 7354
Ninian, St., bp. of Galloway, 4986
Nisbet (John), 3037–38
Nisbett (Norman C. H.), 10447
Nitze (William Albert), 1096, 1672–73, 5973
Niver (Charles), 11937
Noble (Rose), 9326
Noël-Hume (I.), 7761
Nolan (Patrick), 9248
Nordenfalk (Carl), 11938, 11969
Nordman (Carl Axel), 8734, 8905, 11713
Norgate (Kate), 1401
Norman (George Warde), 955
Norris (Edwin), 6946
North (Jeffery J.), 9327
North (Thomas), 8320
Northbourne (Walter Charles (James)), baron, 4264
Nuallain (Tomas Ua), 203
Nuck (R.), 7701
Nuernberger (August Josef), 5274–76, 5338–39
Nugent (William), 789
Nunnaminster, Book of, 5790
Nutt (Alfred), 4895, 6232, 8839
Nyhan (Daniel), 11919

Oakeley (Frederick), 3961
Oakeshott (R. E.), 8735

Oakeshott (Walter Fraser), 11863
Oakley (Thomas Pollock), 5591–94, 5616–19
Ó Briain (Felim), 5145–46
Ó Bríain (Micheál), 639, 4481–83, 6819
O'Brien (Hon. Donough), 1620
O'Brien (Edward), 4649, 4700
O'Brien (Henry), 10537
O'Brien (M. A.), 1162, 4516
O'Brien (Sylvester), 4484
Obser (Karl), 4017
Ó Buachalla (Liam), 2161–62, 2564
O'Carroll (James), 5455, 5595
O'Cavanagh (John Eugene), 7702
O'Ceallaigh (Seán), 790, 4747
Ó Cléirigh (Michéal), 193
O'Clery (Michael), 5218
O'Connell (Daniel J. K.), 3571
O'Connell (Jerome), 10477
O'Connell (Philip), 9778
O'Connor (F. J.), 7404a
O'Connor (Michael), 7986
O'Crowley (James), 9641
O'Curry (Eugene), 204, 2685, 5855
O'Daly (B.), 4844
O'Daly (John), 9554
Odegaard (Charles E.), 2499
O'Dell (Andrew C.), 5901
O'Doherty (John F.), 4660, 5489
O'Doherty (John K.), 2163, 3862
O'Donnell (M. J.), 5620
O'Donnell (Manus), earl of Tyrconnell, 4896
O'Donoghue (Denis), 5108, 6270
O'Donovan (John), 378, 7143
O'Dowd (Peadar), 6820
O'Driscoll (Desmond), 11105
Ó Duígeannáin (Micheál), 2164, 3502
Oess (Guido), 5699a, 5717
O'Farrelly (J. J.), 205
Offler (H. S.), 4057
Ó Fiaich (Tomás), 2165
Ó Foghludha (Risteárd), 4534
O'Foley (Richard), 6821
Ogden (William Sharp), 9234
Ogilvie (George), 3421
Ogilvy (Jack David Angus), 4203, 6983–84
O'Gorman (J. J.), 5490
O'Gorman (Thomas), 1621
O'Grady (John Sheil), 2166
O'Grady (Standish Hayes), 4485
O'Hanlon (John), 3254, 4486, 4845
O'Hanluain (Enri), 9694–96, 9704
O'Hare (Charles M.), 3572, 3962
Ó h Éaluighthe (D.), 4846

Oheix (André), 5194–96
Ohlhaver (H.), 851b
O'Kearney (Nicholas), 4897
Ohrt (Ferdinand), 7534a
O'Keeffe (C. M.), 4748
O'Keeffe (J. G.), 5621
O'Kelleher (Andrew), 4892, 4896
O'Kelly (Michael J.), 10135
O'Laverty (James), 3503
Olden (Thomas), 3908, 4487, 4650, 4945, 5147, 5914, 6271, 11714, 11778
O'Leary (E.), 6140
Olerenshaw (J. R.), 1762
Oliver (Bruce W.), 2743
Oliver (George), 1970a, 7976
Oliver (J. R.), 3422
Oliver (Walter), 6319
O Lochlainn (Colm), 6198
O'Longan (Joseph), 7272
O'Looney (Brian), 7272
Olrik (Axel), 738, 1373
Olrik (Jørgen), 1389
Olsen (Magnus), 4847, 9503, 9819, 9848
Olszewska (E. S.), 2382
O'Mahony (John), 2167
O'Mahony (Michael), 4946
O'Mahony (T.), 2547
O'Mahony (T. J.), 5856
Oman (Charles Chichele), 11625
Oman (Sir Charles William Chadwick), 673, 1204, 1784, 1971, 2297–98, 3960, 5939, 7825, 8861, 8936
Omurethi, 1024, 2168
O'Neil (B. H. St. J.), 956, 8695, 11539
O'Neill (Henry), 10103, 11071
O Neill (Joseph), 5621a
O Neill (Seamus), 6233
O'Nolan (T. P.), 7596
O'Oubhthaigh (Seosam), 6822
Opet (Otto), 2500–01
Opie (Otho B.), 11053
Oppert (Gustav), 448
O'Rahilly (Cecile), 791, 6823
O'Rahilly (Thomas Francis), 792, 793, 1622, 4701, 5739
Orchard (Bernard), 4265
O'Regan (Patrick J.), 4651
O'Reilly (Edward), 2565
O'Reilly (Joseph P.), 10497–98
O'Reilly (Maureen Margaret), 8122, 8135
O'Reilly (Patrick), 3784
O'Reilly (Patrick J.), 2316, 4947, 11154
Orger (J.), 3637
Ó Ríordáin (Seán Pádraig), 7020, 7987–89, 10609, 11715

O'Riordan (J. B.), 5491, 6272
O'Riordan (Michael), 4749
Orkneyinga Saga, 227, 228
Ormerod (George), 1878, 5881, 7807
Ormonde (James Butler), 6th marquis, 4771
Ormonde (L.), 739
Orpen (Goddard Henry), 3504, 6141, 7990–94, 11155
Orwin (Charles Stewart and Christabel Susan), 2713
O'Shaughnessy (D. F.), 4848
Osthoff (H.), 7429
O'Sullivan (James), 8321
O'Sullivan (William), 9249
Oswald, St., king of Northumbria, 4362–65
Oswald (Adrian), 8598, 8650, 11540
Oswald (H. R.), 11189
O'Toole (Edward), 9779, 11716
Ott (J. Heinrich), 4145
Otté (E. C.), 1503
Ottino (Giuseppe), 7164
Otway-Ruthven (Jocelyn) 2841
Oulton (John Ernest Leonard), 3573, 4552
Ouvry (Frederic), 8322–23, 9011
Owen (Aneurin), 2605, 10020
Owen (Edward), 9907
Owen (Elias), 7808
Owen (Leonard Victor Davies), 1879–80
Owen (Robert), 2253, 6947
Owen (Thomas Morgan), 674, 1248, 1323–24, 1623–24, 5915

P (C. D.), 9328
P. (C. R.), 2074
P. (H.), 10654
P. (W. R.), 6948
Paasche (Fredrik), 69
Pace (S.), 4366
Packe (Alfred E.), 9235
Padelford (Fredrick Morgan), 7336
Paden (W. D.), 7640
Paetow (Louis John), 8
Pafford (John Henry Pyle), 379
Page (Elwin Lawrence), 3113
Page (Frances Mary), 3647
Page (John T.), 4332
Page (Samuel), 8696
Page (W. M.), 3831
Page (William), 1805, 1972, 2787–88, 3720, 3832, 5882–83
Paget ( ), Lady, 8510
Painter (Sidney), 7879

Palaeographical Society, 7289

Palgrave (*Sir* Francis), 675, 676, 2383, 4423

Palmer (Alfred Neobard), 539, 2254, 3785, 5916, 7809

Palmer (Charles Ferrers), 1881

Palmer (Hurly Pring), 2075

Palmer (J. Foster), 8840

Palmer (J. Linton), 9393

Palmer (William Mortlock), 7780, 8147a

Pancoast (Henry S.), 2299

Panum (Hortense), 7337

Pape (T.), 10731

Papetti (M.), 7086

Parez (C. H.), 10961

Parish (William Douglas), 2961

Parker (Charles Arundel), 1325, 10804–07

Parker (F. H. M.), 2502

Parker (James), 1179–80, 1882–84, 2076, 3464, 3662, 8401, 10448

Parker (John Henry), 10161–63, 10449

Parkin (Charles), 1567

Parkins (W. Trevor), 7810

Parlin (Henry), 4849–50, 4948–49

Parry (Henry), 243

Parry (John Jay), 133, 1674, 7620

Parry-Williams (T. H.), 2606

Parsons (A. E.), 1675

Parsons (Frederick Gymer), 6589, 8777–81, 8783, 8841

Parsons (H. Alexander), 8937, 9073–74, 9153–54, 9165–68, 9186, 9204–06, 9236, 9250–51, 9329–30

Parsons (Mary Prescott), 271, 272

Partington (S. W.), 1885

Partridge (Charles), 740

Passmore (A. D.), 7826, 8402, 9331, 11007, 11541–42

Paterson (Donald Rose), 2255–56, 6409, 6949–50

Paterson (John Wilson), 8034

Paterson (T. G. F.), 11130, 11156, 11717

Paton (Lucy Allen), 130

Patrick, *St.*, 4553–63, 4594

Patrick (George), 1886

Patterson (James), 4266, 10341a, 10342

Patterson (William Hugh), 4851, 9780, 11664, 11718

Paues (Anna Carolina), 9394

Pauli (Reinhold), 1181, 1249, 1503

Pavey (A. K.), 1887

Payn (Howard), 2300

Payne (F. G.), 2714

Payne (George), 7762, 8181–87, 8697 11543–45

Payne (Joseph Frank), 7471

Peacock (John), 8906, 9125

Peake (Harold John Edward), 380, 3332, 5884, 6199, 7763, 7843, 8403

Pearce (Ernest Harold), *bp. of Worcester*, 3255, 4058

Pearce (J. W.), 4176

Pearman (M. T.), 1888

Pearson (Charles Henry), 677

Pearson (Frederick Richard), 1972a

Pearson (Howard S.), 3529

Pearson (Karl), 7472

Pearson (William C.), 2955

Pease (Howard), 1973

Peate (Iorwerth Cyfeiliog), 2646

Peckham (W. D.), 381, 382, 2964

Pedersen (Holger), 9395–96

Pedler (E. H.), 3833

Peebles (Rose Jeffries), 7373

Peers (*Sir* Charles Reed), 3721, 3891, 10164, 10228–29, 10343, 10353, 10450, 10751, 10919–20, 11970

Pegge (Samuel), 383, 540, 2647, 3239, 3648, 7338, 7535, 10376, 11546, 11600, 11626

Peile (James Hamilton Francis), 4031

Pell (O. C.), 541, 2789, 3073, 3114–16

Pellizzari (A.), 5428

Pender (Séamus), 515, 516, 1025, 3423

Pennington (Edgar Legare), 3530

Pennock (B.), 3324

Penny (James A.), 10708

Pentland (George Henry), 11097

Perceval (Charles Spencer), 384

Perels (Ernst), 5277

Peri Didaxeon, 7418

Perkins (J. B. Ward), 11455

Perret (A.), 5158

Perry (Francis A.), 1715

Perry (George Gresley), 3333

Perry (Marten), 9332

Person (Erik), 9207

Peschel (O. F.), 6273

Pesci (Benedetto), 6215

Petau (Denis), 5596

Peter (Thurstan), 7233

Petersen (Jan), 9208

Petersen (Th.), 11810

Petit (J. L.), 10321

Petit-Dutaillis (Charles), 1374, 2279

Petley (Charles Carter), 11331

Petrie (George), 2169, 7764, 8035–36, 9601, 9867, 9888, 10538, 11719, 11762–63, 11811

Petrie (*Sir* William Matthew Flinders), 957, 958, 8842

Pettigrew (Thomas Joseph), 8420, 9555, 9849, 10962

Pettito (Remo Renato), 5413

Peyron (Amedeus), 7165–66

Pfaendler (Wilhelm), 2648

Pfahler (Georg), 5340

Pfeiffer (Franz), 4367

Pfeilstuecker (Suse), 10058

Pfister (Kurt), 11864–65

Pfleger (Luzian), 4517, 5250, 7051

Pflugk-Harttung (Julius von), 3755, 4564, 5148

Phear (*Sir* John Budd), 1716, 3074, 3117, 3465

Phelps (Joseph James), 10655, 10895

Philip (Alexander John), 1785–87

Philippen (L. J. M.), 4852

Philippson (Ernst Alfred), 3505

Phillimore (Egerton), 244, 517, 7473

Phillimore (William P.), 6524

Phillipps (*Sir* Thomas) *bart.*, 385, 386, 833, 2790, 6320

Phillips (Charles William), 1889, 7765, 7781, 8105–08, 8148

Phillips (D. W.), 7793

Phillips (David Rhys), 7144

Phillips (Edwin Noel Masson), 11027–28

Phillips (G.), 6546, 8281

Phillips (Georg), 2384

Phillips (James), 5063

Phillips (Maberly), 10921–22

Phillips (Walter Alison), 3424

Phillips (William), 1890, 7943

Phillpotts (*Dame* Bertha Surtees), 2649, 3334

Philpot (W. B.), 4059

Phipps (C. B.), 10478

Phythian (John Ernest), 10059

Picken (W. M. N.), 2853, 6031

Pickering (A. J.), 8599

Pickersgill (T.), 9333–34

Pictet (Adolphe), 6463, 6824

Picton (Harold), 10060, 11920

Picton (J.), 8843

Picton (*Sir* James Allanson), 566, 959, 1891, 1974, 2650, 6321, 6410, 6479, 6951, 8844, 10165

Pierce (T. Jones), 542

Piercy (William Coleman), 4950

Pierquin (Hubert), 273, 678, 2280, 3335, 6985

Piggot (John), *jun.*, 741, 9379

Piggott (C. M.), 7844

Piggott (Stuart), 134, 3506, 7446, 7750, 8061, 10984

Pike (Luke Owen), 852, 2385

Pinkerton (John), 4877

Piper (Ferdinand), 4146

Pirenne (Henri), 7116

Pite (Beresford), 10061

Pitman (James Hall), 7371, 7671

Pitt-Rivers. *See* Fox *afterwards* Pitt-Rivers (A. H. L.)

Plaine (Franciscus Beda), 4204, 5079, 5197, 5201, 5212

Planché (James Robinson), 1474, 1504, 1568–69, 3004

Plant (Margery I.), 8043

Plantagenet-Harrison (George Henry de Strabolgie Neville), 2912

Platts (C.), 5109

Plenderleath (William Charles), 1182

Plettke (Alfred), 853, 854

Plucknett (Theodore Frank Thomas), 2386, 3118

Plummer (Alfred), 3336

Plummer (Charles), 1026, 1250, 2566, 4155, 4488–91, 4853–55, 5110, 5740, 5857, 6246, 6274, 7310, 7536, 9556

Plummer (Selby Wetherell), 4320

Pocock (W. W.), 3722

Pogatscher (Alois), 6411

Pokorny (Julius), 3756, 6825–26

Pollard (C. J. K.), 1251

Pollard (H. P.), 6108, 10322

Pollexfen (John Hutton), 9155, 11627

Pollitt (William), 1763–64, 8149–51, 11547

Pollock (*Sir* Frederick) *bart.*, 1204, 2351, 2387–89, 2502a, 2791, 2865, 3221

Polson (A.), 8062

Poncelet (Albert), 5159, 5542–44

Pontifex (Dunstan), 3971

Ponting (C. E.), 10451–52

Ponting (William), 8298–99

Poole (E. H. Lane), 6109

Poole (George Ayliffe), 3677, 10285

Poole (Herbert), 10405

Poole (Reginald Lane), 274, 449–52, 1326, 3574, 4018, 6110, 7234, 9377

Pooler (Lavis Arthur Hill Trevor), 4685

Pope (Thomas S.), 10255

Pope (William), 387, 11029

Porter (Arthur Kingsley), 11072–74, 11157

Porter (J. L.), 9126

Porter (Jerome), 1395

Porter (William), 1327, 6382

Porthan (Henricus Gabriel), **6176**
Poschmann (Bernhard), **5597**
Postan (Michael), **3144**
Poste (Beale), **245, 246, 960, 961, 1975,
    2077**
Potter (Simeon), **1252, 4177, 4229, 5666**
Potthast (August), **9**
Potts (Robert Ullock), **3892, 4060, 8982,
    9521, 10229a–31, 10639**
Poulson (George), **1975a**
Pounds (Norman John Greville), **5952a**
Povey (Kenneth), **4424**
Powel (Thomas), **229**
Powell (Frederick York), **1253, 1570,
    2651–52, 2792**
Powell (J. U.), **2078**
Powell (John Enoch), **2595**
Powell (W. F.), **10376a**
Power (C. J.), **2975**
Power (Patrick), **3425, 3863, 4492, 4856,
    5755, 6200, 6827, 8539, 8600, 8651,
    9642, 9738–41, 9781, 10499, 10539,
    11158–59**
Powicke (*Sir* Frederick Maurice), **453**
Pownall (Assheton), **8983–85, 9012–13,
    9335–36, 11548**
Pownall (T.), **3649**
Pra (Mario dal), **7107**
Praeger (R. Lloyd), **9692**
Pratt (Fletcher), **2301**
Prehn (August), **7703**
Preisandanz (Karl), **7184**
Preisinger (Werner), **5341**
Prendergast (J. P.), **715**
Prentout (Charles), **1475**
Prentout (Henri), **1505**
Preston (Arthur E.), **3621**
Pretyman (J. R.), **2281**
Previté-Orton (Charles William), **679**
Prevost (*Sir* George), **5058**
Price (Frederick George Hilton), **8652,
    8736**
Price (Lewis), **11366**
Price (Liam), **3786, 6828–29, 11160**
Prideaux (E. K.), **10453**
Prideaux (W. F.), **2317, 6412**
Priebsch (Robert Charles), **5809, 5858,
    7235, 7537**
Prigg (Henry), **8152–53**
Prim (Christopher Humphrey), **9714**
Prim (John G. A.), **9715**
Pring (Daniel James), **3531**
Pring (James Hurly), **2744, 6383**
Prins (A. A.), **4147**
Prior (C. E.), **1892**

Prior (Richard Chandler Alexander),
    7395
Prior (W. H.), **543**
Pritchett (J. P.), **10963**
Probert (William), **2607**
Probst (Ferdinand), **5756**
Pryce (John), **3426**
Pryce (T. Davies), **1476, 7880–81**
Ψ **1571, 4951**
Public Record Office, **126, 275**
Puckle (John), **10232**
Pugh (R. B.), **2079, 3281**
Pughe (John M.), **7416**
Pughe (William Owen), **2596**
Puntschart (Paul), **2503**
Purlitz (Friedrich), **2340**
Purser (Olive), **11161**
Purton (W. J.), **3771**
Puttock (James), **8907**

Q. (J. C.), **3787**
Quaile (Edward), **11866**
Quaritch (Bernard), **11867**
Quarry (J.), **9614**
Quennell (Marjorie *and* Charles Henry
    Bourne), **2653**
Quick (Richard), **11764**
Quiggin (Edmund Crosby), **6464, 7355**
Quigley (E. J.), **5757, 7145**
Quine (John), **4652, 6845, 9127, 11223,
    11665**
Quinne (James), **9721**

R. (E. G.), **6480**
R. (E. S. G.), **9187**
R. (W.), *LL.D.*, **3972**
R. (Y. S.), **6547–48**
Raby (F. J. E.), **4267**
Radcliffe (P. Delme), **388**
Radford (A. J. V.), **8938**
Radford (Courtenay Arthur Ralegh),
    **1716a, 2230–31, 3721, 3788–89,
    4987, 8653, 9449, 9585, 9984, 10021,
    10062, 10104, 10423, 10454, 10510–
    12, 10522, 10747, 11258, 11295–96,
    11358, 11392, 11413**
Radford (E.), **4988**
Radford (*Mrs.* G. H.), **1717, 3685**
Radford (W. Locke), **1135, 2080, 6053**
Radnor (Jacob Pleydell-Bouverie), *6th
    earl*, **3242**
Rafn (Charles Christian), **1396, 9450**
Raftery (Joseph), **10099**
Ragg (Frederick William), **389–92, 2828,
    2833, 2835, 2892, 2900**

Raglan (Fitzroy Raglan Somerset), *4th baron*, **962**

Rahn (Johann Rudolf), **11908**

Raine (Angelo), **6986**

Raine (James), **1975b, 4045, 4061, 4321, 8354, 10964**

Ralston (William Ralston Sheddon), **9522**

Ramackers (Johannes), **7087**

Ramsey (*Sir* James Henry), *bart.*, **680**

Ramsay (John), **9867**

Ramsay (Robert Lee), **5703, 5705, 5718–19**

Ramsden (Josslyn Vere), **7977**

Rand (Edward Kennard), **7087a, 7187a**

Randolph (Mary Claire), **7538**

Raper (W. A.), **1418, 9188**

Raphael (Oscar), **8737**

Rashleigh (Jonathan), **8908, 9075**

Rashleigh (Philip), **8909**

Rask (Rasmus Christian Nielsen), **6147, 6177**

Rasmussen ( ), *headmaster at Odense*, **4117**

Rasmusson (N. L.), **9209**

Rason (Ernest), **1375**

Ratti (Achile Ambrogio Damiano) [Pius XI], **7167–68**

Ratton (M. H.), **1655**

Rauschen (Gerhard), **3337**

Raven (John James), **10197**

Ravenscroft (William), **8404–05**

Rawlence (E. A.), **6054–55**

Rawnsley (Hardwicke Drummond), **4268**

Rawson (J.), **3893**

Ray (John E.), **2012–13**

Read (*Sir* Charles Hercules), **8154, 8324, 8379, 8601, 8738–40, 11456–57, 11720**

Reade (George H.), **3790, 9128, 11162**

Reade (Hubert), **6525**

Reader (William), **2973**

Reaney (Percy Hide), **594, 595, 1765, 6032, 6481–89**

Reany (William), **4062**

Réau (Louis), **11868**

Redin (Mats), **596**

Redlich (P. Virgil), **4269**

Redmond (Gabriel), **9742**

Redstone (Vincent Burrough), **1766**

Reed (Harbottle), **11030**

Reed (Trelawney Dayrell), **963–65**

Rees (Alloyn D.), **4450**

Rees (J. Rogers), **7597**

Rees (Rice), **5050**

Rees (William), **2257–58, 5917**

Rees (William Jenkins), **5051**

Reeves (W. P.), **7396**

Reeves (William), *bp. of Down*, **206, 3427–28, 3757–58, 3909, 4857–59, 4952, 5018, 5251–52, 5622, 7277–78, 7311, 7539, 9722, 9782, 11163, 11765–67**

Reeves (William Peters), **9466**

Reichel (Oswald Joseph), **393, 1254, 1376, 1718, 2745, 2793, 2866–67, 3177–83, 3225, 3282, 3466–69, 3874, 6033–34, 6774, 6785–87**

Reid (Herbert J.), **2794**

Reid (R. C.), **7855, 8011–12, 11290**

Reid (R. W.), **8668**

Reid (Rachel Robertson), **3222**

Reinerding (Franz Heinrich), **5342**

Reinhard (J. R.), **2504–05**

Rennell of Rodd (Francis James Rennell Rodd), *2nd baron*, **2887, 2887a**

Renshaw (T. Lloyd), **2976**

Repp (Thorlief Gudmundson), **1396, 9467**

Rethwisch (Ernst), **9697**

Reum (A.), **5650**

Reynolds (D.), **4860**

Reynolds (J. J.), **2081**

Reynolds (Llywarch), **168**

Rhamm (Karl), **2654**

Rhyggyfarch, **5064–65**

Rhys (Ernest), **5065**

Rhys (*Sir* John), **236, 794–96, 1183, 4451, 7621, 8845–46, 9557, 9586–87, 9602–03, 9615, 9643, 9657, 9682–84, 9705, 9725–27, 9743–44, 9783–89, 9820–21, 9830–31, 9889, 9908–13, 9940, 9954, 9985–93, 9997, 10022–28**

Ribton-Turner (Charles James), **2655**

Ricci (Aldo), **6987**

Rice (David Talbot), **10063–64, 10752**

Rice (Richard Justice), **9685**

Rice (Robert Garraway), **8380, 8698**

Richard (Arthur J.), **8075, 9941, 10610**

Richards (Arthur), **9942**

Richards (Melville), **2595a**

Richards (Robert), **3429**

Richardson (Adam B.), **9129**

Richardson (H. G.), **2715**

Richardson (Henry), **10858**

Richardson (James Smith), **8037**

Richardson (L. J. D.), **9558**

Richardson (Ralph), **6907**

Richardson (William H.), **2082**

Richmond (Ian Archibald), **4322**

Richomme (Florent), **1506, 4953**

Richter (Gregor), **5343, 5388**
Rickman (Thomas), **10166**
Rickword (George), **2656, 3093**
Ridgeway (*Sir* William), **7782**
Riemann (Erhard), **854a**
Rietschel (Siegfried), **3184**
Riezler (S.), **5405**
Rigby (T.), **10377**
Riguet ( ), *abbé*, **4751**
Riley (Henry Thomas), **70, 394**
Riley (Marjorie), **8264**
Rimington (Joseph Cameron), **1255**
Ringbom (Lars-Ivar), **11971**
Risk (J. Erskine), **3834**
Ritchie (Alexander *and* Euphemia), **4954**
Ritchie (James), **11332**
Ritter (Otto), **2426, 6322, 6590, 6676, 7653**
Rivière (Jean), **5492**
Rivington (L.), **4020**
Rivoira (Giovanni Teresio), **10105, 10167**
Rix (Michael M.), **10693**
Roach (Thomas), **6591**
Robbins (Michael), **1893**
Robert, *prior of Shrewsbury*, **5111**
Robert (Benjamin), **4627**
Roberts (Askew), **1136**
Roberts (Edward), **10286**
Roberts (Harold Vernon Molesworth), **10168, 10406**
Roberts (R.), **3723**
Roberts (Richard G.), **6696**
Roberts (Thomas), **10029**
Roberts (William John), **10896**
Robertshaw (Wilfrid), **1976**
Robertson (Agnes Jane), **276, 2427**
Robertson (Eben William), **22, 797**
Robertson (G. Philip), **6908, 9840–41**
Robertson (J. Drummond), **9337**
Robertson (James S.), **8540**
Robertson (William Allan), **102**
Robertson (William Archibald Scott), **4063, 4425**
Robinson (C. J.), **2888**
Robinson (*Sir* Charles), **11549**
Robinson (Charles Henry), **5148a**
Robinson (Fred Norris), **2567**
Robinson (George E.), **9927, 9943, 9994, 11393**
Robinson (George Washington), **5278, 5285**
Robinson (John L.), **4518, 10611**

Robinson (Joseph Armitage), *dean of Wells*, **71, 103, 277, 395, 396, 1097–98, 2053, 2083–84, 2318, 3602, 3638, 3973–76, 4064–66, 5112–15, 6347, 10274, 10455**
Robinson (Stanford Frederick Hudson), **5770, 7236, 11939**
Robinson (T.), **8847**
Robson (Isabel Suart), **11550**
Robson (John), **397, 966, 6035, 10378**
Roche (Thomas), **5429**
Rock (Daniel), **3558, 5771**
Rodger (John W.), **11380**
Rodwell (G. E. C.), **4426**
Roe (Helen M.), **10106, 11075**
Roeder (Fritz), **2657, 5701, 6988–89, 7766**
Roesler (Margarete), **6990**
Roessler (Charles), **798**
Roger (James C.), **9890**
Roger (Maurice), **6991**
Rogers (Inkerman), **1256**
Rogers (J.), **3374**
Rogers (John Jope), **8910, 11551**
Rohde (Eleanour Sinclair), **7474**
Rolleston (George), **967, 8083, 8406–07, 8782**
Rolleston (Thomas William), **10500**
Romans (Thomas), **8699, 10344–45, 10910**
Romer (H. G.), **968**
Ronan (Myles V.), **3864, 9790, 10479, 11164**
Roosval (Johnny), **10612**
Roscoe (Thomas), **1507**
Rose (James Dudfield), **10345a, 10875**
Rosenau (Helen), **11921**
Rose-Troup (Frances), **277, 398–403, 1137, 1719–20, 2352, 3119, 3185, 3724, 4035, 4067, 4378, 5116–17, 5918, 6111, 6465, 6780, 6783**
Rositzke (Harry August), **79, 82**
Ross (Alan Strode Campbell), **169, 3507, 5695, 6178, 9457a, 9468, 9480, 9504**
Ross (Alexander), **11552**
Ross (J. Lockhart), **834**
Ross (Marvin Chauncey), **7146**
Ross (Thomas), **8063, 10508, 11333**
Ross (W. J. Calder), **4861**
Rossetti (Benedetto), **5465**
Roth (Bernard), **9252**
Rotheram (Edward Crofton), **9130**

Round (John Horace), **404, 405, 969, 970, 1377, 1419–23, 1572–74, 1767–68, 1772, 2341–42, 2716, 2744, 2746–47, 2795–98, 2829, 2834, 2836, 2874–75, 2884, 2889, 2893, 2924, 2945, 2960, 2965–67, 2977, 2986, 3066, 3075–76, 3120–23, 3186, 3223, 3256, 3283, 3470, 4050, 4068, 6384, 6490, 7882, 7912–14, 7944**
Roussel (Aage), **10513**
Roussel (J.), **5456**
Routh (Theodore E.), **10672, 10694–95**
Routledge (Charles Francis), **3532, 3894, 10233**
Rowe (George), **10379–90, 10965**
Rowe (J. Brooking), **1721**
Rowe (Joseph Hambley), **406, 2799, 2989, 3187, 3224, 4069, 4439, 5118, 5974, 6036–38, 6636**
Rowles (Henry J.), **1285**
Rowley (F. R.), **11031**
Royal Society of Antiquaries of Ireland, **2170**
Rudder (Samuel), **2879**
Rudkin (Ernest Horace), **1424**
Rudkin (*Mrs.* E. H.), **8602**
Rundell (T. W.), **407**
Rundle (S.), **4118**
' Rupicastrensis ', **4270**
Rushe (James Patrick), **3759**
Rushforth (G. Mc N.), **4379, 5119**
Rushton (Gerald Wynne), **5545**
Russell (   ), *Miss*, **971, 1977, 2232, 6909, 7856, 9891**
Russell (Constance), *Lady*, **2085**
Russell (Edward B.), **1625**
Russell (H.), **4878**
Russell (Josiah Cox), **2800, 3094–95**
Russell (Phillips), **1508**
Rutland (James), **8325**
Rutter (J. A.), **2854, 3225–26, 7883–84**
Rutton (William Loftie), **3284**
Ryan (Alice Mary), **3603**
Ryan (John), **799, 1027, 1328, 1626, 2171, 2568, 3430, 3760–61, 3791, 4493, 4565, 4702, 7452, 5253, 7031, 7987**
Rybot (N. V. L.), **1575**
Rydberg (Viktor), **10794**
Ryder (Thomas Arthur), **1894**
Rye (Henry A.), **4427**
Rye (Walter), **1769, 4070, 6491**
Ryland (J. W.), **8296**
Rylands (Thomas Glazebrook), **1978**
Rypins (Stanley I.), **7237**

S., **9131**
S. (C.), **5344, 6549**
S. (R.), **8939, 9237**
Sabbadini (Remigio), **7169**
St. Augustine's abbey, Ramsgate, *Monks of*, **4090**
St. Croix (William de), **8603**
St. Gallen, **11909**
Saint John (James Augustus), **681**
Sainte Marie (   ), *marquis*, **2781**
Salin (Bernhard), **11972**
Salin (Éduard), **1656**
Salis (J. F. W. de), **8940**
Salisbury (F. S.), **8941**
Salmon (E. F.), **6697**
Salmon (John), **3431–32, 10540**
Salter (Herbert Edward), **1895**
Saltmarshe (Philip), **1979–80, 3124**
Salvin (A.), **10198**
Salzman(n) (Louis Francis), **2014, 2842, 2968, 3077–78, 3699, 8375, 10169**
Sanctain, *St.*, **5859**
Sanders (William Basevi), **2816, 2852, 2984**
Sanderson (Joseph), **4628**
Sands (Christopher Nicholson Johnston), *Lord*, **4989**
Sandys (Charles), **3257**
Sanford (Eva Matthews), **7088**
Sansbury (Arthur R.), **8783**
Sansom (J.), **3338**
Sante (Georg Wilhelm), **5345**
Sarabia (José M.), **4271**
Sarfatti (Mario), **1657**
Sargant (W. L.), **972, 1896–97**
Sauer (Joseph), **5254**
Saunders (G. W.), **10456**
Saunders (George), **1806**
Saunders (O. Elfrida), **10065, 11869**
Sauvage (Eugène Paul Marie), **4000–01, 7147**
Savage (Ernest B.), **9822, 9826**
Savage (Henry Edwin), **973, 1138, 3725, 4071, 5696, 5940, 7238, 10170, 10346**
Savage (*Sir* William), **2748**
Sawyer (Frederick Ernest), **2015, 2801, 2969–70, 4019, 6429**
Sawyer (Frederick W.), **7569**
Sawyer (John), **8381–82**
Saxby (Jessie Margaret Edmonston), *Mrs. Henry Linckmyer Saxby*, **8038**
Saxl (Fritz), **10066, 10265, 10795**
Saxton (Austin J.), **3963**
Sayce (Archibald Henry), **10030**
Sayer-Milward (W. C.), **10457**

Sayers (Edward), **6039**
Sayles (George Osborne), **682**
Scanlon (J. F.), **5415**
Scarth (Harry Mengden), **7827–28, 8654, 10136, 11009**
Schaaffs (G.), **9995**
Schannat (Johann Friedrich), **5389–90**
Schapiro (Meyer), **10796, 11870**
Schardt (Alois Jakob), **11871**
Schaumann (Adolf Friedrich Heinrich), **855**
Schell (Paulus), **4368**
Schenkl (H.), **4091**
Scherer (Karl), **5343**
Scherer (Rudolf), *Ritter von*, **5298**
Schererz (C.), **6492**
Scherrer (Gustav), **7178–79**
Schetelig (Haakon). *See* Shetelig
Schiaparelli (Luigi), **7052, 7312**
Schiavo (Alessandro), **4369**
Schieffer (Theodor), **5255, 5345a**
Schipper (Jacob), **4178**
Schirmer (Gustav), **6275**
Schive (C. J.), **8942**
Schlauch (Margaret), **7032**
Schleich (G.), **7667**
Schlutter (Otto Bernhard), **2506, 3932, 7380–81, 7397–98, 7430–34, 7704**
Schmerbauch (Moritz), **5346**
Schmid (Joseph), **3575–76**
Schmid (Reinhold), **2438, 2507**
Schmid (Toni), **4519**
Schmidlin (J.), **5493**
Schmidt (K. Dietrich), **5347**
Schmidt (Ludwid), **885a, 4179**
Schmitz (Hermann Joseph), **5598**
Schmitz (Philibert), **3604**
Schneider (Arthur Carl August), **7108**
Schneider (Joseph), **5391**
Schnepper (Heinrich), **2302**
Schnittger (Bror), **9100**
Schnuerer (Gustav), **5348**
Schoell (Carl Wilhelm), **3433**
Schoenbach (A. F.), **4205**
Schoenfelder (   ), *Oberlehrer in Zittau*, **7089**
Schoepperle (Gertrude), **4896**
Scholle (J.), **5256**
Schove (Derek Justin), **7404b–7405**
Schram (O. K.), **6385, 6493–95**
Schramm (Percy Ernst), **2319–21**
Schreiber (Georg), **5257**
Schreiber (Heinrich), **4272–73**
Schreiner (Katharina), **974**
Schroeder (Carl), **6247**

Schroeder (Edward), **479, 975, 7540**
Schroeer (Arnold), **3605**
Schubel (Friedrich), **5120**
Schubert (Hans von), **3339**
Schuecking (Levin L.), **2343**
Schuette (Gudmund), **856, 976, 977, 1184, 3508, 8848**
Schultze (Walther), **5149**
Schulze (Alfred), **6276**
Schulze (M.), **3509**
Schumacher (Karl Heinz), **7356**
Schwabe (H. O.), **8943**
Schwartz (E.), **3577**
Schwarz (Ignaz), **5349**
Schwerin (Claudius) *Freiherr von*, **2508, 3188**
Scott (A. Boyd), **4653**
Scott (Archibald Black), **835, 3434–37, 4955, 4990–92, 5019–24, 5150, 5494, 5570, 8013, 8849**
Scott (Forrest S.), **1597–98**
Scott (George Digby), **11165**
Scott (George Gilbert), **10234, 10323**
Scott (*Sir* Lindsay), **8024**
Scott (Mary Monica Constable Maxwell), *Hon. Mrs. Joseph Constable-Maxwell-Scott*, **1257**
Scott (W. H.), **9132**
Scott-Gatty (A. S.), **1099**
Scott-O'Connell (D. H.), **11666**
Scouler (John), **8850**
Scrope (G. Poulett), **1258**
Scrutton (Thomas Edward), **2509, 3285**
Scudder (Vida D.), **4157**
Seaby (Allen W.), **10985**
Seaby (Peter John), **8861a**
Seaby (W. A.), **8741**
Sealy (H. N.), **6413**
Searle (William George), **480, 597, 3650**
Seaver (Esther Isabel), **10613**
Sedgefield (Walter John), **978, 1287, 1576, 4162, 6414, 6677**
Seebass (Otto), **5430–40, 7170**
Seebohm (Frederic), **2390, 2658, 2686–87, 2717, 3285–87**
Seebohm (Mabel Elizabeth), *Mrs. Christie*, **2718**
Seeley (*Sir* John Robert), **3533**
Seelmann (W.), **857**
Segger (Arthur Thomas), **10286a**
Seiters (John Ch. A.), **5350**
Selby (John S. Donaldson), **9076**
Sellar (A. M.), **4158**
Selmer (Carl), **6277–79, 9434**
Semple (William), **7857**

Senior (Elizabeth), 11803
Senior (W.), 2391–92
Sephton (John), 6678–79
Sepp (Bernhard), 5392
Serjeantson (Mary Sidney), 7344, 7570
Serjeantson (Robert Meyricke), 4428
Serland (F. S.), 5351
Serrure (Raymund), 8858
Seton (George), 10797
Seul (W.), 7109
Sewell (Augustus Bell), 1981
Sexton (Eric Hyde Lord), 10038, 11076
Sexton (John E.), 4654
Seydl (Ernst), 7090
Seyler (Clarence A.), 6142, 6415
Seymour (St. John Drelincourt), 3792, 5860, 7598–7601, 7654–57
Shahan (Thomas Joseph), 4753, 5457
Sharp (Arthur D.), 4429
Sharp (Samuel), 1898, 9338–39
Sharpe (*Sir* Montagu), 1899, 1900, 2915–16, 3039, 3288
Shaw (F.), 3002
Shaw (Henry), 11872–73
Shaw (James), 6910
Shaw (Samuel), 8986
Shaw (Thomas J.), 4898
Shaw (W. Frank), 6501
Shearman (John Francis), 800, 2172, 2233, 4452, 4686, 5198, 9698–9701
Sheehy (Stephen), 3835
Sheldon (Gilbert), 3340
Shenstone (J. C.), 3040
Shepherd (E. J.), 9340
Shepherd (Geoffrey), 5831
Sheppard (H. E.), 2259
Sheppard (Lewis), 10324, 10327
Sheppard (Thomas), 1982, 5953, 7767–68, 8326, 8355–65, 8513, 8604–05, 8700, 10966–67, 11609–10, 11628
Sherlock (William), 2173, 4520
Sherwin (Gerald Ambrose), 2086
Sherwood (George F. Tudor), 6720
Shetelig (Haakon) 742, 2287, 7769, 8109, 8511–12, 9014, 9823, 10067, 10614, 11190, 11667, 11973–74
Shimmin (Christopher R.), 2198
Shirley (Evelyn Philip), 2973
Shirley (Walter Waddington), 111
Shook (L. K.), 7541
Shoosmith (Edward), 408, 496, 1425–26
Shore (Thomas William), 683, 979–81, 1100, 1139, 1807–09, 2087–95, 2749, 3041, 3125, 3895, 6201, 6592, 6721

Shortt (Hugh de Sausmarez), 8476, 9341–43, 11611
Shrewsbury (John Findlay Drew), 7447
Shrubsole (George W.), 6040
Shurlock (Manwaring), 8327
Sibbald (*Sir* Robert), 830a
Sickel (Theodor), 5571, 7091
Sieveking (I. Giberne), 4430
Sievers (Eduard), 5832, 9397
Sigurdson (John), 1396
Sills (George), 6575
Silver (Thomas), 2322
Silverstein (H. T.), 7658
Simcox (William Henry), 1185, 1259
Simkins (Maud E.), 1788
Simon (James), 9253
Simpson (James), 1983
Simpson (Jesse James), 3145
Simpson (William Douglas), 2234, 3438–39, 3726, 3793–94, 4956, 4993–96, 9892, 10107, 11240, 11334
Simpson (William John Sparrow), 4380, 5213
Sinclair (Clarence), 1984
Singer (Charles Joseph), 4431, 5791–92, 7357, 7368–69, 7413, 7419, 7475–77
Singer (Dorothea Waley), 7368–69, 7420
Singer (S. W.), 5650a, 6160
Singer (Samuel), 7668
Sisam (Celia), 4148
Sisam (Kenneth), 72, 3727, 7239
Size (Nicholas), 2719
Sjøvold (Thorleif), 11668
Skaife (Robert H.), 2997
Skeat (Walter William), 23, 544, 598–600, 607, 1228, 1770, 3086, 5772, 6179, 6323, 6355, 6360, 6386, 6496–97, 6604–07, 6619, 6737, 6722, 6752, 6788–89, 7290, 7358, 7382, 7399, 7569, 7669
Skelton (Joseph), 3126
Skemp (Arthur Rowland), 7542–43
Skene (William Forbes), 247, 801, 836, 1028, 2235, 2323, 3440, 4957, 6112, 6143, 9832, 9861, 9893, 10968
Skinner (Emily), 1722, 6041
Skinner (F. G.), 8655
Skippon (*Sir* Philip), 9133
Skrine (H. D.), 1260
Slack (W. J.), 2720
Slater (D.), 7240
Slater (Gilbert), 2659
Slover (Clark Harris), 1676–77, 6753, 6992
Smail (James), 7858

Smart (T. W. Wake), 3728, 7978
Smart (*Sir* William R. E.), 7477a
Smedt (Charles de), 4092, 4494
Smetham (D. J.), 5892
Smiddy (Richard), 10541
Smirke (Edward), 3146
Smith ( ), *Prebendary of Crediton*, 1723
Smith (A. E.), 11553
Smith (A. L.), 2660, 3147
Smith (Albert Hugh), 80, 81, 601, 1186, 1985–86, 3510, 4148a, 6002, 6324, 6416, 6451, 6638–44
Smith (Aquilla), 9119, 9128, 9134–35, 9138, 9169, 9254–55
Smith (Archibald), 1163
Smith (Arthur), 8606
Smith (Charles Gowen), 2907
Smith (Charles Marshall), 743
Smith (Charles Roach), 2721, 6723, 8084–88, 8155, 8188–93, 8210, 8233, 8421, 8607–08, 9015–16, 9077–78, 10235, 11554–60
Smith (Edward), 278
Smith (G. Le Blanc), 10673–75, 10732–33
Smith (George), 9469
Smith (Gilbert E.), 6799
Smith (Goldwin), 1261
Smith (H. P.), 8701
Smith (Harold Clifford), 11561, 11629
Smith (Henry Ecroyd), 3896, 4432, 8156–57, 9210, 10325, 10656
Smith (Herbert Luther), 11601
Smith (Hubert), 4433
Smith (I. W.), 10876
Smith (Isaac Gregory), 5352
Smith (J. Richardson), 11721
Smith (James A.), 1627
Smith (James Cromarty), 2236
Smith (John), D.D., *minister of Campbeltown*, 4958
Smith (John Alexander), 8514, 8702, 9079, 10923, 11722, 11768
Smith (Joseph Huband), 5902, 8961, 11077
Smith (Lucius), *bp. of Knaresborough*, 3728a
Smith (Martin Linton), *bp. of Rochester*, 3836, 6113
Smith (O. King), 4434
Smith (P. G.), 4524
Smith (Reginald Allender), 5885, 7734, 8130, 8158–60, 8177, 8194–95, 8211–12, 8227, 8254–55, 8267, 8282, 8300–01, 8328–34, 8366–67, 8383, 8408, 8422–23, 8431–32, 8434, 8455–58,

8515, 8609–12, 8703, 8742, 10068, 10690, 11497, 11562–77, 11602, 11612, 11630, 11638–39, 11647, 11669–70, 11720, 11723–24, 11826
Smith (Reginald Anthony Lendon), 3837, 4072
Smith (Roland M.), 837, 2569–72
Smith (Samuel), *jnr.*, 9189, 9344
Smith (Sydney Fenn), 3964
Smith (Walter), 6550
Smith (*Sir* William) and Cheetham (Samuel), 24
Smith (*Sir* William), and Wace (Henry), 25
Smith (Worthington George), 8213, 10753
Smithard (William), 6551
Smithwhite (J. H.), 10347
Smylie (R. Stewart), 4333
Smyth (C. Bohun), 2016
Smyth (Charles), 7241
Smythe (William Barlow), 11769
Snadden (James), 3441
Sneiders (Irène), 4495
Snow (T. B.), 3663
Snowden (C. E.), 497, 498
SNX . P, 4703
Soames (Henry), 3341–43
Soardo (P. C.), 4370
Society of Antiquaries of Scotland, 11671, 11725
Soedergard (Oesten), 1390
Sølver (Carl V.), 2303
Sokoll ( ), 7373a
Solloway (J.), 3344
Sonke (Emma), 7705
Sorby (Henry Clifton), 10171
Sotheby, Wilkinson and Hodge, 8870
Souers (Philip Webster), 11437–38
South (Helen Pennock), 7670
Southern (Richard William), 1397, 3994
Southesk (James Carnegie), *9th earl of*, 9559, 9833, 9862, 9894–95, 9996
Southward (Elaine C.), 7622–23
Spackman (F. T.), 8302
Spain (George R. B.), 8704
Sparvel-Bayly (John Anthony), 744, 1577
Spatz (Wilhelm), 1427
Spaul (J. R.), 1262
Speight (H.), 10969
Spelman (*Sir* Henry), 2429, 3012
Spelman (*Sir* John), 1263, 6180
Spence (Andrew), 4862
Spence (James), 4959

E

Spence (James Lewis Thomas Chalmers), 1810

Spence (John), 838

Spence-Jones (H. D. M.), *dean of Gloucester*, 3442

Sperber (Hans), 9435

Sperling (C. F. D.), 10632

Spicer (F.), 9238

Spiegelhalter (Cecil), 602

Spindler (Robert), 5580

Springer (Anton), 11874–76

Sproemberg (H.), 1187

Spurgeon (Joseph W.), 10199

Spurrell (Flaxman Charles John), 7915–18, 8196

Stack (Gerald), 4655

Stacye (John), 2925

Stafford (L. J.), 5466

Stainer (Charles Lewis), 9345

Stamp (Laurence Dudley), 5953a

Stanbrook, *Benedictines of*, 3655

Standerwick (John W.), 2080

Standish (John), 10754

Stanford (R.), 11877

Stanley (Arthur Penrhyn), *dean of Westminster*, 3965

Stanton (Richard), 4093, 4535

Stapleton (A.), 9346

Stapleton (Thomas), 499, 1578, 3345, 4159–60

Starke (James Gibson Hamilton), 9842

Statham (S. P. H.), 481, 2858–59

Stearns (John M.), 2430

Stebbing (William Pinckard Delane), 1780, 8197–98, 10407

Stedman (Douglas), 7641

Steel (Anthony), 2344

Steele (H. J.), 10734

Steensberg (Axel), 2722

Steenstrup (Johannes Christoffer Hagemann Reinhardt), 745, 1327

Steer (Francis W.), 5981

Stefanović (Svetislav), 7571–72

Stefansson (Jón), 603, 6911, 6993

Steffens (Franz), 7313–14

Steinitz (Francis), 1224

Steinweg (C.), 6248

Stengel (Edmund Ernst), 5369, 5393–95

Stenton (Doris Mary), *Lady Stenton*, 1509, 6586

Stenton (*Sir* Frank Merry), 26, 27, 684, 746–48, 1140, 1264–65, 1510, 1811, 1901–02, 1987–88, 2096, 2661–63, 2860, 2895, 2906, 2908, 2926, 2933, 3013, 3227, 3289, 3622, 3678, 4435, 6202, 6325–26, 6552, 6587, 6694, 6724, 7811, 7885

Stenzel (   ), *Prof. in Breslau*, 5258

Stephan (Adalbert), 5651

Stephan (John), 5353

Stephens (Francis E.), 11098, 11922

Stephens (G. R.), 4436

Stephens (George), 604, 1378, 1628, 9436–39, 9470, 9505–08, 9850, 9896, 10762, 10859–60, 10877, 10970, 11335, 11631, 11726–27

Stephens (George Arbour), 5975

Stephens (Thomas), 229, 248, 249, 1029–30, 6114, 9914, 9944, 9955

Stephens (W. D.), 4436

Stephens (William J.), 11054

Stephens (William Richard Wood), 3838–39, 4073

Stephenson (Carl), 127, 2664, 2750–52, 3014–15, 3189

Stephenson (Mill), 9156

Stephenson (R.), 7783

Stettinger (Richard), 7242

Stevens (Courtenay Edward), 143, 8613

Stevens (Frank), 8478, 8614

Stevens (Joseph), 2723, 8335, 8409–11, 8424

Stevens (William Oliver), 3346

Stevenson (Alexander S.), 11613

Stevenson (Francis Seymour), 3840, 4437, 6105

Stevenson (John Horne), 2585

Stevenson (John Sinclair), 4629

Stevenson (Robert B. K.), 8014, 9211–12, 9897, 11812

Stevenson (W.), 10755

Stevenson (William) 1903, 3897, 5025, 10676

Stevenson (William Henry), 144, 270, 289, 405, 409–13, 454, 545, 982, 983, 1266–68, 1329, 1379, 1428, 1904, 2353, 2450, 2802, 3190, 3228, 6115, 6327, 6387, 6645–46, 6725, 6754, 6800

Stewart (Charles), 3443

Stewart (John), 11267

Stewart (John Lorne), 11728

Stewart (M. J.), 1771

Stewart (Zeph), 7315

Stewart-Brown (R.), 2354

Stirling (James), 8944

Stoddard (F. H.), 7243

Stoessel (Waldermar), 11878

Stoessiger (Brenda N.), 8784

Stokes (   ), *Miss*, 10108

Stokes (Ethel), **1772**
Stokes (George Thomas), **3444, 3795, 4525, 4863, 5495, 7033, 7171**
Stokes (H. F. Scott), **3666**
Stokes (H. G.), **6328**
Stokes (Henry Paine), **3042**
Stokes (M.), **10109**
Stokes (Margaret MacNair), **4864, 5160, 5414, 10110, 10480, 11099, 11166– 70, 11729**
Stokes (Whitley), **207–09, 212, 640, 641, 802, 1031, 1164–65, 2573, 3229, 4496, 4526, 4539–40, 4560, 4595, 4899–4901, 5121, 5218, 5223, 5741, 5861–62, 6234–35, 7421, 7602–03, 7659, 9615, 9644**
Stolberg (Friedrich Leopold zu), *count*, **1269**
Stolze (Max), **6329**
Stone (G.), **6725a**
Stone (Gilbert), **685, 2510**
Stone (Horace J. W.), **7845**
Stone (J. F. S.), **8479**
Stone (J. M.), **10763**
Stone (Percy Goddard), **7979**
Stone (Stephen), **8268–71**
Stone man, *pseud.*, **2927**
Stoney (Constance B.), **3471**
Stonor (Julian), **5122**
Stopes (Charlotte Carmichael), **1629**
Storer (Agnes C.), **4960**
Storm (A. V.), **3347**
Storm (Gustav), **1330**
Storms (Godfrid), **7422, 7544**
Story (R. Herbert), **11336**
Stothard (Charles Alfred), **1477–78**
Stoughton (John), **4149**
Stout (Elizabeth), **8039**
Strabo (Walafridus), **5572**
Strachan (John), **4190, 4902, 5622a–b**
Strachan (Lionel Richard Mortimer), **605, 5078, 7478**
Strasser (Karl Theodor), **1657a**
Stratton (Thomas), **6912**
Streatfeild (George Sidney), **1905**
Strecker (Karl), **4997, 5573, 7053, 7092**
Stredder (E.), **7573**
Street (G. E.), **11827**
Streeter (A.), **4020**
Strobl (Joseph), **7545**
Stroebe (Lilly T.), **3005**
Stroem (Hilmer), **606**
Strunk (W.), *jnr.*, **28**
Strutt (Joseph), **2665–67**
Strzygowski (Josef), **10069**

Stua (Giovanni Pietro della), **4371**
Stuart ( ), *professor, of Aberdeen*, **8541**
Stuart (Dorothy Margaret), **2668**
Stuart (John), **2324, 3796–97, 5026, 8542–43, 9851, 11241, 11779**
Stuart-Douglas (J. A.), **4074**
Stubbs (Charles William), *bp. of Truro*, **1270**
Stubbs (Francis William), **2174, 3798, 4497, 4521, 6830**
Stubbs (J. W.), **3445**
Stubbs (William), *bp. of Oxford*, **2282–83, 2393, 2803, 3016, 3316, 3679, 3729, 3841–42**
Styrap (H. G. Jukes de), **11224**
Suckling (Alfred), **10200**
Sudhoff (Karl), **7423**
Sullivan (*Sir* Edward), *bart.*, **11915**
Sullivan (Joseph M.), **4754**
Sullivan (Richard E.), **5259**
Sullivan (W. K.), **2685**
Sumner (Oswald), **3606**
Surtees (Frederick R.), **3966**
Surtees (Scott F.), **1380**
Sutcliffe (E. F.), **4206, 4274–75**
Sutcliffe (Frank M.), **8656**
Sutherland (Carol Humphrey Vivian), **8911, 8945–46, 11578**
Sutton (Edward), **7945**
Swaen (A. E. H.), **7383, 7706–09**
Swarzenski (Hanns), **7244, 11879**
Swayne (Henry I. F.), **10458**
Sweet (Henry), **104, 5633**
Sweeting (Walter Debenham), **1599, 4121**
Swete (Henry Barclay), **5982**
Swift (Thomas), **5123**
Sydow (Carl Wilhelm von), **6330**
Syers (Henry Sam), **10287–88**
Sylvester (Dorothy), **1906, 5954**
Symonds (Henry), **9170, 9213, 9347–49**
Symons (Thomas), **3580a, 3607–10, 3639**
Sympson (Edward Mansel), **6116, 10709**
Szogs (Arthur), **3148**

T., **9350**
T. (G.), **6790**
Taddy (John), **6417, 8214–15**
Tait (A. C. F.), **10657**
Tait (Edwyn Seymour Reid), **11268**
Tait (James), **414, 1579, 2753–54, 2846, 2877, 2886, 3079–81, 3843**
Talbot (C. H.), **10459–60**
Tallaght, *abbey*, **4498, 5623**
Tallgren (A. M.), **6181**

Tamassia (Nino), 3995
Tangl (Michael), 5266–67, 5279, 5283, 5354–55, 5396
Tankard (E.), 2669
Tanner (Lawrence Edward), 1398, 10275
Tapp (William Henry), 415, 416
Taranger (Absalon), 3348
Tate (George), 10924
Tatlock (John Strong Perry), 135, 4499, 5052, 7574, 7626
Taunton (Ethelred Luke), 3611
Tavernier (W.), 1479
Taxweiler (Richard Karl Wilhelm), 279
Taylor (Alexander Burt), 228, 1630, 6913–14
Taylor (Arthur), 6608
Taylor (Charles Samuel), 1141, 1188, 1271, 1580, 1907, 2097–2101, 2880–81, 3082, 3191, 3534, 3612, 3730–31, 3967–68, 4438, 5941, 7829
Taylor (Edward James), 4323
Taylor (George), 8544
Taylor (George Robert Stirling), 1789
Taylor (Henry), 10658, 10897–98
Taylor (Isaac), 566, 607, 839, 2724, 2804–05, 2998, 3127, 3192, 6331–32, 6388, 6418–19, 6576, 6593, 6726, 9398, 9824–25
Taylor (John), 2102
Taylor (Silas), 3258
Taylor (Thomas), 1724, 3446, 3844–45, 5214
Taylor (Winifred M.), 608
Taylour (Charles), pseud., 11579
Tebbutt (C. F.), 8555, 10133
Techert (Marguerite), 7110
Tellet (F. S.), 6838
Telting (A.), 7546
Tempest (B. C.), 4439
Tempest (E. B.), 10710
Tempest (H. G.), 3799, 7995
Tengstrand (Erik), 6333, 6755
Tengvik (Gösta), 609
Tenhaeff (Nicholaas Bernardus), 5546
Térilis (J.), 4500
Terrett (Ian B.), 3043, 5944a
Tesoroni (Domenico), 1658
Teufelsbauer (Leopold), 4755
Theopold (Ludwig), 73
Théry (P. G.), 7111
Thierry (Jacques Nicolas Augustin), 1429, 1581
Thijm (Petrus Paul Maria Alberdingk). See Alberdingk-Thijm
Thoene (Franz), 7435

Thomas (David Richard), 2260, 9956, 11414–15
Thomas (F. W. L.), 2325, 6915–16, 8064
Thomas (George William), 8336
Thomas (J.), 2103
Thomas (John), 2596
Thomas (R. J.), 6801
Thomas (Thomas Henry), 9945, 10111, 11381, 11394, 11416–17, 11940
Thomey (J. C.), 9751
Thompson (Alexander Hamilton), 3349, 3613, 3732–33, 3846, 4324, 7886, 10266–67, 10380a
Thompson (Charles John Samuel), 7479
Thompson (E. A.), 4687
Thompson (Sir Edward Maunde), 5652, 7316, 11880–83
Thompson (H. V.), 6526
Thompson (James), 8283–85
Thompson (James Westfall), 7625
Thompson (Kate), 5124
Thompson (Pishey), 6003
Thompson (S. Harrison), 5677
Thoms (Alexander), 10514
Thomsen (C. J.), 8947–48
Thomson (Alexander), 9863
Thomson (Alexander P. D.), 7384
Thomson (Ebenezer), 7359
Thomson (Richard), 11884
Thomson (T. Harvey), 4961
Thomson (William), 4962, 11780
Thorkelin (Grímr Jónsson), 1189
Thornber (William), 1989–90
Thorndike (Lynn), 7480
Thorne (William), 3640
Thorogood (A. Jean), 1190
Thorpe (Benjamin), 280, 304, 2330, 2431, 5650a, 6117
Thorpe (Harry), 1908
Thoyts (E.), 10289
Thoyts (Emma Elizabeth), 7846
Thrall (William Flint), 6216, 6236
Thropp (J.), 7770
Thrupp (John), 2670, 7575
Thum (B.), 4180
Thunder (John M.), 2175, 4527, 4865, 4963
Thurnam (John), 1272, 6004, 8368, 8754, 8785, 8493, 11580
Thurneysen (Rudolf), 170, 210, 211, 455, 984, 1101, 2522, 2543, 2574–78, 4501, 4667, 4866, 5624, 6249, 9560–61
Thurston (Herbert), 3296, 3472
Thwaites (Edward), 8862

Tietze-Cohrat (Erika), 7214
Tigernach, *Annals of*, 212
Tikkanen (Johan Jakob), 7215, 11885
Tildesley (Miriam Louise), 8479, 8786
Tille (Alexander), 456
Timerding (Heinrich), 5151
Timmer (Benno Johan), 3350–51
Tindal (William), 3656
Tingey (J. C.), 2920
Tírechán, *bp.*, 4596
Tischendorf (C.), 7188
Todd (James Henthorn), 213, 214, 749,
    1631, 4630, 4756, 5742, 6831, 7279–
    80, 11886, 11941–42
Todd (William Gouan), 3559, 4757
Todière (Louis Phocion), 1511
Toke (Leslie Alexander St. Lawrence),
    3977, 7222
Tolhurst (J. B. L.), 11943
Tolkien (John Ronald Renel), 7642
Toller (Thomas Northcote), 29
Tom (E. N.), 10720
Tomkins (Henry George), 6069–72
Tommasini (Anselmo Maria), 5415
Toms (Herbert S.), 8384
Tonnochy (Alec Bain), 9364
Tononi (A. Gaetano), 5416
Tooker (E. G.), 3734
Torfaeus (Thormodus), 2237
Torr (Cecil), 6042
Torre (Pietro Luigi della), 5496
Tout (Thomas Frederick), 40, 3193
Tower (*Sir* Reginald), 1582
Townend (B. R.), 7547
Townsend (James), 3623
Toy (Sidney), 7887
Toyne (Stanley Mease), 7093
Traill (William), 8040, 8657
Traub (Gottfried), 5356
Traube (Ludwig), 171, 5161, 5280, 7054,
    7112, 7117
Trautmann (Moritz), 7710–19
Travis-Cook (J.), 2999
Traylen (Henry T.), 10290
Treacher (Llewellyn), 2104
Tregelles (S. Prideaux), 145
Treherne (G. G. T.), 9997
Treiter (M.), 281
Trench (Thomas Cooke), 11975
Trench (W. F.), 9651
Trenholme (Edward Craig), 4964
Trethowan (Illtyd), 6056
Trevelyan (George Macaulay), 686, 686a,
    985

Trollope (Edward), 1591, 1909, 3535,
    8337, 10711
Trow-Smith (Robert), 2725
Trusted (Charles J.), 10481
Tucker (W. Trueman), 8338
Tuckett (John), 1725
Tudor (Charles L. R.), 10380b
Tudor (Thomas L.), 1910, 10677–78
Tuffrau (Paul), 6280
Tuomey (J. C.), 9751
Tupling (G. H.), 3898
Tupper (Frederick), *jr.*, 546, 1583, 3352,
    7374, 7720–21
Turchi (Nicola), 10112
Turgis (Suzanne), 1480
Turk (Milton Haight), 2432
Turnbull (John), 5027
Turnbull (W. H.), 10633
Turner (A. G. C.), 2105, 6756–57, 6802
Turner (Cuthbert Hamilton), 5697, 5833,
    7245
Turner (G. J.), 1584, 3128
Turner (J. H.), 4656, 6005–06
Turner (Joseph Horsfall), 1991, 6647,
    9351, 10971
Turner (Sharon), 687, 1585, 8851
Turner (T. H.), 10354
Turner (Thomas M.), 9352
Turner (William), 2304, 7055
Turville-Petre (Edward Oswald Gabriel),
    750
Two Sisters of Notre Dame of Namur,
    4021
Tydecho, 5976
Tyler (F. C.), 4502
Tymms (Samuel), 7784, 8161, 11581
Tynan (Joseph), 2394
Tyrrell-Green (E.), 10523–24

Uhlirz (Mathilde), 5467
Ullrich (H.), 11078
Underdown (H. W.), 6758
Underhill (F. M.), 7980
Underwood (Eric Gordon), 10615
Unger (F. W.), 11887
Unwin (George), 3051
Urry (William), 5698
Urwalek (J.), 4867
Ussher (James), *abp. of Armagh*, 3353

Valentine (Herbert), 10856, 10861
Vallance (William), 8199
Vallancey (Charles), 2579–80, 9604,
    10542
Valroger (Lucien Marie de), 2523

Van der Linden (H.), **7122**
Van Draat (P. Fijn), **4181**
Van Tromp (Harold), **4022**
Varah (William Edward), **3354, 4122, 6007, 6351, 10268**
Varin (Pierre Joseph), **986, 3578**
Varley (Telford), **4075**
Varley (W. J.), **7946**
Varro, *pseud.*, **6803**
Varwell (P.), **1726**
Vasiliev (A. A.), **1659**
Vasmer (Max), **6182**
Vassall (H.), **4346**
Vassall (Harry Graeme), **8743**
Vattelet (Hans), **1512**
Vaughan (Arthur Owen), **803**
Vaughan (Henry F. J.), **518, 519, 1911**
Vaughan (Herbert M.), **5066**
Vaughan (John), **4002**
Vaughan-Williams (Sir Roland Lomax), **3447**
Vaux (W. Sandys Wright), **9214–15**
Vebna, *pseud.*, **4334**
Veitsch (John), **7626**
Venables (Edmund), **1912, 3536–37, 4076, 4150, 6577**
Venables-Llewelyn (*Sir* Charles), **2931**
Vendryes (Joseph), **3511, 4503, 4868, 4903–04, 5067, 5162, 6250, 7034, 7660**
Verbist (Gabriël H.), **5549**
Vernulaeus (Nicholaus), **5512**
Verrier (Jean), **1481**
Verrua (Pietro), **7172**
Victoria and Albert Museum, **10972, 11582**
Vidal (Robert Studley), **1727**
Viëtor (Wilhelm), **9509–11, 11439**
Vigfusson (Gudbrand), **1191, 2199, 9826**
Viglione (Francesco), **104a**
Vigors (Philip D.), **11171**
Vinay (G.), **5497**
Vincent (William Thomas), **6727**
Vinogradoff (*Sir* Paul), **2511, 2671–72, 3083, 3129–33, 3230, 3290**
Vivian-Neal (A. W.), **2106–07, 5125**
Vleeskruyer (Rudolf), **4077**
Vogt (Lorents Juhl), **2176**
Voigt (H. G.), **5260**
Vonderau (Joseph), **5397**
Vries (Jan de), **215**
Vuilhorgne (L.), **1513**
Vulliamy (Colwyn Edward), **7771, 8705**

W. (G.), **9353**

W. (T.), **4440**
W. (W.), **9133**
W. (W. C.), **2876**
Wackerbarth (Francis Diederich), **7339**
Waddell (Helen Jane), **4504, 7034a**
Waddell (J. Jeffrey), **10515, 11337–38**
Waddington (Quintin), **8744**
Wade (John R.), **457**
Wade (W. G.), **1142**
Wade-Evans (Arthur Wade), **146–52, 166, 172, 250, 417, 458, 642, 858, 987–93, 1032, 1992, 2108, 2608, 3448, 4998, 5053–54, 5064, 5068–70, 5126–27, 6144**
Wadmore (Beauchamp), **7947**
Wadstein (Elis), **859, 11440–41**
Wahlund (Carl), **6251**
Wainwright (Frederick Threlfall), **216, 459, 994, 1143, 1273, 1331–33, 1913, 1993, 6145, 6430, 6680**
Wainwright (Thomas), **9354**
Waitz (Georg), **2512, 5284, 5398**
Wake (Charles Staniland), **6008**
Wakefield (Charles), **9190**
Wakeman (Thomas), **251, 252, 2261, 9946, 9957**
Wakeman (William Frederick), **804, 2177–78, 8545, 9791–94, 10501–04, 10569, 11079, 11106–07, 11730**
Walbran (John Richard), **4023, 10355–56**
Walcott (Mackenzie Edward Charles), **3641, 3847–48, 10236**
Walderdoff (Hugo von), **5261**
Walford (Cornelius), **3052**
Walford (Edward Gibbs), **11583**
Walford (Weston Styleman), **10408, 11583**
Walker (Benjamin), **1914, 2978, 3194–95**
Walker (Bernard), **6420, 6553**
Walker (Bryan), **2843–44, 3084**
Walker (Curtis H.), **2395**
Walker (Francis C.), **11442**
Walker (Frederick George), **8162**
Walker (George P.), **5887**
Walker (J. K.), *M.D.*, **2806**
Walker (J. Russell), **10616**
Walker (John), **840, 9136**
Walker (John Cotton), **4758**
Walker (John Holland), **10679**
Walker (John William), **1144, 1155, 7964**
Walker (Joseph Cooper), **7340**
Walker (R. V.), **4869**
Walker (Thomas Henry), **4965**
Walker (Thomas James), **8256, 11672**
Walker (Warren S.), **8706**

Wall (James Charles), 688, 1274, 7888, 10201, 10381, 01617, 10973, 11813

Wallace (J. N. A.), 11172

Wallace-Hadrill (J. M.), 1660

Wallenberg (Johannes Knut), 6118, 6502–03

Waller (Evangelia H.), 520

Waller (John Green), 10172

Waller (Thomas), 9512

Wallis (E. W.), 8852

Wallis (John E. W.), 10899

Wallis (W. Clarkson), 2017, 10409

Wallis (W. Cyril), 10409

Walpole (Spencer), 2200

Walsh (Annie), 751

Walsh (Paul), 217–19, 460, 461, 521, 2179–84, 2688, 4597, 4759, 5919, 6832–33

Walsh (T. A.), 5513

Walshe (Patrick T.), 1033

Walter (Ferdinand), 2284

Walters (Alfred V.), 2109

Walters (H. B.), 3196

Walters (John), 6466

Walton (W. H.), 10680

Walz (John A.), 7722

Warburton (Joseph Robert), 10202

Ward (Gordon), 418–25, 995–97, 1145–47, 1156, 1586, 1790–96, 2018, 2110, 3197, 3642, 3735–36, 3899–3901, 5888–89, 6043, 6119, 8110, 8658

Ward (John), 6553a, 8228–29, 8794, 10681, 11395

Ward (Paul L.), 2326

Wardale (Edith), 8853

Ware (E. M.), 1915

Waring (John Burley), 10113

Warne (Charles), 2111–12

Warner (Sir George Frederic), 4342, 11888

Warner (Richard), 2882, 2885

Warner (Richard Hyett), 4078

Warner (Rubie D.-N.), 5818

Warre (Frank), 10173

Warren (F. C.), 2726

Warren (Frederick Edward), 3231, 3449, 5224, 5743, 5751, 5863–65, 7246, 10114

Warren (Joseph), 11584–85

Warrilow (Joseph B.), 1994

Warriner (Frank), 6681

Wasserschleben (F. W. Hermann), 5599, 5625

Waterhouse & Co., 11731

Waterhouse (G.), 6183

Waterman (Dudley M.), 1994a, 8369, 8418a, 11632, 11673

Waters (Eaton W.), 9645

Waters (Edmond Chester), 500, 501

Waters (Edward George Ross), 6252–53

Waterton (Edmund), 1399, 1592, 10974

Watkin (Aelred), 3664, 4325

Watkin (Hugh Robert), 1728, 6044, 6120, 6421, 6467, 6786, 6791–92, 11032

Watkins (Alfred), 6334, 6389, 7812, 10756

Watkins (Charles Frederic), 10291

Watkins (Oscar Dan), 5600

Watson (Christopher Knight), 426, 8707

Watson (E. W.), 3355

Watson (George), 4123

Watson (James), 1034

Watson (John), 6121, 7889

Watson (William John), 643, 805, 841, 2238, 3512, 4999, 5028, 6804, 6917–22

Watt (Lauchlan Maclean), 3450, 4966

Watt (William G. T.), 8041

Wattenbach (Wilhelm), 5262–63, 7317, 11944

Watts (Thomas), 6390

Watts (William), 6554

Way (Albert), 547, 3737, 7148, 11225, 11586–87, 11732, 11781

Way (R. E.), 11033

Weaver (Frederic William), 2113–14, 4381, 6452, 6759

Webb (Edward Doran), 7247, 11010

Webb (George Herbert), 7481

Webb (Philip Carteret), 2673, 2807

Webster (Charles A.), 3865

Webster (Graham), 1916, 8615, 9137

Webster (W.), 9080, 9171

Wedgwood (Josiah C.), 1917

Wedlake (A. L.), 9355

Weerd (Hubert van de), 5550–52

Weidmann (Franz), 7180

Weigall (Arthur Edward Pearse Brome), 30

Weightman (Jane), 282

Weiland (Ludwig), 860

Weir (W.), 10757

Weisbach (Werner), 11889

Weisweiler (H.), 4230

Welby (Sir Alfred Cholmeley Earle), 482, 2909, 6468

Welby (E. M. E.), 6009

Welch (F. B.), 6594–95

Wells (Benjamin W.), 4024, 4631, 7094

Wells (William Charles), **9157, 9356–57**
Wellstood (Frederick Christian), **8296**
Welzhofer (Karl), **4191**
Wentz (Walter Yeeling Evans), **7604**
Werner (August), **5357**
Werner (Karl), **4276, 7095**
West (Andrew Fleming), **7096**
Westell (William Percival), **1918, 11614**
Weston (G. F.), **1995**
Weston, *afterwards* Hunter-Weston (Gould Read), **11733**
Westphal (Johannes), **6335**
Westropp (Hodder Michael), **2689, 10543–44, 11734**
Westropp (Thomas Johnson), **1632, 2157, 2170, 2185–86, 2328, 3451, 3513, 3910, 4870, 6073, 6237, 7605, 7996–8001, 9795, 10505, 10545, 11782, 11814**
Westwood (John Obadiah), **7248, 9523– 24, 9834, 9915–20, 9928–31, 9947, 9958, 9965, 9998–10003, 10031, 10035, 11034, 11350, 11367–68, 11373, 11402–03, 11418, 11770–71, 11890–92, 11923**
Wethered (F. T.), **427**
Whale (Thomas William), **2115, 2808–10, 2868–70, 2946–47**
Whatmore (A. W.), **1919–21, 6057, 6555–58**
Wheater (W.), **1996**
Wheatley (Henry Benjamin), **2811**
Wheatley (Sydney Williams), **4079, 7922**
Wheaton (Henry), **752**
Wheeler (G. H.), **112, 153, 483, 4657, 6391**
Wheeler (H. A.), **11735**
Wheeler (Henry), **11173**
Wheeler (Lucy), **3738**
Wheeler (*Sir* Robert Eric Mortimer), **1802–03, 1812, 7847, 8669**
Wheeler (W. H.), **1922**
Whelock (Abraham), **2407, 2433**
Whimster (Donald Cameron), **7772**
Whincopp (William), **11588**
Whistler (Charles Watts), **936, 998, 1275, 1334, 6010, 6058, 7576, 8516–17**
Whitaker (Thomas Dunham), **1997**
Whitaker-Wilson (Cecil), **1812a**
Whitbourn (Richard), **9090, 9358, 11633**
Whitbread (L.), **4207, 4335, 4441, 5653, 6184, 7723, 9513**
White (Caroline Louisa), **5654**
White (Charles Harold Evelyn). *See* Evelyn-White

White (G. H.), **1600**
White (G. M.), **8659**
White (H. T.), **2305**
White (Henry Julian), **7200**
White (Hugh Gerard Evelyn). *See* Evelyn-White
White (John Davis), **2187–88**
White (Jon Manchip), **1102**
White (Newport John Davis), **4557–59, 4563, 4566, 4760**
White (R. H.), **11035**
White (Robert), **3996**
Whitehead (J. G. O.), **7948**
Whitehead (John Livesay), **2116**
Whitelaw (J. W.), **6923**
Whitelock (Dorothy), **31, 73a, 610, 1381, 2434–35, 2461, 2513, 2674, 3538, 5655, 5810, 5812**
Whiting (B. J.), **6185**
Whiting (Charles Edwin), **3665, 3489, 4025, 4277–78, 7201, 10348**
Whiting (W.), **8198, 8616**
Whitley (H. Michell), **2855, 8385–87**
Whitley (T. W.), **428**
Whitley (W. T.), **6203**
Whitley (William Thomas), **1922a, 6122**
Whitman (Charles Huntington), **7385–87**
Whitney (J. P.), **3539**
Whittingham (A. B.), **1773**
Wichmann (Johannes), **5667, 5720**
Wickham (W. A.), **10900**
Wicks (A. T.), **2117**
Wiedemann (H.), **5264**
Wieland (M.), **5265**
Wigmore (John H.), **3997**
Wilcock (Peter), **4164**
Wilda (Wilhelm Eduard), **2514**
Wilde (W. R.), **11815**
Wilde (*Sir* William Robert Wills), **7606, 11642, 11674**
Wildhagen (Karl), **462, 5702, 5721–23**
Wildman (William Beauchamp), **2118, 3933, 6760**
Wildridge (T. Tindall), **10292**
Wilkie (James), **2239, 4522, 6281**
Wilkins (C.), **1035**
Wilkins (David), **2429, 2436, 3294, 3356**
Wilkins (E. P.), **8425**
Wilkins (William), **10326**
Wilkinson (Bertie), **1382–83**
Wilkinson (J. J.), **10878**
Wilkinson (John), **2119, 2820**
Wilkinson (*Sir* John Gardner), **10004, 10174**
Wilkinson (Joseph), **8163**

Wilkinson (Thomas Turner), **6011–11a**
Willard (James Field), **1**
Willard (Rudolph), **5798–5800, 5819–21**
Willett (Erhest H.), **9188, 9216, 9359**
William I, *king*, **1430**
William, *of Jumièges*, **1514**
William, *of Malmesbury*, **3666, 4031–32**
William, *of Poitiers*, **1515**
Williams (Albert Hughes), **806**
Williams (B.), **5773**
Williams (Benjamin), **2345, 6123–25**
Williams (Blanche Colton), **2611**
Williams (C.), **9948**
Williams (Edward), **2596**
Williams (Emily Octavia), **4442**
Williams (Geoffrey S.), **3902**
Williams (Harry Franklin), **10**
Williams (Hugh), **3452–53**
Williams (*Sir* Ifor), **173–75, 644, 1148, 1661, 1998, 6952, 9921–22, 9932, 9949, 9959, 10014, 10021, 10032**
Williams (J. F.), **2812**
Williams (John), **1335, 8518**
Williams (John), *ab Ithel*, **3006, 3454, 7416, 8546, 8708, 9958, 10034**
Williams (Jonathan), **7813**
Williams (Laurence Frederic Rushbrook), **2437, 3739**
Williams (Mary), **7035**
Williams (Philip), **10424**
Williams (Richard), **7341**
Williams (Robert), **8854**
Williams (Rowland), **3540**
Williams (Stephen Joseph), **2595**
Williams (Sterling de Courcy), **2189, 11174**
Williams (T.), **3541**
Williams (W.), **1276, 5128**
Williams (W. I.), **9360**
Williams (William), **9745–46**
Williams-Freeman (J. P.), **1276a**
Williamson (Edward William), *bp. of Swansea*, **5055, 7249**
Williamson (F.), **999, 3096, 6559**
Williamson (James Alexander), **689**
Williamson (James Mann), **5358**
Willibald, *St., bp. of Eichstadt*, **6217**
Willibaldus, *presbyter*, **5285–88**
Willis ( ), *18th-c. writer*, **1384**
Willis (Cloudesley S.), **8459**
Willis (F. M.), **1000, 7830**
Willis-Bund (John William), **1923, 2262, 2987, 3455, 3740, 3762–63, 3866, 4453, 5056, 7773, 10035**

Willms (Johannes E.), **7360**
Wills (Samuel J.), **9588**
Wilmart (André), **4151, 4208, 4442a, 5707, 5724, 5726, 5729–30, 7097**
Wilson (Arthur Ernest), **10001–02, 8388, 8617, 11589**
Wilson (Daniel), **1036, 8709, 9898–99, 11339, 11772, 11783–85**
Wilson (F. R.), **10357**
Wilson (George Maryon), **1924**
Wilson (Henry Austin), **2329, 3960, 5726, 5758, 5774, 5793**
Wilson (J.), **1192**
Wilson (James), **429, 1999, 2856, 6012**
Wilson (James Mauricc), **10327**
Wilson (R. M.), **74**
Wilson-Barkworth (Arthur Bromby), **2000, 2991**
Wimmer (Ludvig Frands Adalbert) **9399**
Winbolt (Samuel Edward), **1003, 8618**
Winchester, *Hyde abbey*, **3741**
Winchester, *Newminster*, **3741**
Windeatt (Edward), **9361**
Windele (John), **9241, 9540, 9605, 9646, 10570, 11191, 11736–37**
Windisch (Ernst), **1037, 7548**
Windle (*Sir* Bertram Coghill Alan), **1004, 11175**
Winfield (*Sir* Percy Henry), **2396**
Wingfield-Stratford (Esmé), **690**
Wingrave (Wyatt), **8433**
Winkelmann (Eduard), **691**
Winmill (Joyce M.), **3542, 4279, 4372**
Winnington-Ingram (A. R.), **6596**
Winterfeld (Paul von), **5574–75**
Winters (William), **75, 2813**
Winton, *pseud.*, **2120**
Wise (Francis), **1192a**
Wise (John Richard), **2121**
Wise (Thomas Alexander), **3514, 10546**
Wissig (Otto), **5359–60**
Wittkower (Rudolf), **10066**
Woebling (Gustav), **5289**
Wood ( ), *Canon*, **4443**
Wood (Alfred Cecil), **1925**
Wood (G. W.), **11192**
Wood (George A.), **7724**
Wood (James), **9514**
Wood (James G.), **2035**
Wood (James George), **3969, 4444, 6045, 6953, 7814–15**
Wood-Martin (William Gregory), **3515, 8660**
Woodruff (Charles Eveleigh), **1336, 3643, 3850, 3903**

Woodward (Bolingbroke Bernard), **8619**, **10203**
Wooldridge (Sidney William), **5890–92**
Wooler (Edward), **10879**
Woolf (Henry Bosley), **611–13**
Woolley (Reginald Maxwell), **5762**
Woolrych (E. B.), **484**
Wordsworth (Christopher), **7549**
Wordsworth (J.), **9451**
Wordsworth (John), *bp. of. Salisbury*, **7202**
Workman (Herbert Brook), **3614**
Wormald (Francis), **4152**, **5775**, **11893–95**, **11945–46**
Wormonocus. *See* Wrmonoc
Worringer (Wilhelm), **11896**
Worsaae (Jens Jacob Asmussen), **753**, **754**, **11590**
Worth (Richard Hansford), **6793**
Worth (Richard Nicholls), **1729–34**, **3198**, **5920**, **6046**, **6794**
Wotke (F.), **4553**
Wotton (William), **2609**
Woulfe (Patrick), **645**
Wrdisten, *abbot of Landévennec*, **5199**
Wrenn (Charles Leslie), **614**, **1149**, **7250**
Wright (Arthur G.), **3516**
Wright (Cyril Ernest), **32**, **41**, **283**
Wright (George), **1776**
Wright (George R.), **6469**
Wright (Joseph), **3232**
Wright (Thomas), **33**, **113–14**, **692**, **1005**, **1038**, **1593**, **2675–77**, **2755**, **4080**, **4094**, **6217a**, **6994**, **7149–50**, **7406**, **7577–78**, **7661**, **7774**, **8089**, **8200**, **8234**, **8620**, **8710**, **8855**, **9138**, **9440**, **10175–76**, **11591**
Wright (William), **8787**
Wrmonoc, *of Landévennec*, **5200–01**
Wroblewski (Leonhard), **2438**
Wrottesley (F. J.), **1926**
Wrottesley (*Hon.* George), **430**, **548**, **3044**
Wuelcker (Richard Paul), **33**, **4445**, **5725**, **6995**
Wuerdinger (A.), **2439**
Wuerdinger (Hans), **2397**, **1515**
Wulf (Maurice de), **6996**
Wulfgeat, *of Donnington*, **2462**
Wulfstan, *II abp. of York, St. and homilist*, **5811–12**
Wulfstan, *monk of St. Swithuns, Winchester*, **4003–04**, **4012**
Wurdestinus. *See* Wrdisten

Wyatt (Alfred John), **431**, **7725**
Wyatt (James), **1927**
Wyatt (*Sir* Matthew Digby), **11897**
Wyld (Henry Cecil Kennedy), **6682**
Wylie (William Michael), **8090–91**, **8235–36**, **11592**
Wyndham (Henry Penruddocke), **2980**
Wynne-Edwards ( ), *canon*, **2263**

X., **6126**

Y. (D.), **2885**
Y. (E. H.), **1516**
Y. (X.), **9515**
Yarborough (J. Cooke), **10461**
Yardley (E.), **7627**
Yates (O. V.), **10659**
Yeatman (John Pym), **2861**, **8856**
Yorke (P. A.), **10115**
Young (C.), **10975**
Young (Ernest), **2516**
Young (G. M.), **2122**
Young (George), **3742**
Young (*Sir* George), *bart.*, **2123**
Young (George Malcolm), **1006**
Young (Hugh W.), **8711**
Young (J. L.), **5921**
Young (J. P. W.), **10177**
Young (Jean I.), **755**, **7726**
Young (Matthew), **8747**, **8771**

Z., **6761**
Zachrisson (Robert Eugen), **615–19**, **1007**, **6336–39**, **6361**, **6392–94**, **6422–24**, **6470–72**, **6648–50**, **6698**, **6728**, **6762**
Zehender (W. von), **10547**
Zehetbauer (Fritz), **5361**
Zehrs (C.), **5362**
Zettinger (J.), **5626**
Zézas (Spyridion G.), **2398**
Zimmer (Heinrich), **176–78**, **620**, **842**, **1662**, **3149**, **3456**, **4704**, **4871**, **5744**, **6282**, **7036–37**, **7056**, **7550**, **7607–08**
Zimmermann (Benedikt Ernst Heinrich), **11898–99**
Zimmermann (J. A.), **5498**
Zimmermann (Otto), **5656**
Zinkeisen (Frank), **2399**, **3017**
Zoepfl (Heinrich), **2355**
Zupitza (Julius), **3615**, **3934**, **4153**, **4182**, **5657**, **5794**, **7551–52**, **7579**

II. SUBJECT AND TOPOGRAPHICAL INDEX

Abban, *St.*, *2nd abbot of Hy-Kinsellagh*, 4784

Abbo, *of Worcester*, 52

Abbotsbury, Dorset, 3718

Aber-, 6847, 6855

Abercorn, West Lothian, 11304, 11333

Aberdeenshire (Early Christianity in), 3436, 3439 : (place-names), 6884, 6905. *See also* Aboyne, Auquharney, Buchan, Cé, Dunecht, Farnell, Inverurie, Lymphanan, Maiden stone, Mar, Monymusk, Newton stone, Rhynie, Strathbogie.

Abernethy, Perthshire, 9894, 10546, 10550, 11276.

Aberpergwn, *Book of*, 248

Abingdon, Berks. (abbey), 3616–23 : (charters) 347 : (cemetery) 8398 : (wheel-cross) 10982

Abinger, Surrey, 7970

Abington Pigotts, Cambs., 8570

Aboyne, Aberdeenshire, 9886, 9893

Abson, Glos., 10596

Abury, Wilts., 10452

Acca, *bp. of Hexham*, 4040

Achavrole, Dunbeath, Caithness, 11679

Ackergill, Caithness, 8496–97, 8788–90

Aclea, *battle* (851) : *synod* (782) [?= Oakley, Hants.], 6081, 6084, 6126

Adam, *Penance of*, 5839

Adamnam, *St.*, *9th abbot of Hy*, 4879–83, 5776, 7267 : (reliquary), 4109, 11802 : (vision), 7644, 7650, 7657, 7659–60. *See also* Cáin Adamnáin

Addingham, Cumb., 10834

Adeliza, *sister of William I*, 1578

Aed Dub MacColmáin, *bp.-abbot of Kildare*, 4832

Aedan MacGabrain, 1013

Aedh Mac Bric, *St.*, 4823

Aedh Oirnidhe, *king of Ireland*, 6138

Ægelwine [moneyer], 9319, 9328

Ælfheah, *St.*, *abp. of Canterbury*, 4429

Ælfric, *abbot of Eynsham*, 5637–57, 5669, 7239 : (Colloquium), 5627, 5650a, 5653, 5657 : (festermen), 3200, 3217 : (Lives of saints), 4414–45,

4147, 4153, 5637 : (vocabulary), 5652

Ælfric, *alderman of Mercia* (seal), 9367

Ælfric, *bp. of Hereford* (grant to, 944), 368

Ælfsius, *abbot of Burgh* (*Peterborough*), 5875

Ælfwald I, *king of Northumbria* (coins), 9032

Ælfwald II, *king of Northumbria* (coins), 9049.

Ælle, *king of Sussex*, 948, 968, 987, 6096, 6107

Aenach Carman [pagan festival], 2558, 3504.

Aenach sites, 6073

Ængus, *the Culdee, bp. of Clonenagh*, 4762 : (Calendar or Félire of), 209, 4501

Aera Dionysiana, 447–48

Aestel, 11458, 11537

Æthelbald, *king* (coins), 9088–89

Æthelbald, *king of Mercia*, 1103 : (charter to Woodchester, Glos.), 284 : (letter from St. Boniface), 5813 : (Privilege of, 742), 426

Æthelberht, *king* (coins), 9085

Æthelberht, *St.*, *king of East Anglia*, 1120, 4385, 4413, 4444, 8965 : (coins), 3965–66

Æthelberht I, *king of Kent* (baptism), 3532 : (Canterbury and Paris), 1637 : (court of), 893 : (grant to Sandtun), 422 : (laws), 2445, 2449, 2495, 3209

Æthelberht II, *king of Kent* (charter to Romsey, 740), 1792

Ætheldreda, *St.*, 4397, 4405, 4407

Æthelfleda, 1277

Æthelgar, *2nd bp. of Crediton*, 3327

Æthelheard, *abp. of Canterbury* (coins), 8969, 9015

Æthelheard, *king of Wessex* (charter, Devon), 1685

Æthelingadene, *battle* (1001), 1349

Æthelmund [minister of Uhtred] (grant of land to, 770), 302

Æthelred I, *king*, 1171 : (coins), 8887, 8891, 8899

Æthelred II, *the Unready, king*, 83 : (charter to Bradford-on-Avon, 1001), 379 : (charter to Burton abbey, 1002–4), 330 : (charter to Farleigh Hungerford, 987), 396 : (charter to Hampstead), 356 : (charter to Stanton, Hunts., 1012), 384 : (charter to Westminster), 339 : (charter to Westwood, Somerset, 987), 396 : (charter to Wyke Regis, Dorset, 988), 294 : (coins), 9139–57, 9159, 9168, 9171, 11688 : (grant of Rammesleah to Fécamp), 2006, 2012 : (laws), 2442 : (treaty with Vikings, 994), 1306.

Æthelred, *king of Mercia* (charter to Woodchester, Glos.), 284 : (charter to Dunne and her daughter), 393

Æthelred I and II, *kings of Northumbria* (coins), 9018–19, 9027–28, 9032–33, 9038, 9044, 9056, 9073, 9076

Æthelred, *earl of Fife and abbot of Dunkeld*, 1616

Æthelred, *sub-regulus of Mercia* [son-in-law to Alfred], (coins), 8992

Æthelred-Mucil [father-in-law to Alfred] 1266

Æthelswith, *queen of Mercia*, 11622

Æthelwald, *bp. of Dunwich* (seal), 9372, 9376

Æthelwald, *king of Mercia* (correspondence with Aldhelm), 1110

Æthelweard I, *ealdorman of Wessex* (Chronicle of), 44, 70, 1264 : (tomb of, Mortimer), 2032

Æthelweard, *king of East Anglia* (coins), 8887, 8891

Æthelwig, *abbot of Evesham*, 3653

Æthelwold, *St., bp. of Winchester*, 3594, 3599, 4047, 5584, 5631, 7139, 7148

Æthelwulf, *king* (charter, Canterbury, 837), 418 : (charter om Homme, Devon, 846), 3119 : (coins), 8883–84, 8958–59, 9081, 9085 : (genealogy), 477

Ages of the World, 7346, 7568

Aghabulloge, co. Cork, 9630

Aghadoe, co. Kerry, 9660

Aghagower, co. Mayo, 10560

Aghaleague, co. Mayo, 9768

Aghaloughan, bog of, co.Antrim, 11718

Aghalurcher, co. Fermanagh, 3905

Aghowle, co. Wicklow, 10487

Aglish, co. Kerry, 9666

Agned, Mons, 1047, 5967

Ahenny, co. Tipperary, 11120, 11158

Aherlow glen, co. Tipperary, 11127

Aicill, *Book of*, 2276, 2519, 2524–80 *passim*

Aidan, *St., bp. of Ferns*, 4805, 4838, 4869

Aidan, *St., bp. of Lindisfarne*, 4036, 4048, 4074, 4134

Ailbe, *abbot of Emly* (Rule), 5621a

Aileach, co. Donegal, 2152, 2163, 2554

Aireran, *the wise, St.*, 5855

Airghialla, 2133

Alba (name), 6862

Alban, *St.*, 4117, 4120, 4419

Alcaston moat, Salop, 1890

Alchred, *king of Northumbria* (coins) 9041

Alcuin, 4261, 5649, 6957, 7057–97, 11846a

Aldate, *St.*, 4400

Aldbrough, Yorks, 9473, 10376

Aldeby (Domesday : Leic.), 6024

Aldfrith, *king of Northumbria*, 50, 1112, 1115, 1122, 1142, 6959, 6964, 7022 : (coins), 9057

Aldhelm, *St., 7th bp. of Sherborne*, 1107, 3911–34, 4148a, 6971, 7343 : (correspondence with Æthelbald, king of Mercia), 1110 : (crosses), 10992 : (legal studies), 2361 : (riddles), 7671, 7677, 7680–81, 7702. *See also* Sherborne

Aldhelm, *St.*, ' juxta Werham ' (church of), 3902

Aldhun, *bp. of Chester-le-Street (and Durham)*, 4051

Aldingbourne, Sussex, 2964

Aldingham-in-Furness, Lancs. (motte), 7957, 7959–60, 7963

Aldred, *scribe*, 7140

Aldreth, *battle* (1071) [?site], 6099

Aldwulf, *king* (charter to Lindfield, 765), 376

Alexandria (Tin trade with, 7th c., A.D.), 3146

Alfege, *St. See* Ælfheah

Alfred, *ætheling*, 1371

Alfred, *king*, 1193–1276, 5886 : (as man of letters), 1206, 1209, 1225, 4176–78, 5658–67, 5720, 6961, 6964 : (charter to Chertsey), 318 : (charter to North Newenton, Wilts., 892), 366 : (coins), 8884, 8887, 8891, 9009, 9091–9100, 9276 : (date of death, 899) 454, 1267 : (dates, regnal, of), 439 : (geography of), 6146–85 : (jewel of), 11495, 11550,

Alfred, *king (continued)*
11593–11602 : (laws), 2423, 2432, 2443, 2447 : (letter on educational policy), 6979–80 : (manor house of, Mudgeley), 10136 : (priviledge of, 898), 426 : (proverbs of), 7662–64, 7669–70 : (will of), 431, 2053, 2456–58, 5918, 6069–72

Alfred, *king of Northumbria. See* Aldfrith

Alfriston, Sussex, 8375, 8378, 8574, 8746, 11589

Alfritha, *daughter of Alfred the Great*, 1197

Alhstan, *bp. of Sherborne* (ring), 11626

Alkborough, Lincs., 6565

Alkelda, *St., of Middleham*, 4421

Alkest, Isle of Man, 6841

Alkmund, *St.*, 4415

All Cannings, Wilts., 2065

Allen, co. Kildare (hill of), 2166 : (battle, 718), 1164

Almondbury, Yorks., 7950

Alnmouth, Nhd., 9480

Alnwick, Nhd., 10914

Alod, 3107

Alsace, 7051 : (cult of St. Brigid in), 4517

Altar, 10139 : (cutting of 5 crosses on), 10621

Alured, *the Marshall*, 6036

Alverstoke, Hants. (charter, 948), 315, 362

Amber, 7505, 8119, 8177, 11462, 11505, 11552, 11679, 11702

Amesbury, Wilts, 2079, 3281

Amiatinus, Codex, 3585, 5679, 7188–7202, 7226, 11830, 11846a

Amounderness hundred, Lancs., 6680

Ampney St. Peter, Glos., 10596

Amusements, 2648, 2666

Andérida, and forest, Sussex, 3031, 6096

Andreas (Kirk), Isle of Man, 11195–96, 11203, 11225

Aneirin, 229–30, 237, 240, 242, 247

Angeln, 843–60 *passim*

Anglesey, 2244, 10524 : (inscriptions), 10021 : (personal names), 644 : (sculpture), 11351–58. *See also* Llanfachreth, Llangwyllog, Penmon, Penrhos Llugwy.

Anglo-Saxon Chronicle, 51, 76–104a, 438, 441, 449, 6308 : (MS. A), 77–78, 80–81, 96, 99, 100, 102, 104, 433 : (MS. B), 88 : (MS. C), 79, 83, 88 : (MS. D), 76, 84, 89, 95, 98 : (MS. E), 78, 82, 95, 102, 447 : (MS. F), 87, 95, 101, 101a-b : (MS. G), 92

Anhalt Morgan Gospels, 7244

Angels (names of), 7563

Anianus, *St.*, 5251

Animals, 7375–87 *passim*, 7575 : (Doe, course makes monostic boundary), 3697 : (Dog, resuscitated), 4503 : (ferret), 7384 : (forest), 3026 : (in ecclesiastical literature), 4459, 4504, 7559 : (in personal names), 561 : (in place-names), 6309, 6801 : (weasel), 7726

Anlaf. *See* Olaf

Annales Cambriae, 244, 517, 865, 867, 951, 5057, 6133

Annals, *Irish*, (cattle mentioned in), 7606 : (comets mentioned in), 7404 : (dating of), 461 : (in MS. Cotton Titus A. XXV), 181–82 : (names in), 208, 641 : ('Three Fragments'—MS. Brussels, Bib. Royale, 5301–21), 186, 215–16, 1168

Anstie Bury, Surrey, 7968

Antrim, *county* (crosses), 11128, 11143 : (place names), 6808, 6822. *See also* Aghaloughan (bog of), Armory, Budore, Connor, Cushendall, Dunluce, Nendrum, Portglenone

Apocrypha, Irish, 5846–47, 5860

Apollonius, of Tyre (O.E. version), 7579

Appleby, Old, Westm., 10809

Aquhollie, Kincardine, 9895

Aquitaine (relations with Ireland), 1634

Aran islands, co. Galway, 2185

Arbogast, *St., bp. of Strasburg*, 5240

Arbory, Isle of Man, 9820

Arculf, 6204–05, 6217a

Ardagh, co. Limerick (brooches), 11691–92 : (chalice), 10084, 11686, 11691–92, 11729

Ardboe, co. Tyrone, 11110

Ardderyd, *battle of* (c. 573), 1010, 6112

Ardilaun, co. Galway, 3772

Ardmore, co. Waterford, 9733, 9735, 9743, 10486, 10570

Ardoileán, co. Galway, 10494

Ardpatrick, co. Limerick, 2125

Ardstraw, co. Tyrone, *see of*, 3862

Argh [place-names], 6381, 6386

Argoed, *kingdom of*, 1826

Argyllshire (invasion by Picts, 736 and 741), 1163 : (Norsemen in), 2203 : (place-names), 6864 : (sculpture), 11242–50. *See also* Ballinaby (Islay), Bhreacain cave (Jura), Carn nan Bharraich (Oronsay), Coll (island

Argyllshire (continued)
of), Colonsay (island of), Dunadd,
Eileach an Naoimh (island of),
Gigha (island of), Iona (island of),
Islay (island of), Isle of Saints,
Keills, Kilbride, Kildalton (Islay),
Kildonan bay (Kintyre), Kilmartin,
Kiloran bay (Colonsay), Kintyre,
Oronsay (island of), Tiree (island of)
Arild, St., 4420
Armagh, 2145, 3383, 3400, 3427, 3758,
3909, 6831, 9782, 11130, 11157,
11717
Armagh, Book of, 184–85, 201, 4567–97
passim, 7278, 11714
Armagh, county (Brigid's crosses in),
11156. See also Armagh, Clonarb,
Tynan
Armoy, co. Antrim, 10568
Arms, armour, 1464, 3006, 8670–8744,
11964
Army, Danish, 2298
Arne hill, Berks., 8395
Arran, Bute, 2201, 9873. (Holy Isle,
remains on), 4847, 5001, 9890,
9898–99 : (Kilpatrick cashel—early
Christian settlement), 3363 : (place-
names), 6850, 6854
Arrest, 2491
Arreton, I.o.W., Hants., 8418
Arrow valley, Herefordshire, 7948
Arthur, king, 962, 1011, 1039–1102, 1297,
2264, 7590, 7609–27 : (chronology
of), 458 : (place-names), 6937 :
(propaganda), 1663–74 : (saints
and), 4143, 5052 : (sites), 5955–76
Arthuret, Cumb., battle (c. 573), 1010,
1017, 6112, 10840
Arthurlee, Renfrewshire, 11307
Arundel, Sussex, 10637
Arundel Penitential, 5586
Arundel Psalter, 5699a, 5717
Ashburton, Devon, 1687
Ashdown, battle (871), 1168a, 1169–70,
1179–80, 1182, 1192, 1192a, 6095,
6106
Ashfield, Great, Suffolk, 10629
Ashingdon (Assandun), battle (1016),
1346, 5977–82
Aslockton, Notts, 8696, 8794
Aspatria, Cumb., 10816, 10819
Asprington, Devon, 6791
Assart-land, 2696, 2698
Asser (Joannes), bp. of Sherborne, 105–
114

Assicus, St., bp. of Elphin, 4808
Asthall, Oxon, 8263
Aston, Berks. (charter, 801), 380
Aston, Oxon., 3271
Aston, Warw., 2974–75
Aston Cantlow, Warw., 8294
Aston on Salwarpe, Worcs., 7245
Astrology, 7498, 7502
Astronomy, 7400–06
Ath Da Ferta [Ford of the grave], 6138
Athanasian Creed, 5827
Athelney, Isle of, Somerset, 1211 :
(abbey), 1274, 3711
Athelstan, king, 69, 1278–79, 1290, 1297,
1304, 1677a, 3338, 3460, 5086 :
(charter to North Newenton, Wilts.,
933), 366, 388 : (charter to St.
Buryan, 943–spurious), 403, 1696 :
(charters to Worcester), 395 : (chro-
nology), 439 : (coins), 9102–38
passim : (endowment of college at
St. Buryan), 286 : (grant to Malmes-
bury, 931), 8461 : (grant to Wilton
abbey, 937), 357 : (laws), 2414 :
(relics), 4112–13 : (statutes), 3049
Athelstan I (son of Egbert), king of
East Anglia, Kent, etc. (coins), 8968,
8977, 8981, 8983–85
Athlone, co. Westmeath, 9756, 11150
Auckland St. Andrew, co. Durham,
10872, 10874,
Aughascribbagh, co. Tyrone, 9792
Aughton, Lancs., 10900
Augiestin, Irish writer, 206
Augury, 7482
Augustine, St., 3935–69, 6206 : (Oak),
3520, 3959, 3969
Aultagh, co. Cork, 9784
Auquharney, Aberdeenshire, 8668
Aurora borealis, 7405
Aust, 3967–68
Aveland, Lincs., 6062
Axeholm, Isle of, Lincs., 6574, 6577
Axminster, Devon (Cyneheard buried at)
1137
Aycliffe, co. Durham, 10879
Aylesbury-road, co. Dublin (mound),
8530–31
Aylesford, Kent, lathe of, 3197
Ayre, Orkney (broch), 8032
Ayrshire (sculpture), 11315. See also
Fardenreoch, Girvan

Badanoð Beotting (will), 2460
Badbury rings, Dorset, 5960, 5964

Badby, Northants., **11583**

Baden (missionaries in), **5254**

Badon, *Mt.*, *battle*, **140, 153, 1039–41, 1053, 1060, 1070, 1081, 1094, 5955, 5958–60, 5963–64, 5969, 5975, 6083**

Baginbun, co. Wexford, **9967, 9996**

Baginton, Warw., **8292–93, 8584**

Bail, **2491, 2507**

Bain, Lincs. [river], **6438**

Baithen, *St.*, *2nd abbot of Iona*, **5027**

Bakewell, Derbs., **10663, 10675, 10681**

Balance-beam, **8647, 8655**

Baldred, *king of Kent*, (coins), **8962–63, 8970**

Baldred, *St.*, **5012, 5026**

Baldricus, *abbot of Bourgueil*, *abp. of Dol*, **1520, 1533, 1560**

Balladoyne, Isle of Man, **8508**

Ballaghmoon, *battle* (903 or 908), **1309**

Ballaqueeney, Isle of Man, **8525, 9820, 9822**

Ballavarkish, Isle of Man, **11214**

Ballinaby, Islay, Argyllshire, **8498, 8791**

Ballinderry crannog, co. Westmeath (gaming-board), **8524, 8638, 10603**

Ballinderry Lough, co. Westmeath, **9763**

Ballingarry, co. Limerick, **9758**

Ballintaggart, co. Kerry, **9658, 9660, 9668**

Ballinvoher, co. Kerry, **9669**

Ballyboodan, co. Kilkenny, **9646, 9706, 9711**

Ballycattern, co. Cork, **7988**

Ballycrovane, co. Cork, **9621**

Ballyholme, co. Down, **11645, 11647**

Ballyknock, co. Cork, **9620, 9644–45**

Ballymorereigh, co. Kerry, **9679**

Ballymote, *Book of*, **9590–91**

Ballyvourney, co. Cork, **10135, 11136**

Ballywiheen, co. Kerry, **10495**

Balsham, Cambs., **10622, 10628**

Baltinglass, co. Wicklow, **9768**

Bamburgh, Northumberland, **1935**

Bampton, Oxon., **10161**

Banffshire. *See* Kirkmichael

Bangor, Carnarvonshire, **2250, 3785, 3851, 8800, 9101**

Bangor, co. Down, **3770, 4801, 8509**

Bangor, *Antiphony of* [Bobbio MS.], **5761, 5764, 5852, 5854, 7277**

Banquo (?identity of, and of Fleance), **1627**

Banstead, Surrey, **8450**

Bantry, co. Cork, **11116, 11172**

Banwell, Somerset, **2097**

Baptism, **5351** : (pagan), **3492**

Bardney, Lincs., *abbey*, **3733**

Bards, **6998–99, 7023, 7340**

Bardsey, Yorks., **1946**

Barham downs, Kent, **8200, 8749**

Barholme, Lincs., **10264**

Barintus [?=St. Barri], **3481**

Barkwith, East and West, Lincs., **1823**

Barlaston, Staffs., **8310, 8334**

Barnaan Cuilawn, **7581**

Barnack, Northants., **10276, 10287–88, 10714**

Barnafeadog, co. Louth, **9719**

Barnetby-le-Wold, Lincs., **6562**

Barnett coin collection, **8863**

Barnstaple, Devon, **1677a, 2743, 3177** : (mint), **9290, 9311, 9322, 9354**

Barra, island of, Inverness-shire, **6848a, 8518, 11335**

Barrington, Cambs., **8111, 8118, 8163, 11482, 11821**

Barrow, Leic., **2613**

Barrow-on-Humber, Lincs., **6564**

Barrows and burials, heathen [as landmarks in A.–S. charters], **343–45, 357, 7742**

Barrymore castle, co. Cork, **9638**

Barton [place-name], **6351, 6781**

Barton-on-Humber, Lincs., **1827, 5991, 8365, 10260–61, 10268**

Barton Stacey, Hants., **2087**

Basingstoke, Hants., **8423**

Basingwerk, *Book of*, **238**

Basset down, Wilts., **8474**

Baston, Lincs., **8337**

Bath, **1321a, 2039–41, 2098, 2115, 3712, 6733, 8654, 10996, 11006**

Bath Forinsecum, Somerset, *hundred of*, **2115.**

Bath Forum, Somerset, *hundred of*, **2044**

Battersea, Surrey, **2031, 6611, 8083**

Battle, Sussex, *abbey*, **3716, 10384** : (charters), **305** : (hidation), **3079** : (roll of), **552, 1558**

Baudri, *de Bourgueil*. *See* Baldricus

Bavaria (Irish art in), **10109** : (Irish missionaries in), **5225–26, 5228, 5334–35**

Bawtry, Notts., **8719**

Bayeux tapestry, **51, 1431–81, 1560**

Beacons, **2305**

Bealach Leachta, co. Cork, *battle* (978), **2167**

Bealin, co. Westmeath, **9764, 11117**

Bealings, Little, Suffolk, **8675**

Beards, 2636

Beaworth find [pennies of William I.], 8872, 9219, 9225–26

Beccles, Suffolk, 6473

Becfhola, *wooing of* [7th c. saga], 1159

Beckermet, Cumb., 10835, 10852

Beckermont, Cumb., 9471, 9505

Bedale, Yorks., 10941

Beddington, Surrey, 8437, 8444, 8548

Bede, 4154–4279. *See under the various subdivisions*: *also*: 437, 456, 879, 1062, 3944, 3949, 4317, 7468: (chronology of Ecclesiastical History), 451: (Death song), 4148a, 5638: (geography of Ecclesiastical History), 5879: (library of), 7142: (name), 620: (penitential of), 5583: (personal names in), 606, 4172: (place-names in), 4227, 6301: (riddles), 7720

Bedford, 1927, 8205, 8634: (battle of, 571), 11497, 11524: (mint), 9350: (place-name), 6599, 6603

Bedfordshire, 1866, 1892: (cemeteries), 8201–15: (charters), 336: (Danes in, 921), 1305: (devastation of, 1065 and 1066), 1355: (Domesday) *see* Domesday (Beds.): (earthworks), 7937, 7947: (place-names), 6602, 6604: (water-mills), 2690. *See also* Bedford, Elstow, Felmersham, Kempston, Leagrave, Leighton Buzzard, Luton, Milton Bryan, Risinghoe, Sandy, Sheepwalk hill, Toddington

Bedminster, Somerset, 2100

Bedwig (in West Saxon genealogies), 465

Bedwyn, Wilts, 2029, 2034: (battle, 675), 6083: (mint), 9273

Beeston Tor, Staffs. (coin find), 8884, 11565

Beg-Eire, co. Wexford (St. Ibar's monastery), 4819

Belcoo, co. Fermanagh (brooch), 11704

Belladooan, co. Mayo, 8803

Bellafago, William de, *bp. of Thetford*, 4070

Bells, 3768, 7682, 11738–72, 11781

Belvoir, Leics., 7944

Benedict, *St., of Aniane* (Epitome of), 5589

Benedict, *St., of Nursia* (Rule of), 5578–79, 5584

Benedict Biscop, *abbot of Jarrow*, 3579

Benedictional of abp. Robert of Jumièges [at Rouen], 5753, 5774, 11924, 11931, 11943

Benedictional of St. Æthelwold, 11924–25, 11931–32, 11943

Benen, *Sts.*, 4812

Benfleet, Essex, 5980, 7916

Benignus, *St., of Armagh*, 4823

Bennington, Long, Lincs., 11477

Benniworth, Lincs., 8581

Bensington (Benson), Oxon., 2045

Bentham, Yorks., 10945

Benty Grange, near Monyash, Derbs., 8216, 8227

Benwell, Nhb., 11468

Beoc, *St., of Wexford*, 4864

Beorhtric, *king of E. Anglia* (coins), 8986

Beorhtric, *king of Wessex* (coins), 9084

Bearhtwulf, *king of Mercia* (coins), 8958–59, 8961, 9015

Beowulf (links with Mercia), 1108–09: (manuscript, Cotton Vitellius A XV), 7224, 7237, 7250: (name), 611

Berach, *St., abbot*, 4845

Beranburh, *battle* (566), 6083

Berchan, *prophecy of*, 756

Berechtwine (name), 633

Beretchert, *St., of Tullylease*, 3430, 4773, 4857, 9634

Bergholt, West, Essex, 11627

Berin, *St. See* Birinus

Berkeley, Glos., 10688: (mint), 9220, 9274

Berkeley, Roger de, 1340

Berkshire, 2104, 3521: (archaeology of), 7763, 8389–8411: (barrows), 343–44: (charters), 347: (Domesday) *see* Domesday (Berks.): (earthworks), 7843, 7846: (name), 301, 6713, 6720: (paganism in), 3493: (place-names), 6706, 6712, 6722, 6724: (pottery), 8577: (roads), 6188, 6199: (sculpture), 10978, 10982–85. *See also* Abingdon, Arne hill, Ashdown, Aston, Besselsleigh, Betterton, Blewbury, Boxford, Brightwell, Coleshill, Cookham, Earmundslea, Frilford, Garford, Hampstead Marshall, Hurley, Kintbury, Lamborne, Lockridge, Mackney, Mortimer, Newbury, Reading, Roeburgh hundred, Shefford (East and West), Shefford Woodlands, Silchester, Sotwell, Speenhamland, Sunninghill, Sutton

Berkshire (continued).
Courtenay, Swallowfield, Theale, Tilehurst, Wallingford, Wantage, Welford, Wittenham (Long)
Berla laws, 2558
Bermondsey, Surrey (coins), 8903
Bernicia (boundary), 5923, 5925, 5940 : (name), 20a
Berts [Domesday manor, Sussex], 6043
Berwickshire (place-names), 6872. See also Black dykes, Cockburn law, Coldingham, Hoprig (Cockburnspath), Hordwell
Besselsleigh, Berks., 2695
Betchworth, Surrey, 2708
Betha Colmáin, topography of, 5919
Betterton, Berks., 8409
Beuno, St., 5126
Beverley, Yorks., 1970a, 1975a, 10363, 3712a
Bewcastle, Cumb. (cross, inscription), 9453–69, 9495 : (cross, sculpture), 10038, 10767–89, 10835 : (wheel dial), 527
Bexhill, Sussex, 10638
Bexley, Kent (dyke near), 7838
Bhreacain cave, Jura, Argyllshire, 11721
Biarmia, 6163a–65, 6178, 6181
Bibliothèque National, Paris (A.–S. MSS. in), 53
Bibury, Glos., 10690
Bickington, High, Devon, 3338
Bidford-on-Avon, Warw., 8296–97, 8747–48
Bidston, Cheshire, 1828
Bifrons, Kent, 8176, 11615
Billingham, co. Durham, 10366
Bilton, Yorks., 10964, 10968
Bindon hill, battle (614), 1124
Bind-runes, 11196
Bingley, Yorks., 10944, 10969
Biohchandoune (site), 304, 6117
Birel [female servant], 3209
Birinus, St. bp. of West Saxons, 3803, 4033, 4046, 4075
Birmingham, Warw., 1815, 1908, 1914, 2974–76
Birsay, Orkney, 1618, 9885, 11260
Birstall, Yorks., 10930
Birtley, Nhd., 10909
Birton, Worcs. (A.–S. sundial at), 529
Biscovey, Cornwall, 11049
Bishops, appointment of, 3835

Bishopstone, Sussex, 10390, 10393, 10404 : (sundial), 538, 547
Bixlea, Sussex (grant by Offa, 772), 408
Bjoerke, Norway, 11603
Black Book of Chirk, 2600
Black Dykes, Berwickshire, 7850
Black Rood of Scotland, 4108, 4123
Blackheath, Surrey, 6612
Blackrock brooch, 11707
Blackwell, Derbs., 10673, 10676
Blæce, 7429
Blaitmaic, St., of Iona, 4763, 4871
Bledlow, Bucks., 8309, 8637, 11607
Blegywryd, Book of, 2595, 2595a
Blewbury, Berks., 2082, 8393
Blickling Homilies, 5795–5800
Blockley, Worcs., 8286
Blood covenant (Celtic), 2682
Boarhunt, Hants., 3125, 10426, 10439
Bobbio Missal, 5726–30, 5752
Bobbio, monastery, 5416, 5458–67 : (library), 7151–72 : (manuscripts), 5761, 5850, 7277 : (scriptorium), 7172, 7302, 7314
Bockerly dyke, 892, 7840
Bodmin Gospels, 3208, 3213, 3229, 5686, 7233
Boedan, St. (bell), 11748
Boldgetæl, 2443
Boley hill, Rochester, Kent, 7922
Bolney, Sussex, 10386
Bonchurch, I. of W., Hants., 2116
Boniface, St., 4392, 5148a, 5266–5362 : (birthplace), 925, 5353 : (letters), 72, 5266–79, 5292, 5313, 5360, 5813 : (riddles), 7700
Book of Armagh. See Armagh, Book of
Book of Conquests (or Invasions) of Ireland. See Leabhar Gabála
Book of Deer. See Deer, Book of
Book of Dhimma. See Dhimma, Book of
Book of Rights [Irish]. See Leabhar na gCeart
Book of the Dun Cow. See Leabhar na Huidre
Bookland, 257, 3118–19, 3128–29, 3132, 3210
Book-right, 3108
Borh [pledge], 2498
Borhtriming, 2448
Boroma [Irish fine], 802, 2557
Borough English, 2735, 3203
Boroughs, 2727–55
Borstall horn, 3233–34
Borthwick Mains, Roxburgh, 9897

F

Bosbury, Herefordshire, 11764
Bosham, Sussex, 2011, 10387, 10394
Boston, Lincs., 1922a
Bosworth Psalter, 5714, 7222
Bosworth-Toller (additions to diction-
    ary), 29
Botany (in A.–S. charters of Wilts.), 306,
    346
Bothamsall, Notts., 7926
Botl [place-names], 6401
Botley, Hants. (discovery of ship at),
    2286
Botolph, *St.*, 4408, 4437, 6122
Bough, Rathvilly, co. Carlow, 11716
Boultypatrick, co. Donegal, 4660
Boundaries, 268, 277, 3697, 5922–41,
    6398, 7856, 7984, 8810a. *See also*
    Offa's dyke
Bourne Park, Kent, 7919
Bourton-on-the-Water, Glos., 6342, 8610,
    10116, 10124
Bow, Midlothian, 8047
Bowcombe down, I.o.W., Hants., 8417,
    8425
Boxford, Berks., 10430
Bracklaghboy, co. Mayo, 9726, 9755, 9784
Brackley, Northants. (coin), 8995
Bradbourne, Derbs., 10664–65, 10675
Braddon, Kirk, Isle of Man, 11198,
    11200, 11213, 11225
Braden, Wilts., *forest of*, 3667
Bradford, Yorks., 1981
Bradford-on-Avon, Wilts., 2062–63, 3887,
    10410–24, 11005 : (charter, 1001),
    379
Brailsford, Derbs., 10668
Bramham, Yorks., 11454
Brampford, Devon (charter), 398
Brampton, Little, Herefordshire, 2887
Bran ditch, Cambs., 7776–77, 7780, 8140,
    8758 : (massacre at, 1010), 1360
Brandon, Suffolk, 1759
Branscombe, Devon, 1714
Branwalatr, *St.* [Brelade], 4114, 5086
Bray, co. Wicklow, 11165
Breach down, Kent, 7919, 11462
Breadalbane, Perthshire (brooch), 11720c :
    (place-names), 6918
Breamore, Hants., 10438
Breastagh, co. Mayo, 9723–24, 9768, 9789
Brechin, Forfar, 10546, 10548, 10566
Brecknockshire (castles, 10th c.), 8071 :
    (inscriptions), 9923–32, 9935 : (sculp-
    ture), 11416–18. *See also* Brecon,
    Crickhowel, Llanddetty stone, Llan-

devaelog, Llanfeigan, Llangorse,
    Llywel, Patrishow, Pentyr-Poeth,
    Pen-y-Mynnid, Trallong
Brecon, Brecknock, 2258
Breedon-on-hill, Leic., 10691, 10693–94
Breguoin (Mons Agned) [?=High
    Rochester), 5967
Brehon laws, 2520, 2524–80 *passim*, 2586,
    2689, 7458
Bréifne, *kingdom of*, 2164
Brelade, *St.* [Branwalatr], 4114, 5086
Brendan, *St., abbot of Clonfert*, 3769, 6205,
    6238–82
Brent, Somerset (grant of, to Glaston-
    bury, 663), 342
Brentford, Devon (charter), 398
Bressay, Shetland, 9882, 11259, 11263–64
Breteuil, *laws of*, 2401–02
Bretha Nemed (law of the priviledged
    classes), 2571
Bretwaldas, 2266, 2333–34
Brian, *of Brittany, earl of Cornwall*, 1579
Brian, *king of Munster*, 1301
Brian Borumha, *king of Ireland*, 1632 :
    (name), 634 : *See also under* Clontarf
Briavel, *St.*, 5099
Bricklehampton, Worcs., 8302
Bride [parish], Isle of Man, 11206, 11214
Bridekirk, Cumb., 9458, 9495, 9500,
    9502, 10819
Bridell, Pembrokeshire, 9972, 9974, 9977,
    10016
Bridge, Kent, 8195
Bridgend, Glam., 11393
Bridgford, East, Notts., 10315, 10745
Bridgford, West, Notts., 1903, 1921
Bridgnorth, Salop, 4433, 6524, 7925
Bridle-bit, 8628, 8652, 11463
Bridport, Dorset (mint), 9347, 9349
Brie, 5449
Brigg, Lincs. (discovery of ship at), 2285
Brigham, Cumb., 10814
Brighthampton, Oxon., 8258, 8260, 8268–
    69
Brighton, Sussex, 2017
Brightwell, Berks. (charter), 333
Brigid, *St.*, 2136, 4505–22, 4757, 5133,
    5501, 5834, 5836, 11823–25 : (crosses),
    11156
Brigstock, Northants., 10280
Brihtnoth, *abbot of Ely*, 3727
Brihtnoth, *ealdorman* (buried at Ely, 991),
    1320
Brihtric, *king of Wessex* (charter to Aston,
    Berks., 801), 380

Brihtric(?father to Gundreda de War-
enne), **496**
Brihtricestan, Devon (manor of), **6111**
Brioc, *St.*, **5079**
Brislingcote, Burton, Staffs., **11466**
Bristol, Glos., **2099, 2101–02** : (mint)
9268, 9306 : (museum), **11684**
Britford, Wilts., **10458–60**
Brittany, **931, 1541, 1638, 1651–52, 5163–**
5214, 6218–26 *passim*
Brittas, co. Kilkenny, **9712**
Britway, co. Cork, **10483**
Britwell, Wilts., **10991**
Brixham, Devon, **1726**
Brixworth, Northants., **1887, 10281,**
10285–86, 10289, 10291, 11472
Brize Norton, Oxon., **8266**
Broadchalke, Wilts., **8463, 8768, 10998**
Broadstairs, Kent, **8177**
Brocaidh, *St. and bp.*, **4776**
Brochs, **7730, 8015–64, 8623, 8657, 11261**
Brockworth, Glos., **1818**
Brodie, Moray, **9895**
Bromfield, Cumb., **10811, 10813**
Brompton, Yorks., **10965**
Brooches, **3140**. *See* in sections ceme-
teries and jewellery, *passim*
Brookborough, co. Fermanagh, **9753**
Broomfield, Essex, **8154**
Brough, Westmorland, **9508**
Broughton Gifford, Wilts., **2119**
Broughton Poggs, Oxon., **8257, 8259**
Broyle, Sussex, **11608**
Bruges, **11823–25**
Brunanburh, *battle* (937), **1282, 1284,**
1291, 1302, 1307, 1310, 1334, 5983–
6012, 8914 : (place-name), **6349**
Brunemue (site), **6115**
Brunswick reliquary, **9429, 9431, 9433,**
9438–39
Brussels cross (inscription), **9425, 9427,**
9432, 9457a
Brut y Saeson, **243**
Brut y Tywysogion, **234–35, 244**
Brychan documents, **250**
Brychan, *St. and king*, **5041, 5073, 7590** :
(genealogical evidence), **510**
Buchan, Aberdeenshire, **3421**
Buckets, **8621, 8626–27**
Buckfast, Devon, *abbey*, **3709**
Buckinghamshire, **1855, 8328** : (con-
version), **3541** : (Danes in), **1842** :
(Domesday) *see* Domesday (Bucks.):
(dykes), **7833** : (11th c.), **1840** :
(hundreds), **3163–64a** : (place-

names), **6583, 6587**. *See also* Bled-
low, Desborough castle, Elles-
borough, Iver, Mentmore, Newport
Pagnell, Risborough, Stone, Tap-
low, Tickford, Whaddon chase,
Wing, Wycombe (High)
Buckland, Glos., **1821**
Buckland Denham, Somerset, **8429**
Budleigh, East, Devon, **1690, 1716**
Budoc, *St.*, **5104** : (name), **622**
Budore, co. Antrim, **11664**
Buern Brucecarle, **1167, 1647**
Buidhean [bell of Strowan], **11772**
Builders, building, **10169, 10172, 10176,**
10327, 10513–14 : (measurements),
523
Bulwick, Northants., (coins), **8983**
Bumpstead, Steeple, Essex, **11723**
Buncton, Sussex, (grant from, 791), **304**
Buraburg, *bishopric of*, **5236, 5322**
Burbage, Derbs., **10680**
Burbage, Wilts., **2034**
Bures, Essex, **7896**
Burford, Oxon., **6342, 10744**
Burgage tenure, **2735, 3247, 3250–51**
Burgesses, Domesday. *See* Domesday
Burgh, *abbey of*. *See* Peterborough
Burgh castle, Suffolk, **1766, 5215, 7910,**
8989
Burghal hidage, **3063, 3067**
Burghead, Moray, **3907, 8055**
Burghs. *See* Boroughs
Burgred, *king of Mercia* (coins), **7535,**
8884, 8887, 8891, 8897–98, 9000–01,
9005, 9009 : (spurious charter to
Crowland, 868), **394**
Burh-geat-setl [in Law of Promotion],
2450
Burmarsh, Kent (charters), **423**
Burnett, Somerset, **11480**
Burning [at stake], **2504**
Burnley, Lancs., **5998–99**
Burnswork, Dumfriesshire, **5984, 5996,**
6001
Burra, Shetland, **11262**
Burradon, Nhd., **8704**
Burray, island of, Orkney, **11688**
Burrian, N. Ronaldsay, Orkney (broch),
8040, 8657
Burt, co. Donegal (coins), **9126**
Burton, Staffs, *abbey* (cartulary), **117, 430:**
(charter from Æthelred II), **330**
Burwell, Cambs., **8134, 8238, 8747, 8758,**
8760, 8771
Bury [place-names], **6405, 6417**

Bury Psalter, 5724
Bury St. Edmunds, Suffolk, *abbey*, 3624–
    29 : (charter under William I), 327 :
    (grants from Edward the Con-
    fessor), 325 : (Harlowbury given
    to), 1354 : (survey of estate, temp.
    Leofstan), 328. — *borough*, 4741a
Bute, 2216, 3394. *See also* Arran (Holy
    Isle, Kilpatrick, King's cross, Lam-
    lash), Milport, Rothsay, St. Blane
Buttermere, Cumb. (mill), 2719
Buttington, Montgomery, *battle* (894),
    1248, 2246, 5915, 6088, 8796
Byrhtferth, *of Ramsey*, 61, 64, 71, 4042,
    7348, 7357, 7361–69
Byrhtnoth, 1313, 1316 : (date of death,
    10. viii. 991), 440
Bywell, Nhd., 10367, 10907
Byzantium (art influence), 1649, 10063,
    10585–86 : (immigration to), 1659 :
    (influence—glazed ware), 8587 : (re-
    lations with, 7th–10th, c.), 1649–50

Cadbury, Somerset, 1045, 1097, 7746,
    7870
Cadoc, *St.*, 5028, 5097
Cadwalla, *king of Wessex. See* Cædwalla
Cædmon, 367, 4423, 4431, 4440, 9455,
    9463 : (metrical paraphrase : ms.),
    7243, 11928, 11930 : (name), 568
Cædwalla, *king of Wessex* (charter, hun-
    dred of Manwood), 381 : (charter
    to Selsey monastery), 382 : (' Epita-
    phium Ceadwallae '), 1117
Caellwic, Cornwall, *manor of*, 406, 6120
Caenby, Lincs., 11655
Caer Iuden (site), 5972
Caerleon, Mon., 2261, 11389
Caerwent, Mon., 2245
Caher Island, co. Mayo, 3774, 10500
Caherelly, co. Limerick, 11141
Cahirciveen, co. Kerry, 9673
Caillin, *St.*, 4788, 4806, 11758
Caimin, *St.* (Psalter of), 7264
Cáin Adamnáin, 2556, 2563, 2568
Cáin Eimíne Báin, 7536
Cainneach [Canice], *St.*, 4771, 4781,
    4837, 4840
Caio, Carmarthenshire, 8669
Cairn valley, Dumfriesshire, 6897
Caistor, Lincs., 8314, 9449
Caithness, 2237 : (brochs in), 8022,
    8042–43, 8056, 8058 : (ecclesias-
    tical history), 3364 : (Ninianic
    foundations), 3434 : (Norse colon-

isation of), 2212 : (sculpture),
    11303. *See also* Achavrole, Acker-
    gill, Dunbeath, Freswick Links,
    Latheron, Ousdale, Reay, Skitten,
    Wick
Calbourne, I.o.W., Hants., 6063.
Caldale, Orkney (coins), 9158
Calder [river], 6447
Caldy island, Pembrokeshire, 6927, 9975,
    9995, 9999, 10002, 10023
Caledones (in 9th c.), 1191
Caledonians (name), 627
Calendars, 265, 526, 5518, 5531, 5534,
    5569, 5759, 5773, 5775 : (10th c.,
    in MS. Cotton Tib. B V), 528 :
    (Robert of Jumièges' Missal : *q.v.*) :
    (York, metrical), 4151
Calf of Man, 11201
Callan mountain, co. Clare, 9761
Cambridge, 1749, 2733, 2747, 7137–38,
    7904, 8135, 8145, 8162, 8756, 10621,
    11821 : (Girton College cemetery),
    8121–22
Cambridge Psalter, 5702
Cambridgeshire, 1740, 1744, 1747, 1754,
    8810a : (cemeteries), 8120 : (Danes
    in), 1300, 1308 : (Domesday) *see*
    Domesday (Cambs.) : (dykes),
    7775–84 : (first English settlement
    of), 905 : (forests), 3042 : (place-
    names), 6492, 6496 : (religious
    houses), 3699 : (sculpture), 10627.
    See also Abington Pigotts, Balsham,
    Barrington, Bran ditch, Burwell,
    Cambridge, Cheveley, Cottenham,
    Cratendune, Ely, Foxton, Friday
    Bridge, Hauxton, Hildersham, Lin-
    ton, Orwell, Shudy Camps, Soham,
    Stapleford, Thorney, War ditches,
    Waterbeach, Whittlesey mere, Wil-
    braham (Little), Wood Ditton
Cambusnethan, Lanark, 11328–29
Camel, West, Somerset, 10993, 10999–
    11000
Camelford [*Gafulforda*], *battle* (823), 6101
Camelot, 1045
Camerton, Somerset, 7515, 8428, 8430,
    11465, 11700
Camin, *St.*, 7270
Camisedale [?=Greenhow, Yorks.],
    6079
Camlan, *battle* (?537), 1079, 5971, 5976
Cammeringham, Lincs., 10709
Campden, Chipping, Glos., 1819
Campodonum [?=Doncaster], 6121

Camus-juxta-Bann, co. Derry, **11135**

Candida Casa, **4974–99**, *passim. See also* Ninian, *St.*

Canfield, Great, Essex, **7893**

Canice. *See* Cainneach, *St.*

Canna park, Devon [field-name], **6792**

Cannington, Somerset, **2053, 8517**

Cano, *son of Gartnán* (7th c. Saga), **1159**

Canon law, **3389, 5361, 5576–5626.** For Rule of Columbanus, *see* Columbanus

Canones Hibernici (Cambray), **196**

Canterbury, **1779, 1789, 3815, 3850, 3861a, 11504, 11569–70** : (archbishops), **4053, 4063** : (their coins), **8946, 8949, 8964–80** *passim* : *see also* under individual archbishops : (Benedictional), **5762** : (Canterbury versus York), **3344, 3817** : (cathedral), **3810, 10205, 10215** : (its library), **313, 5698** : (charter, Dudda's land, 837), **418** : (Christ Church), **3632–36, 3638–39, 3642–43, 3901, 4063** : (coin-hoard), **8894** : (forgeries, c. 1070) *see under* Lanfranc : (Gospels), **7241** : (libraries), **7136** : (mint), **9308** : (Psalter), **5713, 5721, 5723** : (St. Augustine's abbey), **3630–31, 3637, 3640–41, 4060, 4063, 8653, 9521, 10141, 10211–12, 10216–18, 10229–31, 10236, 10639, 11945** : (St. Martin's), **3893–94, 10206, 10233** : (St. Mildred's), **3892, 3899** : (St. Pancras' chapel), **10211** : (school of illumination), **11836a**

Cantoche [Domesday : Quantock], **6028**

'Cantucton,' Somerset, **2053**

Canute, *king. See* Cnut

Capel Brithdir, Glamorgan, **9944, 9948, 10016**

Capel Mair, Carmarthenshire, **9985, 10018**

Capelrig cross, Renfrewshire, **11318**

Capheaton, Nthb. (bowl), **8564**

Capitula Caroli, **48**

Car dyke, Cambs., **7779, 8644**

Caradoc, *Chronicle of*, **248**

Carannog, *St.*, **5074**

Carantoc, *St.*, **5029, 5114, 5116, 5125**

Cardiff, Glamorgan, **2255, 6939, 11395**

Cardiganshire, **2262** : (saints), **5034** : (sculpture), **11411.** *See also* Lampeter, Llanarth, Llanbaddarn Fawr,

Llanddewibrefi, Llandyssil, Llanfechan, Llangwyryfon, Llanwnws, Penbryn, Tregaron

Cardinham, Cornwall, **11043**

Carew, Pembrokeshire, **9967, 9971, 9984, 9996, 10022, 11400**

Carham, Nthb., *battle* (1018), **1602**

Carisbrooke, Hants., **6704, 6723, 7973**

Carlisle, Cumb., **1949, 3952, 4290, 8492, 9462, 9477, 10825, 10829, 10835, 10838** : (lost churches in diocese), **3374** : (patron saints of diocese), **4133**

Carlow, *county. See* Bough (Rathvilly), Crosslow, Killoughternane, St. Mullins, Tuckamine

Carmarthen, *museum*, **9982**

Carmarthenshire (Celtic saints in), **6218** : (inscriptions), **9960–10004** : (place-names), **6938** ; (sculpture), **11359–68.** *See also* Caio, Capel Mair, Cenarth, Conwil Gaio, Craig Gwrtheyrn, Dolau Cothy, Eglwys Cymmyn, Egremont, Eiudon, Gelli-Dywell, Hen Gapel, Llanarthney, Llanbeidy, Llandeilo, Llanfallteg, Llansadyrnin, Llanwinio

Carn Conaill, *battle* (645), **1165**

Carnarvonshire. *See* Bangor, Clynnog, Dinas Emrys, Festiniog, Llystyn Gwyn, Penmachno, Treflys, Tremadoc

Carno, Montgomery, *battles* (949 and 1077), **1614, 1624, 2252**

Carns, hill of, co. Roscommon, **2311**

Carrick-on-Suir, co. Tipperary, **9772**

Carshalton, Surrey, **8439**

Carthage, *St., of Lismore. See* Mochuda

Carthaigh, Clann, **2150**

Carucate, **2789, 3066, 3069, 3073** : (fiscal) **3072** : (Staffs.), **3059**

Cartmel, Lancs., **1938**

Cashel, co. Tipperary, **2187–88** : (Calendar of), **4802** : (diocese), **3861** : (Right of the king of), **2272**

Cassington, Oxon., **8264**

Castell Villia, Pembrokeshire, **9965**

Castle [place-names], **6621**

Castle Acre, Norfolk, **7890, 7902, 8114, 8123, 11573**

Castle Bellingham, co. Louth, **9717**

Castledermot, co. Kildare, **2126, 10562, 11166–67**

Castle Eden, co. Durham (vase), **8559**

'Castle of Cornwall,' **1701**

Castle Rising, Norfolk, **10198** : (mint), **9321**

Castletimon, co. Wicklow, **9747, 9751**

Castleton, Derbs., **1826**

Castor, Northants., **11660**

Castreton [Domesday : ?=Flint], **6040**

Cathach of St. Columba, **7251–56, 11790**

Cathaldus, *St., of Taranto*, **5410**

Catraeth, (Kaltraeth, Kaltraez), *battle*, **229, 237, 1960–62, 1975, 1998, 5972, 6114**

Catrail, **7853–54, 7856, 7858**

Catterick, Yorks., **8346**

Cauldrons, **8625**

Cavalry, Viking, **2288, 2301**

Cavan, *county*. *See* Cloughoughter, Drumlane, Dungimmin (Lower), Mullagh, Slanore

Cave, South, Yorks., **8360**

Cavenham, Suffolk, **8148**

Caw, *of Pictland*, **1011, 1078**

Cé, Aberdeenshire, **6857**

Ceadda, *St. See* Chad

Ceallachán, *king of Cashel*, *See* Cellachan

-*ceaster* [place-names], **6395**

Ceawlin, *king of Wessex*, **900, 902, 907a, 6080**

Cedd, *St., bp. of the East Saxons*, **4037**

Celibacy, **2485, 3472**

Cellach, *St., bp. of Killala*, **1161, 4485, 4772**

Cellachan, *king of Cashel*, **1295, 1328**

Celliwig (site), **5966, 5968**

Cenarth, Carmarthenshire, **9976**

Centwine, *king of Wessex*, (grant of Crucan to Glastonbury), **2083**: (grant of West Monkton to Glastonbury, 682), **326**

Cenwulf, *king of Mercia* (coins), **8882–83, 8902, 8956, 9010, 9015, 11552, 11695** : (seal), **9369**

Ceolfrid, *St., abbot of Wearmouth and Jarrow*, **3585**. *See also* Amiatinus, Codex

Ceolnoth, *abp. of Canterbury*, **3815, 8882, 8884, 8961**

Ceolwulf I, *king of Mercia*, (coins) **8989, 8993–94, 9016**

Cetball mac Muirecáin, *king of Leinster*, **2153–54**

Cerdic, **888** : (genealogy), **469, 921** : (Mons Badonicus and), **1081** : (name), **550**.

Cerdicesora (site of), **889, 916, 950**

Cereals, **2703, 2706a, 2711**

Ceredigion, **2251**

Cern [river-name], **6461**

Cerne, Dorset (giant), **3506**

Cerne, *Book of*, **5776a–77, 5786, 5789, 5793, 7247**

Cerney, South, Glos., **10682**

Cerrig-y-Druidian, Denbigh, **8567**

Cert Ríg Caisil (Right of the king of Cashel), **2272**

Chad, *St., bp. of Lichfield*, **3527, 4037, 4039, 4056, 4071, 4077–78, 4111** : (Gospels of), **5678, 5683, 5696, 7238, 7249**

Chadlington, Oxon, **8265**

' Chalices, stone,' **8552, 8600**

Chancery (?existence under A.-S. kings), **405, 412, 2267**

Chancton farm, Sussex (coins), **9181, 9184, 9336**

Charaton, Cornwall, **6031**

Charlcombe, Somerset, **2054**

Charlemagne, *emperor*, **1635** : (in Northumbrian annals), **1181** : (league with Scotland), **1641**

Charms. *See* Magic

Charters, **253–431, 6125, 6194, 6338, 9377**. *See also under* places concerned and grantors

Chavenage, Glos., **8234**

Cheadle, Cheshire, **10655**

Cheam, Surrey, **8676**

Checkley, Staffs., **10733**

Cheese [place-names], **6396**

Cheldis [Domesday manor, in Craven], **6037**

Chelsea, *councils of*, **3332**

——, (place-name), **6610**

Cheltenham, Glos., **3280, 6579**

Chepstow, Monmouth, **1878**

Chertsey, Surrey (inscription), **9522**

——, *abbey*, **3723, 3728, 9460** : (charters), **318**

Cherwell [river], **8741**

Cheshire, **1885** : (church dedications), **4128** : (Domesday) *see* Domesday (Cheshire) : (place-names), **6511, 6518, 6521, 6671** : (rural settlement), **1906** : (sculpture), **10640–59** : (woodland), **3043**. *See also* Bidston, Cheadle, Chester, Eddisbury, Hilbre, Kirby (West), Macclesfield, Neston, Overchurch, Prestbury, Sandbach, Shotwick, Upton, Wirral

Chessell downs, I.o.W., Hants., **8420**

Chessmen, 11447
Chester, 1847, 1851, 1868, 1891, 1916, 2354, 2738, 10313 : (coin-hoard), 8568, 8906, 9115, 9124–25, 9137, 9150, 9360, 10652, 10658 : (mint), 9280, 9296, 9300, 9320, 9353, 9360 : (Saxon earls of), 1876
—— St. Werburgh's abbey (charters), 397
Chester-le-Street, co. Durham, 3813, 3829, 4282, 10877
Cheveley, Cambs. (deed of exchange and Domesday entry), 295
Chew Stoke, Somerset, 11001
Chichester, Sussex, 297, 8617, 9096, 10634 : (see of), 3838–39, 3848, 4050
Chilham, Kent, 8632
Chilterns, 1888, 3089, 7927
Chilwell, East, Notts., 6023
Chingford, Essex, 1767
Chippenham, Wilts., 2061, 3269 : (mint), 9331
Chipping and market, 3137
Chirk, Black Book of. See Black Book of Chirk
Chislehampton, Oxon., 2928
Chithurst, Sussex, 10397
Christmas. See Yule
Chrodegang, Rule of, 5589–90
Chronology, 432–62
Chulmleigh, Devon, 6787, 6789
Church Island, co. Kerry, 11122
Church Stretton, Salop, 7930
Churchdown, Glos., 1820
Churchscot, 3469–70
Ciaran, St., of Clonmacnoise, 4761, 4779, 4792–93, 4820, 7603 : (crozier of), 11774
Ciaran, St., of Ossory, 4770, 4804, 4837
Ciaran, St., bp. of Saigir, 4485, 4797, 4839, 4841
Cilda [moneyer], 9273
Cill, cillín, 8539, 10471
Cillitona [Domesday : Devon], 6041
Cill-Sleibhe-Cuillinn [Kilslieve], co. Armagh, 3790
Cinque Ports, 2278 : (charters), 311
Cirencester, abbey (charters), 386
Citta [place-name], 6400
Clane, co. Kildare, abbey, 3795, 4520
Clare, county (Aenach sites), 6073 : (cahers [stone forts] of), 7998, 8001 : (churches), 3451 : (ring forts), 8001. See also Callan mountain, Dysert O'Dea, Inchiquin,

Kilfenora, Killaloe, Magh Adhair, Scarriff, Scattery island, Vi-Fearmaic
Claughton hall, Lancs., 11657
Clausentum, Hants. (coin), 8957
Clavering, Essex, 7560
Clayton, Sussex, 10399
Clede Mutha [built by Edward the Elder, 921], 6142, 6145
Clement, St., 4391a
Clermont casket. See Franks casket
Clether, St., 5083
Cleveland, Yorks., 2988, 6620, 8804
Clibberswick, Unst, Shetland, 11671
Clickhimin, Shetland (broch), 8027, 8029
Clifton, Glos., 3267
Clifton, Great, Cumb., 10832, 10838, 10853
Clifton-on-Teme, Worcs., 1852
Climate, 7347
Clog-an-Edachta [bell of St. Patrick], 508, 11765, 11767, 11807
Clog an oir [bell shrine of St. Senan], 11814
Clog Mogue [bell of St. Mogue], 11753, 11756
Clog-na-fullah [bell of blood], 11753
Clog-na-Righ [bell of St. Caillin], 4806, 11758
Clog-oir [bell of St. Senan], 4831
Cloghanecarhan, co. Kerry, 9676
Clogher, co. Tyrone, 2145, 11129, 11805
Clonarb, co. Armagh, 11163
Clondalkin, co. Dublin, 2173
Clonea, co. Waterford, 10499
Clones, co. Monaghan, 10503
Clones Missal, 5757
Clonfert, co. Galway, 3854
Clonmacnoise, King's County, 3776, 3778, 3781, 3791, 8665, 9794, 10505, 11080–87 : (brooch), 11687
Clonmel, co. Tipperary, 9772
Clontarf, battle (1014), 1607, 1609, 1612–13, 1620–21, 1626, 1631–32, 7525.
—— (pin from), 11646, 11663
Cloonmorris, co. Leitrim, 9775
Cloughoughter, co. Cavan, 7982
Clovesho [?site], 6092, 6100, 6105
Cloyne, co. Cork, 2124, 10556
Clydai, Pembrokeshire, 9973, 9986
Clyde (Norsemen on), 2203
Clydesdale (place-names in), 6863
Clynnog, Carnarvonshire (sundial at), 535

Clyst [place-names], 6785
Cnósl, 2643
Cnut, *king*, 1359, 1367–68, 1378, 1384 :
  (charter for Fécamp), 358 : (charter,
  Hazelhurst, Ticehurst, 1018), 419 :
  (coins), 9068, 9158–71, 9283, 9351 :
  (dual with Edmund Ironside), 1365:
  (grant to Pusey family, Pusey horn),
  3241–42 : (laws), 2406, 2410, 2413,
  2415, 2420–21, 2434, 2438 : (writ,
  1020), 369
Cnytel, 557
Coates, Notts., 10750
Cobham, Surrey, 8689
Cockan, Yorks. [lost hamlet], 1976
Cockburn law, Berwickshire, 8057
Codex Amiatinus. *See* Amiatinus, Codex
Codford, Wilts., 10989
Coemgen, *St. See* Kevin
Coenwulf, *king of Mercia. See* Cenwulf
Coercion, Irish, 2555. *See also* Fasting
Cóic Conara Fugill, 2576
Colchester, Essex, 7911, 7913, 10187,
  10188a : (Domesday of), 2874 :
  (mint), 9293, 9352
Cold Eaton, Derbs., 11445
Cold Harbour, 6340, 6350
Coldingham, Berwick, 3715, 3726, 3794,
  3796, 6668
Coldoch, Perthshire, 8063
Coleby, Lincs., 10710
Coleshill, Berks., 8402
Colga, *St., of Clonmacnoise*, 5855
Colga, *St., of Kilcolgan*, 4786
Coliberti [tenure], 3244
Coll, Argyllshire, 6885, 11728
Collingham, Yorks., 9494, 9510, 10954,
  10962
Colman, *St., missionary*, 5244, 5246
Colman, *St., of Cloyne*, 4774, 4866
Colman, *St., of Mayo*, 4789
Colmán, *Maic Lúachain, St.*, 4833
Colman Uacluasaigh, *St.*, 5835
Cologne, *Irish monastery*, 5241
Coloman, *St.*, 4867
Colonies (Kentish in A.–S. England),
  683 : (Scandinavian in Eastern Eng-
  land), 748
Colonsay, Argyllshire, 2213, 8480, 8506,
  8511, 11641
Colour, 7351, 7353, 7360, 7491
Coludes burh, 6086
Columba, *St.*, 4884–4966 : *also*, 1027,
  3379, 3396, 3758, 3764, 5016, 7405,
  7522, 7524, 10515 : (Altus prosator)

5853 : (Cathach : Psalter), 7251–56:
  (obit of), 435, 3560 : (reliquary of),
  11334, 11790, 11799 : (Rule), 4929 :
  For Ninian-Columba controversy,
  see 4974–99, *passim*
Columbanus, *St.*, 5417–98, 5554, 5565,
  5719 : (Penitential and Rule), 5419,
  5422–25, 5429–35, 5439–40, 5469,
  5475, 5595, 5608
Columkille, *St. See* Columba, *St.*
Colyton, Devon, 11030
Combs, 8623, 8630–31, 8634, 8646, 8656
Combwich, Somerset, 8516
Comets, 7404
Comgall, *St., abbot of Bangor (Ireland)*,
  4794, 4801
Commendation, 3008, 3014, 3245
' Companions of the Conqueror,' 1538
Compass, Viking, 2303
Compensation, 2521
Composition for crime, 2524–25, 2530
Compton, Surrey, 2028
Compton Verney, Warw., 11546
Computus, 7348 : (Welsh), 7355
Conaille-Muirthemhne, *kingdom of*, 2160
Conal, *St.*, 5017
Conall, *king of Dalriada*, 6136
Conall, *St.*, 4851
Conan, *St., bp.*, 5005
Confession formulas, 5314, 5823
Congar, *St.*, 5087, 5095, 5112–13, 5115
Conisborough, Yorks., 7954
Conisholme, Lincs., 10699
Connaught, 2180, 4672 : (kings of),
  2179, 2311
Connor, co. Antrim, 9606–10, 9768,
  9784, 9786, 11113
Consecration of churches (ceremonial),
  3313, 5861
Constantine, *St.*, 5029
Consuetudo regis, 2620
Conveyance, 2470
Conwil Gaio, Carmarthenshire, 9960
Cookham, Berks., 2037, 2123
Copford, Essex, 741, 10190
Copister broch, Shetland, 8025
Copplestone, Devon, (charter, 974), 387,
  11025 : (cross), 11023, 11025, 11029,
  11033
Corann, *battle* (701 or 702), 1160
Corbridge, *battles* (913/5, 918), 1331
Corby, Northants. (3 hides belonging to
  Malcolm Canmore), 292, 3097
Corentin, *St., 1st bp. of Quimper*, 5196
Corfe, Dorset, 1296

Corhampton, Hants., (sundial), 547
Cork, 7017, 9632, 9639, 9646: (monastery), 3779
Cork, *county* (churches), 3904a, (inscriptions), 9611–46: (place-names), 6809, 6818: (round towers), 10554: (sculpture), 11114–16. *See also* Agh-abulloge, Aultach, Ballycattern, Ballycrovane, Ballyknock, Bally-vourney, Barrymore Castle, Bantry, Bealach Leachta, Britway, Cloyne, Cork, Glenwillen, Glounaglach, Greenhill, Gurranes, Imokilly, Kil-cullen, Kinneigh, Knockshan-awee, Leades, Monataggart, Mount Music, Rathcanning, Rathcobane, Ross, Rosscarbery, Rus-Glas, Spike Island, Tullylease, Watergrasshill, Yougal
Cormac McCullinan, *bishop-king of Cashel*, 4809
Cornage. *See* Horns
Cornard, Little, Suffolk, 1745
Cornély, *St.*, 5163
Corney, Cumb., 10852
Cornwall, 6020, 6036, 6038: (architecture, ecclesiastical), 10517, 10519, 10522: (archaeology), 7747, 8431: (Arthur in), 1063–64: (bishopric), 3446, 3807, 3833, 3844–45: (boundary with Devon), 5922, 5933–34: (Brittany, relations with), 1638, 5184: (charters), 334: (coins), 8918: (Domesday) *see* Domesday (Cornwall): (early history of), 1689: (earthworks), 7965: (hundreds), 3152, 3187: (inscriptions), 9563–88, 9910: (mills), 2694: (place-names), 6924–53 *passim*: (roads), 6190: (saints), 4118, 5029–5128 *passim*, 5184: (sculpture), 11036–54: (topography), 5920. *See also* Biscovey, *Caellwic*, Cardinham, Charaton, Cubert, Gulval, Lanhadron, Lanteglos-by-Camelford, Launceston, Lewan-nick, Mawgan, Menscryfa, Padstow, Penhawger, Perranporth, Phillack stone, Quethiock, St. Allen, St. Buryan, St. Cleer, St. Helens (Scilly Isles), St. Kew, St. Michael's Mount, St. Neot stone, Scilly Isles, Tintagel, Tregoney, Trevena, Trewhiddle, Waterpit down
Coronation, 22, 1321a, 1327, 2306–29, 2338: (oath), 2315

Corscombe, Dorset, 2019
Cosmology, 7119–22, 7493
Costume. *See* Dress
Cot, Cote [place-names], 6364, 6371
Cotswold, 1907
Cottenham, Cambs., 3268
Cottesmore, Rutland, 8274, 8276
Cotts, the, co. Wexford, 9768, 9771
Coulsdon, Surrey, 8445, 8447, 8454
Councils and Synods (Church), 3293–94, 3316, 3323, 3356: (Chelsea), 3332: (Hertford), 3293: (Mag-Léna, 632), 3573
Countisbury, Devon, 1694
Coutances (Geoffrey de Montbray), *bp. of*, 1370, 2113, 2940
Coventry, Warw., 1829, 1846, 1853
——, *abbey*, 1853: (charters), 319, 359, 414, 428
Cowbridge, Glam., 11387
Cow-lore, 7606
Cowrie shells, 7515, 7520
Craig Gwrtheyrn, Carmarthenshire, 8070
Cramond, Midlothian, 11631
Cranat, *St.*, 4853
Cranborne, Dorset, 3728, 7844, 7978
Crayke, Yorks., 7768, 8513
Crediton, Devon, 1692, 1720, 1723, 1725, 3183, 3874: (bishopric), 3834: (bishops of), 4392: (charters), 321, 401, 407, 862
Cremation, 8080, 8082, 8091, 8546
Creodantreow, site, near Crediton, 6076
Cressage, Salop, 3936
Crickhowel, Brecknock, 9924, 9931
Cricklade, Wilts., 6750, 11003: (mint), 9259, 9319, 9328
Cringleford, Norfolk, 10625
Croft, Yorks., 10963
Crofton, Yorks., 10943
Cromm Cruaich [idol], 3486, 3502
Crondall, Hants., (coins), 8899, 8911
Cronk Conoly, Lezayre, Isle of Man, 8537
Cronk Keeillane, Isle of Man, 10520
Cronk yn How, Isle of Man, 6841, 8522
Cropredy, Oxon., 4443
Crosby Ravensworth, Westmorland, 1995
Crosscanonby, Cumb., 10808, 10816, 10822, 10855
Crosslow, co. Carlow, 9767
Crowle, Lincs., 6093, 10702–04

Croy, Inverness. *See* Mains of Croy
Croydon, Surrey, 2020, 6699, 8449 : (coins), 8882, 8887, 8891
Croyland, Lincs., *abbey*, 3644–50 : (charters), 312, 394, 1831 : (miracles at Waltheof's tomb), 1596, 1599
Croziers, 3768, 4844, 11456, 11773–85, 11796
Cruach Mac Dara, co. Galway, 10482
Cruc (place-names), 6415
Cruc(t)an, Somerset, 5878 : (grant of, to Glastonbury, by Centwine), 2083
Cruet, 8639
Crundale down, Kent, 11544
Crundels, 3098
Cúán ua Lothcháin, 1622
Cubert, Cornwall, 9563, 9578
Cuby, *St.*, 5077
Cuerdale find, 5992, 8640, 8871–78, 11507, 11590
Culcheth, Lancs., 1978
Culdees, 3428, 3752, 3755, 3757, 4927 : (Rule of), 5622
Culebath [liturgical fan], 11778
Cumb [place-names], 6365
Cumberland, 1942, 1948, 1950, 1954, 1969, 1983, 1999 : (ancient monuments, inventory), 10041 : (archaeological survey of), 7745 : (charters), *see* Gospatric : (dedications to St. Kentigern), 5009 : (Domesday) *see* Domesday (Cumb.) : (place-names), 6651, 6677, 6681 : (sculpture), 10808–61 : (Teutonic settlements), 887. *See also* Addingham, Aspatria, Arthuret, Beckermet, Beckermont, Bewcastle, Bridekirk, Brigham, Bromfield, Buttermere, Carlisle, Clifton (Great), Corney, Crosscanonby, Dacre, Dearham, Distington, Eaglesfield, Fluskew Pike, Gilcrux, Glassonby, Graymoor hill, Harrington, Hazel-Gill, Hessilgill crags, Isell, Keswick, Liddell, Penrith, Plumbland, Rockcliff, St. Bees, Scotby, Stanwix, Walberthwaite, Whitbeck, Workington
Cumbria, 2232, 8493 : (A.–S. relations with), 1977 : (Manx names in), 6834
Cummain, *St.*, *bp. of Clonfert*, 4800
Cummean (hymn), 5856 : (penitential), 5613, 5618, 5625
Cunningsburgh, Shetland, 9879, 9896
Cunomorus stone, Castle Dore, Cornwall, 9585

Cunwal, *St.*, *bp. of Tréquier*, 5195
Curia Regis, 2339
Curig, *St.*, 5101
Curragh, the, co. Kildare, 2136
Cushendall, co. Antrim (coins), 8961
Cuthbert, *St.*, 4280–4325 : *also*, 1932, 1956, 4134, 6082, 7134, 10056 : (Gospel Book of), 5693, 7230 : (pallium of), 1635 : (pectoral cross), 11514 : (pennies), 9043
Cuthburga, *St.*, *foundress of Wimborne*, 4402, 4404
Cuthman, *St.*, 4396, 4434, 4436
Cuthred, *king of Kent* (coins), 8963
Cuthwini, *bp. of Leicester*, 11836
Cuthwulf, *bp. of Hereford* (charter of, 840), 341
Cuthwulf, *West Saxon leader*, 871, 919
Cwm Clais, Glam, 8075
Cwm Glöyne, Pembrokeshire, 9998
Cymmer [place-names], 6803
Cyneheard, *brother of Sigeberht, king of Wessex*, 1105, 1123, 1130, 1133a, 1137, 1149
Cynete, *battle* (1006), 6083
Cynethryth, *queen of Mercia*, 1114
Cynewulf, *bp. of Lindisfarne*, 4391
Cynewulf, *king of Wessex*, 1105, 1123, 1130, 1133a, 1137, 1149
Cynffic, Glamorgan, 9630
Cynren, 2644
Cynuit, *battle* (878), 1272 : (?=Countisbury), 6075

Da-(place-names], 6817, 6825
Dacre, Cumberland, 10373, 10827, 10857–58
Daegsastan, *battle* (603), 6114, 6139
Dagenham idol, 3516
Dál Fiatach [Ulster population group], 2127
Dalbeattie, Kirkcudbright, 8007, 8491
Dalcassians, co. Clare, 2328
Dalkey, co. Dublin, 10498
Dalmahoy, Midlothian, 8014
Dalmeny, West Lothian, 11471
Dalriada (brooch), 11675 : (inauguration of kings of), 2325
Damhnat, *St.*, 4844
Damnonia, *kingdom of*, 59, 5905
Danbury, Essex, 7915
Dancing procession [Echternach], 5516, 5528, 5545
Danegeld, 2631, 2673, 2796, 2954

Danelaw (conversion of), 3538 : (English and Danish elements in), 2612, 8815 : (social and economic history of), 2661, 3289 : (sokemen of), 3206, 3227
Danes in Anglesey 2244
Danes' dyke , Yorks. , 7834
Danes' skins, 714, 740–41
Danesfield, Watton, Herts., 6108
Darenth, Kent, 10208, 11469
Darerca-Moninne, *St.*, 3790
Darley, Derbs., 10669, 10678
Dartford, Kent, 8196
Dartmoor, 3019, 6772 6793
Dating of charters, 281
Daventry, Northants. (charter 944), 368
David, *St.*, 5057–70
Dawlish, Devon, 1698
Deal, Kent, 8197, 8547, 8753
Dean, forest of, Glos., 3029, 3038, 6045
Dearham, Cumb., 10812, 10814–15, 10818, 10849, 10860
Decies, the, co.Waterford, 6200, 6827, 8600
Declan, *St.*, *of Ardmore*, 4856
De consuetudine monachorum, 3599, 3605
Decuman, *St.*, 5106, 5115
Dedications of churches, 4081, 4128, 4142, 4150, 4324, 4347a, 4400, 4474, 4873, 4875, 4878, 5009, 5036, 5038, 5045, 6219 : (ceremonial for), 3313, 5905 : (stones), 4125
Deddington, Oxon. (coin), 8995
Deer, *Book of*, 188, 5837, 7266, 7271, 7274–75
Deer, Aberdeenshire, *monastery*, 3794
Deerhurst, Glos. (early history of), 3868, 4429 : (font), 10689 : (granted to Westminster by Edward the Confessor), 3731 : (Saxon church and chapel), 3888, 10237–55, 10318 : (Saxon house), 10118, 10126
Degen, (*Irish*) *bp.*, 4815
Deil's dyke, Galloway, 7849, 7850a, 7855, 7857
Deiniol, *bp. of Gwynedd*, 5072
Deira (boundary), 5923, 5925–26, 5940
Delgany, co. Wicklow (coins), 8892
Demesne, ancient, 2271, 2271a, 2761
-*den* [place-names], 6376
Denbighshire (Domesday) *see* Domesday (Denbigh) : (place-names), 6952. *See also* Cerrig-y-Druidion, Gorsedd Wen, Gresford, Llanfwrog, Llangollen, Rhuddlan, Ruthin

Deneholes, 7921
Denisesburn, *battle* (634), 6085
Dentune [Domesday manor : Sussex], 6039
Deodred, *bp. of London* (will of), 3825
Deorham, *battle* (577), 870, 881, 914, 954
Deorman, *of London* [Domesday tenant in capite], 2911
Derby, 10673 : (mint), 9264, 9288–89, 9295, 9316–17, 9323 : (place-name), 6543, 6551, 6553a, 6555 : (Red Book of), 5751
Derbyshire, 1848, 1913 : (cemeteries), 8214–29 : (Domesday) *see* Domesday (Derbs.) : (earthworks), 7934 : (place-names), 6420, 6529, 6535–37, 6542–44, 6553, 6559 : (sculpture), 10660–81. *See also* Bakewell, Benty Grange (near Monyash), Bradbourne, Brailsford, Burbage, Castleton, Cold Eaton, Darley, Derby, Dove (river), Eyam, Fernilee hall, Foremark, Ingleby, Melbourne, Mugginton, Newton (King's), Norbury, Northworthy, Repton, Rowsley, Stapenhill, Stapleford, Staveley, Strines, Tideslow, Tideswell, Tissington, Wilne, Winster, Wirksworth
Dering (*Sir* Edward), *bart.*, [17th c. antiquary], 283, 309
Derry, *county*. *See* Camus-juxta-Bann, Dunalis stone, Fahan
Desborough, Bucks., 7936
Desborough, Northants., 8238–39
Déssi, 1018a, 1025
Dettic and Deorulf, 5323
Devenish (island), lough Erne, co. Fermanagh, 10134, 10502
Devil [sculpture], 10592, 10859, 11070
Devil's dyke, Cambs., 7776–77, 7783–84.
Devil's dyke, Galloway. *See* Deil's dyke
Devil's dyke, Sussex, 8752
Devizes, Wilts., *museum*, 8465–66
Devon, 1677a–1734, 3150, 5929, 6033, 6046, 8432 : (Alfred and Devon), 1210, 1254 : (boroughs), 2727, 2733 : (boundary with Cornwall), 5922, 5933–34 : (boundary with Somerset), 5928 : (castles of Conqueror in), 7972 : (Celtic Devon), 1693 : (charters), 334, 393, 400 : (Christianity in), 3304 : (coins)

Devon (*continued*)
    8938 : (Domesday) *see* Domesday
    (Devon) : (Hubba's invasion, 878),
    1256 : (hundreds), 1682, 3151, 3161,
    3177–83, 3185, 3187 : (inscriptions),
    9562, 9910 : (Irish invasion, 1068),
    1519 : (mints), 9297 : (parishes,
    formation of), 1707 : (place-names),
    6763–94 : (religious houses), 3692a,
    3693 : (river names), 6431, 6472 :
    (roads), 6191 : (saints), 4129 :
    (Saxon conquest of), 863, 891, 925,
    942, 1682a, 1685 : (sculpture),
    11011–33 *passim* : (surnames), 602 :
    (villani), 3202. *See also* Ashburton,
    Asprington, Axeminster, Barnstaple,
    Brentford (Brampford), Brixham,
    Buckfast, Chulmleigh, Colyton,
    Copplestone, Countisbury, Crediton,
    Dartmoor, Dawlish, Dolton, Exeter,
    Exminster hundred, Exmouth, Far-
    del stone (Ivybridge), Harberton,
    Hartland, Heavitree, Hempston
    (Little), Hemyock, Holcombe, Hul-
    ham, Ilfracombe, Kenwith, Kers-
    well (Abbot's and King's), Lifton,
    Luppitt, Lustleigh, Lydford, Lynton,
    Molton (South), Newton Abbot,
    Newton St. Cyres, Norton, Nymet,
    Nympton, Okehampton, Ottery St.
    Mary, Paignton, Pilton, Pinhoe,
    Plympton, St. Marychurch, Sal-
    combe Regis, Seaton, Sidbury, Sid-
    mouth, South Hams, Sticklepath,
    Stoke Canon, Tavistock, Tawton
    (Bishop's, hundred of North,
    South), Tiverton, Torbay, Torquay,
    Totnes, Werrington, Widworthy,
    Wonford, Wray
Dewsbury, Yorks., 9493
Dhimma, *Book of*, 7269
Dials, wheel, 527
Dicuil, 7041, 7043–44, 7048, 7400–01
Dieppe (A.–S. remains found near), 8090
Digby, Lincs., 10707.
Dinas Emrys, Carnarvonshire, 8067
Dinsdale, co. Durham, 10876
Dīre, 2577
Disciples (A.–S. list of 70), 7564
Diserth, Radnor, 11408
Disme, 7398, 7430
Distington, Cumb., 10819
Distress [law], 2534–35, 2541
Dittisham, Devon, 1728
Divine king, 7567

Doccus, *St.*, 4816
Doe [course makes boundary of monas-
    tic land], 3697
Dog, resuscitated, 4503
Dolau Cothy, Carmarthenshire, 9963
Dolgelly, Merioneth, 9956
Dolton, Devon, 11011, 11015–16, 11024
Domangart, *king of Dalriada*, 1080
Dombec, 2381
Domesday, 575, 1377, 1521, 1546, 2756–
    2999, 3116–17, 3120, 3246, 3283 :
    (boroughs and burgesses), 2730–32,
    2741, 2745, 2751 : (churches in),
    2777, 2787–88, 2794, 2806, 2866,
    2927, 2936, 3461, 3464, 3470, 3889,
    3895, 10405 : (commemoration,
    1886), 120, 126 : (commendation
    in), 3014 : (custody of), 115, 124–
    25 : (the document), 115-27 :
    (finance of), 2658, 2796 : (forest and
    woodland), 3019, 3021–25, 3030,
    3034–35, 3040, 3042–44 : (geo-
    graphy), 5872, 5942–54 : (hidage),
    3057, 3062–63, 3065, 3068–70, 3073,
    3075–76 : (hundreds), 3158, 3190,
    3192, 3198 : (leuca or lug of), 2793 :
    (measures of land), 3112, 3114–15,
    3121–22, 3127 : (mills), 2690, 2692,
    2694, 2704, 2707–08 : (owners of
    land in Cleveland), 2988 : (pigs),
    2700 : (place-names), 6329, 6366–
    68 : (plough-team), 2699, 2710,
    2715, 2720, 2724 : (rural population),
    2757, 2800, 3205, 3225–27, 3259 :
    (sites), 6013–46 : (sokemen), 3214 :
    (tillage), 2693, 2725 : (vills), 5947a :
    (vineyards), 2716, 2721 : (wool),
    3145. [By shires], (Beds.), 2690, 2821,
    2825–29 : (Berks.), 2821, 2830–
    34, 5948 : (Bucks.), 2818, 2821,
    2835–36 : (Cambs.), 2837–44, 3042,
    5943 : (Cheshire), 2822–23, 2845–
    49, 3043, 6518 : (Cornwall), 1724,
    2694, 2850–55, 3244, 5952a, 6020,
    6036, 6038 : (Cumberland), 2819,
    2822–23, 2856 : (Denbigh), 2822 :
    (Derbs.), 2819, 2857–61 : (Devon),
    2694, 2862–70, 3019, 5949, 5953a,
    6033, 6046 : (Dorset), 2770, 2783,
    2871 : (Essex), 2716, 2872–76, 3075,
    5944, 6032 : (Flint), 2822, 2877, 6040 :
    (Glos.), 1580, 2818, 2878–81, 5881,
    5941, 6045, 6585 : (Hants.), 2707,
    2776, 2821, 2882–85 : (Hereford),
    2886–89 : (Herts.), 2818, 2821,

Domesday (*continued*).
2890–93 : (Hunts.), 2741, 2894–95, 3024 : (Kent), 1785, 2777, 2820, 2896–2900, 3247 : (Lancs.), 2819, 2822–24, 2901–04, 6679 : (Leicester), 2905–06, 5946 : (Lincs.), 1587, 2819, 2907–09, 3025 : (London), 2911 : (Middlesex), 2818, 2821, 2910, 2912–16, 3065, 3288 : (Norfolk), 2817–20, 5944–45, 6019 : (Northants.), 2921–24, 3076, 5942 : (Notts.), 2819, 2925–27 : (Oxon.), 2818, 2928–29 : (Radnor), 2930–31: (Rutland), 2819, 2905, 2907, 2932–33 : (Shropshire), 2720, 2934–36, 5946a, 5954, 6025 : (Somerset), 2113, 2782, 2937–47, 3057, 3712, 5950 : (Staffs.), 2948–50, 3044, 3062, 6016 : (Suffolk), 2951–55, 5944–45 : (Surrey), 2708, 2777, 2820–21, 2956–60 : (Sussex), 2776–77, 2820, 2961–70, 3070, 3078–79, 3154, 6687, 10405 : (Warw.), 2971–78, 3194–95, 5947, 5952 : (Westmorland), 2819, 2822: 2824 : (Wilts.), 2979–83, 3035, 5951, (Worcs.), 2984–87, 5942a, 5945a : (Yorks.), 2819, 2822, 2824, 2988–99, 3069, 5953, 6027, 6635, 6647. *See also* under individual towns and villages concerned

Domnach Airgid, 7258, 11805, 11811
Donaghmore, co. Down, 11145
Dinaghmore (Maynooth), co. Kildare, 9702–05
Donaghmore, co. Limerick, 10496
Donard, co. Wicklow, 9786
Donatus, *St.*, *bp. of Fiesole*, 5409, 5416
Donegal, *county* (brooches, etc.), 11715 : (crosses), 11128. *See also* Aileach, Boultypatrick, Burt, Fahan Mura, Glencolumbkille, Inishowen, Inishkeel, Tory island
Donnan, *St.*, 5000, 5019
Doonfeany stone, co. Mayo, 9792
Dorchester, Dorset, 11478 : (Domesday return for), 2871
Dorchester, Oxon., 8677
Dores, Inverness, 11313
Dorking, Surrey, (coins), 8907
Dornoch, Sutherland, 6846
Dorset, 2023, 2049, 2111–12 : (bishopric), 3824 : (charters), 348 : (church dedications), 4142 : (Domesday) *see* Domesday (Dorset) : (manors), 2027, 3265 : (mints), 9302, 9318,

9348 : (Normans in), 1536 : (place-names), 6729, 6739, 6755, 6762 : (roads), 6192 : (Saxon mark, *mearc*), 5938 : (sculpture), 11012–35 *passim* : (surnames), 571 : (Welsh in), 2069. *See also* Abbotsbury, Badbury rings, Bindon hill, Bridport, Cerne Abbas, Corfe, Corscombe, Cranborne, Dorchester, Gillingham, Hamworthy, Hardown hill, Iwerne valley, Milton abbey, Ockford, Portland, Purbeck, Shaftesbury, Sherborne, Studland, Sutton Waldron, Toller Fratrum, Wareham, Whitchurch Canonicorum, Whitcombe, Wimborne, Winterbourne Steepleton, Wyke Regis, Yetminster
Double monasteries, 3580
Doughmaksone, co. Mayo, 9789
Douglas, Isle of Man (Woodbourne coin-hoard), 9114, 9127, 11658, 11662, 11665
Dove, river, Derbs., 6439
Dover, Kent, 1774, 3736, 8185, 10219, 10222, 10232, 10234, 11576, 11635 : (attack on, 1067), 1572 : (library), 7136 : (mint), 9256
Dowdeswell, Glos. (grant of land at, to Worcester monastery), 329
Dower, 2464
Down, *county*, 4685 : (crosses), 11143 : (St. Patrick in), 4085. *See also* Ballyholme, Bangor, Donaghmore, Downpatrick, Drumgolan, Maghera, Mahee (Inis), Saul, Scraba mt.
Down, *diocese* (pagan monuments in), 3503
Downpatrick, co. Down, 4634, 4639, 11111
Downton, Devon, 6067
Downton, Wilts., 2058, 10450
Dragons, 7574, 7612, 7742, 10878, 11265, 11398
Draughtsmen, 8423, 11445
Draycott-in-the-Moors, Staffs., 6018
Dress, 2628, 2665, 3000–17, 6955, 10989
Dress-fasteners, 8660
Driffield, Little, Yorks. (burials), 8363, 8774 : (moot-hill), 6061, 6068 : (ring from), 11621, 11628 : (tablet to king Aldfrith in, 705), 1115, 1122, 1142
Drinclean [law term], 2444
Drink, 2624, 7459
Drogheda, co. Louth, 3775, 9718, 11719

Dromiskin, co. Louth, 3798

Drostan, *St.*, 5020

Droxford, Hants., 8414–15

Druim Ceat, *convention* (575), 1027

Drumcliff, co. Sligo, 11159

Drumcoltran, Kirkcudbright, 8722

Drumcullin, King's County, 11161

Drumgolan, co. Down, 11109

Drumlane, co. Cavan, 3784

Drumloghan, co. Waterford, 9730, 9734, 9744, 9746

Drummin, co. Roscommon, 9774

Drummond Missal, 5748

Drung Hill, co. Kerry, 9665

Dryhtinbéag [law term], 2441

Dublin, 2171, 2176, 3864, 6815, 9787, 10485, 11164, 11680 : (Gospels), 7257 : (Scandinavian kingdom of), 715 : (see of), 3858, 3864 : (Trinity College, Ogam inscribed stones at), 9787

Dublin, *county* (architecture, ecclesiastical), 10501, 10504. *See also* Aylesbury Road, Clondalkin, Clontarf, Dalkey, Dublin, Dún Laoghaire, Ireland's Eye, Island-bridge, Killiney, Kilmainham, Liffey valley, Rathdown (half-barony), Tallaght

Dubricius, *St.*, 5088, 5128, 6223

Ducklington, Oxon., 8270

Duel, 2529

Duggleby howe, Yorks., 8340

Duleek, co. Meath, 2155

Dumbartonshire. *See* Luss, Rosneath

Dumbleton, Glos., 6581

Dumfries (name), 6923

Dumfriesshire (Celts in), 2238 : (forts, camps and motes), 8005 : (Norse influence in), 2205 : (place-names), 6853, 6869, 6923 : (relations with Cumberland), 1969 : (sculpture), 11251–58. *See also* Burnswork, Cairn valley, Dumfries, Dungarry fort, Dunragit, Friar's Carse, Hoddom, Kirkconnel, Nith Bridge, Nithsdale, Ruthwell, Torbeckhill

Dun [place-names], 6397

Dunadd, Argyllshire, 2325

Dunalis stone, co. Derry, 9765

Dunbar, East Lothian, 8523

Dunbel, co. Kilkenny, 9706, 9708, 9715

Dunblane, Perthshire, 11270

Dunbolg, co. Wicklow, *battle* (594), 1024, 1033

Duncan II, *king of Scots* (charter to Durham, 1094), 288

Dun Cow, *Book of the.* *See* Leabhar na Huidre

Dunecht, Aberdeenshire, 9874

Dunfallandy, Perthshire, 2324

Dungal, 5133, 7042, 7045, 7053–54

Dungarry fort, Dumfriesshire, 8011

Dungimmin, Lower, co. Cavan, 9759, 9778

Dunhill, co. Waterford, 9741

Dunkeld, Little, Perthshire, 11740

Dún Laoghaire [Dunleary=Kingstown], co. Dublin, 9762, 9790

Dunleer, co. Louth, 9718

Dunloe, co. Kerry, 9652–57, 9660

Dunluce, Antrim, 2147

Dunmore cave, co. Kilkenny, 8797

Dunnichar loch, Forfar [=Nechtanesmere], 1143

Dunragit, Dumfriesshire, 8012

Dunrobin, Sutherland, 8543

Dunsætes, *laws of the*, 2408

Dunstan, *St., abp. of Canterbury*, 22, 52, 3658, 3970–77, 4043, 7222, 7318

Dun Telve, Invernesshire [broch], 8046

Dun Voradale, Raasay, Skye, 8052

Dunwich, Suffolk (mint), 9330

Durham, *city and cathedral*, 1967–68, 3315, 3813–14, 3829, 10372 :(Bishops' borroughs), 2737 : (castle), 1952 : (Liber Vitae), 5313, 7218 : (library), 7134–35, 7231, 10868, 11946 : (mint), 9313 : (place-name), 6670 : (Ritual), 5766, 5772, 5829 : (sculpture), 10862, 10868–70

Durham, *county* (architecture, ecclesiastical), 10359–62, 10366, 10372, 10374 : (ethnology), 8844 : history, ecclesiastical), 3591 : (monasteries), 3696 : (place-names), 6663, 6669, 6673–75 : (river names), 6460 : (sculpture), 10862–79. *See also* Auckland St. Andrew, Aycliffe, Billingham, Castle Eden, Chester-le-Street, Dinsdale, Durham, Escombe, Gainford, Greatham, Hartlepool, Jarrow, Lanchester, Monkwearmouth, Norton, Pittington, Sadberge, Seaham, Sockburn, Sunderland

—— Symeon of. *See* Symeon, *of Durham*

Durness, Sutherland, 2214

Durrow, King's County, 2189, 11167, 11174 : (Book of), 5679, 11927, 11929, 11939

Duston, Northants., **8243, 11606**
Dympna, *St.*, *of Gheel*, **4803**
Dyrham, *battle* (577). *See* Deorham
Dysert, co. Limerick, **10549**
Dysert O'Dea, co. Clare, **11132, 11153**

Eachtra Conaill Gulban, **1020**
Eadberht, *king of Kent*, **1146**
Eadburga (letter from Wynfrith to), **72**
Eadgifu, *queen to Edward the Elder*, **1336**
Eadred, *king*, (charter to Alverstoke, 948), **315, 362** : (coins), **9120–38** *passim* : (grant of land in Merstham, 947), **2698**
Eadric, *of Laxfield* [falconer to Edward the Confessor], **1372**
Eadwig, *king*, **2330** : (coins), **9121–38** *passim*
Eadwine, *Psalter*, **5721, 5723**
Eaglesfield, Cumb., **8721**
Ealderman, **3219**
Ealdwulf, *heretoga of S. Saxons* (grant by, 791), **304**
Ealhstan (grant to, of land at Stanton, 958), **299**
Ealu-scerwen [deprivation of ale], **2619**
Eanbald, *abp. of York* (coins), **9018–19, 9033, 9074**
Eanred, *king of Northumbria* (coins), **9018, 9027–28, 9033, 9038**
Eanswith, *St.*, **4103–04, 4110, 4425**
Earls Barton, Northants., **10277, 10286a, 10292**
Earmundslea, Berks., **3620**
Earnley, Dorset [place-name], **6735**
Easby, Yorks., **10955, 10966, 10972**
Eashing, Surrey (burials at), **1003**
East Anglia (bishops), **3825** : (Celtic population in), **8822** : (coins), **8964–86** *passim* : (commendation), **3008, 3245** : (conversion of), **3528** : (forest and wood land), **3023** : (free peasantry), **3205** : (kings), **1166, 1742** : (pottery), **8563** : (royal genealogy), **471** : (villani), **3212**
East Lothian (place-names), **6906.** *See also* Dunbar, Milton, Morham.
East Saxons, *kingdom of*, **969–70, 1748, 1765, 1771, 1801, 2656, 3093, 5932.** *See also* Essex
Eastbourne, Sussex, **2007, 3168, 8370, 8385–87, 8670**
Eastburn, Yorks., **8359**
Easter (date of) *see* Paschal controversy

Easthope, Salop (exchange of land, 901), **310**
Easton, Great, Essex, **7899**
Eastry, Kent, **6501, 8556**
Ebbesbourne Wake, Wilts., **8464, 11617**
Ecbright stone, **1229**
Ecclesfield, Yorks., **10953**
Eccleshall, Yorks., **1991**
' Ecclesia ' [in Domesday Book], **2767**
Ecgfrith, *king of Northumbria* (coins), **9055**
Ecgwine, *1st abbot of Evesham*, **3654–55**
Ecgwine, *bp. of Worcester*, **4043, 4080, 4432**
Echternach, **5516, 5528, 5530, 5541, 5545**
Eckington, Worcs., **1844**
Eclipses, **7404a–b**
Edburg, *St.*, **4416**
Edderton, Ross, **11301**
Eddi, **4008–09, 4024**
Eddisbury, Cheshire, **7946**
Eden's hall, Berwickshire [broch], **8057**
Edgar, *ætheling*, **1571**
Edgar, *king* (charter, St. Werburgh's, Chester, 958), **397** : (charter, Copplestone), **387, 11025** : (charter, Ely, second foundation), **285, 303** : (charter, Ely, forgery), **291** : (charter, Hampstead), **356** : (charter, Nymed, 974), **387** ; (charter, S. Denis, 960), **375, 411** : (charter, Send, 962), **369** : (charter, South Hams), **402** : (charter, land at Stantun, to Ealhstan, 958), **299** : (charter, Sunbury, 962), **369, 415–16** : (charter, Westminster), **339** : (coins), **8956, 9101–38** *passim*, **11688, 11710** : (commendation to), **1329** : (coronation), **22, 1321a, 1327** : (coronation order), **2326** : (Edgar-Ælfðryð story), **1289, 1303** : (establishment of monasteries), **3586** : (laws), **2408** : (monastic reforms), **3352, 3594, 3607, 3609, 5576** : (poems in A.-S. C.), **97** : (relics), **4119** : (?rowed on Dee), **1323–24, 1327**
Edgbaston, Warw., **2974–75**
Edgware, Middlesex, **2910**
Edinburgh, **2222, 6860**
Edington, Wilts., *battle* (878), **1221–22, 6047–58**
Edith, *St.*, **4409, 4442a**
Edith, *Swanneck*, **1344**

Edlingham, Nhd., **10916**
Edmonton, Middlesex, **8739**
Edmund I, *king* (coins, **9106–37** *passim*, **9329** : (Danes of York &), **1288** : (grant to Ælfric, bp. of Hereford), **368**
Edmund II, *Ironside, king*, **1384** : (dual with Cnut), **1365** : (sons of), **1353**
Edmund, *St., king of East Anglia*, **1173–74, 3627, 4326–35, 4411** : (coins), **8887, 8891, 8906, 8956, 9134**
Ednam, Roxburghshire, **11768**
Edred, *king. See* Eadred
Edstone, Yorks., (sundial), **547, 9512**
Education, **269, 6954–7037,** *passim*
Edward, *ætheling*, **1575, 4969**
Edward [I], *the Elder, king* (Alpine son-in-law), **1326** : (chronology), **432, 439, 459** : (Clede Mutha [*burh*] built by), **6142, 6145** : (coins), **8906, 9104–35** *passim*, **11688** : (grant to Asser), **2059** : (laws), **2381, 2435** : (letter to, re. Fonthill), **313** : (Scots &), **1333** : (site of his peace negotiations with Guthrum), **6091**
Edward [II], *the Martyr, king*, **1296, 1322, 3589, 4411** : (coins), **9141, 9150**
Edward [III], *the Confessor, king*, **1341, 1350, 1385–99, 7450, 7472** : (arms), **11956** : (charter to Chertsey), **318** : (charter to Coventry), **319** : (charter to Waltham), **3729** : (coins), **9171–90, 9293, 11956** : (grants to Bury), **325** : (grant to Malvern), **3737** : (grant to Nigel, huntsman : Borstal horn), **3234** : (grants to Westminster of Deerhurst & Pershore), **3731** : (jewellery, from his coffin), **11536, 11579** : (laws), **2418, 2499** : (officers), **2341** : (relics), **4105, 4119** : (ring legend), **1399, 7560** : (seals), **9363** : (Westminster writs), **2478**
Edwin, *king of Northumbria* (relics), **4122, 4432**
Edwin, *son of Edward the Elder*, **1303**
Edwold, *St.*, **4403**
Edwy, *king. See* Eadwig
Edzell, Angus, **11312**
Egbert, *abp. of York* (coins), **9041** : (penitential), **5577, 5580, 5585**
Egbert, *king*, **406, 1190, 6120** : (coins), **8882, 8902, 8959, 8977, 9082, 9086, 9090** : (grant to Sandtun), **422** : (privilege of, 830), **426**

Egilsay, Orkney, **10507**
Egilssaga, **1334, 1958, 6185**
Eglwys Cymmyn, Carmarthenshire, **9970, 9997**
Egremont, Carmarthenshire, **9988**
Egwin. *See* Ecgwine
Eia (or Eye), next Westminster, **3284**
Eifel, **5525**
Eigg, island of, Inverness, **8731**
Eileach an Naoimh, island of, Argyllshire, **10506**
Eirík Blódöx, *king of York. See* Eric Bloodaxe
Eiudon, Carmarthenshire, **11361, 11363, 11367**
Eldad, *St.*, **4400**
Elent [Domesday,Cornwall], **6026**
Eliseg's pillar, near Llangollen, Denbigh, **991, 10008, 10030, 10034, 11413**
Elkington, South, Lincs., **8589, 8595a, 8615**
Ellandun, *battle* (825), **6083, 6102–03**
Ellendune, Wilts. (boundaries), **2071**
Ellesborough, Bucks., **8304, 8787**
Elloughton, Yorks., **8365**
Elmet, Yorks., *kingdom*, **1936, 1963, 1997**
Elmham, *bishopric*, **3819, 3822, 3840**
Elmham, North, Norfolk, **8592, 8607, 10180–82, 10202**
Elmham, South, Suffolk, **10194, 10197, 10200, 10203**
Elsmwell, Yorks., **8342**
Elphin, *diocese* (patron saints in), **4474**
Els- [place-names], **6418**
Elstob (Elizabeth) [biography], **35**
Elstow, Beds., **10736**
Elves, elfshot, **7489**
Ely, Cambs. (Ely Fields cemetery), **8119, 8694** : (jewellery from isle of Ely), **11476, 11531** : (place-name), **6477** : (Saxons in isle of), **1756**
Ely, *monastery*, **2645, 2840, 3699, 3708, 8745, 10624** : (Brihtnoth buried at, 991), **1320** : (charters), **285, 303** : (Land pleas, William I), **2497**
Embroidery. *See* Textiles
Emer, *Wooing of*, **7595**
Emlagh, co. Kerry, **9660, 9682**
Emly, *Lord* [shrine], **11792**
Emma, *queen*, **1343, 1351**
Emscote, Warw., **11484**
-en [personal names], **6402**
Enda, *St.*, **4765**
Endellion, *St.*, **5078**
Endowments, church, **3464, 3466**

Enville, Staffs., 7556
Eogan Bél, *king of Connaught*, 1014
Eolla, *bp. of Selsey* (ring), 11616
Eorcenwald, *bp. of London* [founder of Chertsey abbey], 3738
Epidemics, 7436–47, 7451, 7536
Epping, Essex (forest), 3020
Epworth, Lincs., 6093
Erc, *daughter of Loarn*, 509
Erdington, Warw., 2975
Erfurt, *Schottenkloster*, 5256
Ergyngfield, *kingdom*, 5936
Eric Bloodaxe, *king of Norway* & *of York*, 1283, 1299, 1307: (coins), 8956, 9111
Erigena (Johannes Scotus), 6965, 7098–7112
Eriskay, island of, Inverness, 8730
Ériu [name], 6819, 6826
Erne, Loch (shrine), 11794, 11808–09
Eschatology, 7643–61
Escombe, co. Durham, 10334–44 *passim*, 10866
Esher, Surrey, 8438
Essex 1753, 1772, 5892, 6032, 8158: (antiquities from, in Ashmolean museum), 8132: (architecture, ecclesiastical), 10179–10201 *passim*: (boundary with Mercia), 5932: (conversion), 3542: (Domesday), *see* Domesday (Essex): (earthworks), 7895, 7901: (forest & woodland), 3040, 5877: (hidation), 3075: (moot sites), 6060: (personal names), 594: (place-names), 6481–90: (river names), 6434: (settlement of E. Saxons in), 969–70: (vineyards), 2716. *See also* Bergholt (West), Benfleet, Broomfield, Bumpstead (Steeple), Bures, Canfield (Great), Chingford, Clavering, Colchester, Copford, Danbury, Easton (Great), Epping forest, Fryerning, Greenstead, Hadstock, Harlowbury, Maldon, Maplestead (Great), Mersea, Navestock, Ongar, Pleshy, Prittlewell, Rayleigh, Rickling, Rockford hundred, Saffron Walden, Shoebury, Southend, *Sunecastre*, Waltham abbey, White Notley, Wicken Bonhunt, Witham, Ythancaester.
Estochelia [Domesday : ? = Leigh Barton], 6029
Estrecilleuelle [Domesday : ? = Chilwell, Notts.] 6023

Estriyhoiel [Domesday], 5881
-et [place-names], 6366
Ethandun, *battle* (878), 1234, 1243, 1251, 1258, 1260, 1272, 1275, 6047–58, 6083
Ethel-. *See* Æthel-
Ethnology, 8804–56
Eucharist, 3296, 3307, 3337, 4258, 5849
Eudo, *dapifer* [chief steward to William I], 1548
Evercreech, Somerset, 8426
Evesham, Norfolk [near Bungay], 8619
Evesham, Worcs., *abbey*, 2470, 3651–56: (charter of Ecgwine, 714), 3654: (chartulary, MS. Harl. 3763), 548: (grant of Wrottesley, Staffs., to, 1072), 332
Evie, Orkney, 8030
Evil eye, 7486, 7520
Ewald, *SS.*, 5235
Ewell, Surrey, 8441, 8451, 8459, 9156
Ewelme, Oxon., 8267, 8461
Ewias Harold, Herefordshire, 1565, 7931
Exchequer, 2342
Excommunication, 2488
Exeter, 1703, 1710, 3872, 7976, 11019, 11031: (Benedictional) 5770: (cathedral library and its mss.), 7125, 7150, 7219, 7228, 7236: (charters at, 938–1069), 323: (Martyrology), 4131: (mint), 9299: (monastery of SS. Mary and Peter), 3693, 3724
Exeter Book, 7219, 7240: (riddles of), 7611–7726 *passim*
Exminster hundred, Devon, 3180, 3282
Exmouth, Devon, 1697
Exodus, 5676
Exorcism, 3497, 7516–17, 7549
Eyam, Derbs., 10675
Eye, Suffolk, 7909, 9372

Fabrics. *See* Textiles
Fachtna, *St.*, 3773, 3865, 5914
Færbena [peasant], 3216
Fahan Mura, co. Donegal, 3768, 4862, 9766
Fairford, Glos., 8230–31, 8233, 8235–36, 8627, 11592
Fair Isle, Shetland, 8514
Falconer, falconry, 1372, 2641, 7685
Falstone, Nhd., 9481, 9514, 10909
Family (A.-S.), 2657, 2662: (Celtic), 2678–79: (family law), 2516, 2540
Famine fevers, 7442
Fanchea, *St.*, 4790, 4813, 4843

G

Fardel stone (Ivybridge), Devon, 9577
Fardenreoch, Ayrshire, 11302
Farleigh Hungerford, Somerset (charter, 987), 396
Farley Chamberlayne, Hants., 2021
Farne islands, 4322, 4325, 6653
Farnell, Aberdeen, 11306
Farnell, Angus, 11312
Farthing down, Surrey, 8445, 8447, 8449a
Fasting [Irish], 2538–39, 2546, 2567
Fasts, 3362, 4095
Faussett collection, 8089, 8191, 8607
Faversham, Kent, 5889, 8171, 8182, 8184, 8189, 11543, 11558, 11577
Fécamp (charter of Cnut), 358
Fechin, St., of Fore, 3772, 4523–27, 11769
Feckenham, Worcs., 6512
Feighin, St., 4791
Felgerde [= polipodium], 7396
Felix, St., bp. of Dunwich, 4044, 4055
Felmersham, Beds., 8577
Felony, 2474
Felton, Salop, 3276
Fens, The, 1743, 1755–56, 1922, 5872, 5927, 6494, 6530, 7562
Ferbane, King's County. See Gallen priory
Ferghil. See Virgilius, bp. of Salzburg
Fergus, St., 5013
Fermanagh, county, 2181. See also Aghalurcher, Brookborough, Devenish (island), Galloon, Inismacsaint, Killadeas, Lisnaskea, Topped mountain, White island (Lower Loch Erne)
Fernilee hall, Derbs., 10662
Ferns, co. Wexford, 3856
Ferret, 7384
Ferriby, South, Lincs., 8326, 10706, 11486
Ferring, Sussex, 2964
Ferrybridge, Yorks., 8678
Festaen dic, 7838–39
Festermen, 3200, 3217
Festiniog, Carnarvon, 8720
Fetcham, Surrey, 8440, 8446
Fethanleag, battle (584) [? = Fotherley, Staffs.], 907a, 6080
Fethard, co. Wexford, 9967, 9996
Fetteresso, Kincardine, 8527, 8541
Feudalism, 3007–17
Feuillien, St., 5217, 5219
Fiacc, St., bp. of Hy-Kinsellagh, 4780
Fiacre, St., 5157
Fian, St., 5406
Fiddington, Somerset, 10596

Fiecc, St., 4574, 4625
Field names, 6425–30 : (Devon), 6792 : (Glos.), 349 : (Hants.), 353 : (Lancs.), 6680 : (Somerset), 350 : (Staffs.), 6522 : (Worcs.), 6512 : (Yorks.), 6027, 6627, 6634
Field System, 2691
Fife (history of), 2239 : (place-names), 6876. See also Inchcombe, Largo, St. Andrews, Shenchy dyke
Filey, Yorks., 6645
Filkins, Oxon., 8257
Fillan, St., 5014, 11742, 11752, 11757 : (crozier of), 11773, 11776, 11779–81, 11783–85
Finan, St., 4821
Finbar, St., of Caithness, 4529, 5021
Finbar, St., of Cork, 4528–35, 7017
Findchua, St., 4836
Finglesham, Kent, 8198
Finistère (conversion of), 5176
Finkley, Hants., 8424
Finnian, St., 4849, 4865, 5969, 6832
Finnsburuh fragment, 6966
Fintan, St., abbot of Dromin, 4849–50, 4948
Fintan, St. of Rheinau, 5556
Fintan Máeldub, St., 4795
Firma burgi, 2753
Firma unius noctis, 2621, 3189
Firth, Orkney, 8030
Fish, fishponds, 2695, 2706, 7379
Fitzsimon (Henry) : his Catalogue of Irish saints, 4464
Five Boroughs, 1319
Flabellum, 7556
–flæd [suffix], 605
Flambard (Ranulf), bp. of Durham (crozier of), 11777
Flamborough, Yorks., 6626
Flanders (relations with), 1642
Flannacán mac Cellach, king of Bregha 2156
Flannan, St., of Killaloe, 4828–29
Flawford, Notts., 1919
Fleam dyke, Cambs., 7776–77
Flint (Domesday) see Domesday (Flint) : (sculpture), 11369–74. See also Maen Achwyfan, Mold, St. Asaph
Fljótsdæla saga, 7580
Florence, of Worcester, 51
Florentius, St., bp. of Strasburg, 5240
Fluskew Pike, Cumb., 11670
Foclut [St. Patrick], 4658–67
Foesl, 2643

Folchart-Psalter [St. Gall], 11904
Folkestone, Kent, 8620, 8779
Folkland, 3118–19, 3128, 3130–31, 3210
Folk moots, 2625
Fonthill, Wilts. (charter), 313
Foods, 2628, 2703, 7451, 7462, 7466
Ford, Sussex, 10400
Fordoun, Kincardine, 11297
Fordwich, Kent, 1777
Fore, co. Westmeath, 4525
Forecynren, 2644
Foreign connections, 1002, 1015, 1127, 1633–62
Foremark, Derbs., 8222
Forest and woodland, 3018–44, 3667, 5870, 5877, 6292 : (animals), 3026 : (Arthurian), 7611 : (Domesday), 3019, 3021–25, 3030, 3034–35, 3040, 3042–44 : (flora), 1391 : (laws), 2420, 2502, 3026
Forfarshire, or Angus (forts and camps), 8004. *See also* Brechin, Dunnichar loch (Nechtanesmere), Edzell, Farnell, Glamis, Inchbrayock, Lethnott, Linlathen, Lochlee, Monifieth, Nechtanesmere, Restenneth, St. Vigeans
Forrœpe [=assart-land], 2696, 2698
Fort St. Mary, Man, 8795
Forteviot [?=Fortren], Perthshire, 6143: (bell), 11741
Fothad, *Rule of*, 5622
Fortingall, Perth (bell), 11742
Fosse, Belgium, 5500–01
Fotherley, Staffs. [?=Fethanleag], 907a, 6080
Four Masters, *Annals of the*, 189, 200, 218, 521
Fowlis Wester, Perth, 11338
Foxcote manor, Andoversford, Glos., 8232
Fox's Castle, co. Waterford, 9737
Foxton, Cambs., 8121, 8759
Fraech, *St.*, *of Cloone*, 4830
Framfield, Sussex, 6693
Franchises, 2481
Frankpledge, 2492, 2498
Franks (intercourse with), 1656, 1660
Franks casket, 9491, 11419, 11423–42
Frech, *St.*, 4618
Freckenham, Suffolk, 1758
Frediano, *St.*, 5407, 5409
Fremund, *St.*, *son of Offa*, 4443
Freswick Links, Caithness, 8497, 10119, 10123

Friar's Carse, Dumfriesshire, 8562
Friday Bridge, Cambs., 6476
Frideswide, *St.*, 4426, 4435
Fridolin, *St.*, *of Seckingen*, 5553, 5555, 5557
Frilford, Berks., 8390, 8394, 8406–07, 8782
Frisia, Friesland, 844, 858, 1633, 1633a, 1640, 5234, 5238, 5509, 8835, 8893 : (place-names, in England), 6306, 6495
Frithwald, *sub-regulus of Surrey* (charter to Chertsey abbey : founder, 666), 318
Frodingham, North, Yorks., 10947
Frostenden, Suffolk, 1761
Fryerning, Essex, 2872
Fulda, *abbey*, 5342, 5363–98, 7183, 7187, 11831, 11898 : (shrine of Boniface at), 5290, 5332, 5343, 5363. — *Landesbibliothek*, 5320, 5343
Fulgentius, *St.* (Rule), 3590
Fuller brooch, 11474
Funshog, co. Louth, 4813
Funta [place-names], 6403
Funtington, Sussex, 6684
Furness, Lancs., 1938, 1947, 7959
Furnishing [of early Scottish church], 3409
Furniture (Viking), 6955
Fursey, *St.*, *abbot of Lagny*, 3769, 5215–24
Fylde, Foreland of the, Lancs., 1990, 6665
Fylfot. *See* Swastika

Gafol, 2506
Gafulforda [823, ?site], 6101
Gaimar (Geoffrey), 56, 464, 1105–06, 1167, 1289
Gainford, co. Durham (coins), 8890, 9009
Gaisa, 2533
Galewood, Northumberland, 8349
Gall, *St.*, 5498, 5554, 5560–75
Gallen priory, Ferbane, Offaly, 8799, 9752, 11108, 11142, 11149
Gallerus, oratory of, co. Kerry, 3908, 9660
Gallican liturgy, 5851
Galloon, co. Fermanagh, 11147
Galloway, 2211, 2220, 11257 : (crosses), 11289 : (Norse influence in), 2205 : (place-names), 6891, 6902, 6903a
Galway, 2131, 11699

Galway, *county* (cyclopean churches), 10490 : (inscriptions), 9647–51. *See also* Aran islands, Ardilaun, Ardoileán, Clonfert, Cruach MacDara, Galway, Inchagoill (Lough Corrib), Iniscaltra (Lough Derg), Kilbannon, Kilmacduagh, Kiltiernan, Roscam, Ross Hill

Gaming-board, 8524, 8638, 10603, 11204, 11657

Garford, Berks., 8401

Gargrave, Yorks., 10961

Garland of Howth [Gospels], 7260, 11941–42

Garranes, co. Cork, 7987

Garranmillion, co. Waterford, 9728

Garraun, co. Waterford, 9710

Gattonside, Roxburghshire, 10923

Gavelkind, 3247, 3253, 3257–58

Gawain, 1093. *See also* Gwalchmei

Gedney, Lincs., 6575

Geld, geld inquests, 2854–55, 2863–64, 2866, 2868, 2938–39, 2999, 3225

Gelli-Dywell, Carmarthenshire, 9976, 9994

Gellyburn, Perthshire, 11273

Genealogy, 17, 85, 463–521, 4736

Genesis, 5669, 5671, 5674–75, 11875

Geoffrey, *of Monmouth*, 128–35, 168, 584, 1663–65, 1670–71, 1673–74, 7590, 7613, 7620, 7624

Geoffrey, *of Montbray, bp. of Coutances*, 1370, 2113, 2940

Gerardine, *St.*, 5004

Geréfa, 2411, 2426

Germanus, *St.*, 4387, 4442, 5102, 6223

Gesail Gyfarch stone, Carnarvonshire, 10026

Gesiths, 3218

Gigha, island of, Argyllshire (find of Viking balance and weights in), 524 : (inscriptions), 9878, 9889

Gilcrux, Cumb., 10819

Gildas, 136–53, 436, 878, 1039–41, 1043–44, 1095, 1101, 5082, 5100, 5103, 5113, 5171, 5183, 5188, 5194, 5670 : (Lorica), 5785, 5788, 5791–92

Gilds, 280, 2642, 3045–52, 3593, 3889

Gilling, Yorks., 6649

Gillingham, Dorset, 11013

Gimingham, Norfolk, 2917

Girvan, Ayrshire, 11326

Giso, *bp. of Wells*, 4049

Giudi [site], 6137

Glamis, Angus, 11325

Glamorgan, 2242, 2256, 6097, 6949 : (camps, Danish), 8072 : (inscriptions), 9933–49 : (place-names), 6942–43 : (sculpture), 11375–95. *See also* Bridgend, Capel Brithdir, Cardiff, Cowbridge, Cwm Clais, Cynffic, Kenfig, Llandough, Llangefelach, Llanrhidian, Llantrisant, Llantwit Major, Loughor, Margam, Margam mountain, Merthyr Mawr, Ogmore, Port Talbot, Womanby

Glasgow (monuments near), 11299 : (name), 2232, 6848

Glass, 8556, 8558, 8573a, 8574, 8601, 8606, 8611, 8618, 11471, 11552, 11683, 11689, 11698, 11702, 11712, 11728

Glasserton, Wigtown, 11293

Glassonby, Cumb., 10832, 10836, 10838

Glaston, Rutland, 8280, 11525

Glastonbury, Somerset (place-name), 6741–42, 6753 : (Saxon church), 3869 : (saints, Celtic), 5084

Glastonbury, *abbey*, 2046, 2084, 2108, 3657–66, 4087, 6992, 10448, 10450, 10454–55, 11004, 11009 : (Arthur and), 1066, 1098, 1668–69, 1672, 1676–77 : (charters), 324 : (David, St., and), 5070 : (grant of Brent to, 663), 342 : (grant of Cruc(t)an to, by Centwine), 2083 : (grant of West Monkton to, c. 682), 326 : (visit of Brigid), 4518

Glenawillen, co. Cork, 9616

Glencolumbkille, co. Donegal, 11160

Glendalough, co. Wicklow, 3786, 9748–49

Gleneagles, Perthshire, 9875

Glenfais, co. Kerry, 9661–62

Glengarry, Inverness, 6859

Glenluce, Wigtown, 11291

Glenlyon, Perth (bell), 11742

Glen Parva, Leic., 11548

Glenquoich, Argyll, 6859

Glenn Mama, *battle* (1000), 6134, 6141

Glentworth, Lincs., 10262

Gloucester, 1864, 10752 : (abbey of St. Peter), 3688 : (mint), 9337 : (priory of St. Oswald), 3349, 10320 : (witan at, 1048), 1364

Gloucestershire, 1894, 2057, 4025a : (art and architecture), 10043, 10318 : (boundaries), 5939, 5941 : (cemeteries), 8230–36 : (charters), 296, 349 : (Christianity, early, in), 3534 :

Gloucestershire (continued).
(Danes in), 1188 : (Domesday) see Domesday (Glos.) : (field names), 349 : (hidation), 3082 : (in 8th c.), 1141 : (jurisdiction of abps. of York in), 3349 : (Norman settlement of), 1580 : (place-names), 6582, 6584–85, 6588, 6591, 6594–96 : (Saxon Glos., geography), 5874 : (sculpture), 10682–90 : (woodland), 3027 : (wool trade), 3145. See also Abson, Ampney St. Peter, Berkeley, Bibury, Bourton-on-the-Water, Bristol, Brockworth, Buckland, Campden, Cerney (South), Chavenage, Cheltenham, Churchdown, Cirencester (abbey), Clifton, Dean (forest of), Deerhurst, Dowdeswell, Dumbleton, Fairford, Foxcote manor, Gloucester, Hampton (Little), Henbury, Kemerton, Leckhampton, Lypiatt, Mattesdune, Newent, Oaksey, Prestbury, Stroud, Tewkesbury, Westbury, Winchcombe, Woodchester

Glounagloch, co. Cork, 9636
Glynde, Sussex, 8603
Glywysing, kingdom, 2241
Gobnata, St., 4810
Gobnet, St., abbess of Ballyvourney, 4798, 4846, 10135
-god, -got [suffix], 556, 615
Godalming, Surrey, 10432
Godfrey, of Malling, 1586
Godiva, 472, 1829, 7566
Godmanchester, Hunts., 6608
Godmundeslaech [=Gumley, Leic.], 6552
Godwin, earl of Wessex, 1357–58 : (pedigree of), 463, 482. (seal), 9371
Gokstad ship, model (Manx Museum), 2293, 2304
Gold, Irish, 11696, 11736–37
Goldborough, Yorks. (coins), 9214
Golden Gospels, 7225, 11867
Golden valley, Herefordshire, 6015 : (castles), 1565 : (Norman occupation), 1565
Golspie, Sutherland, 9870, 9895, 11308
Gore, hundred, 3156
Goring, Sussex, 8381
Gormgal, abbot of 'Ard-oilén, 4802
Gorsedd Wen, Denbighshire, 8528
Gortatlea, co. Kerry, 9667
Gosforth, Cumb. (cross), 10607, 10762, 10798–10807

Gosforth, Nhd., 10371
Gospatric, earl of Bernicia, 1543 : (charter of), 316, 389–92, 429
Gosport, Hants., 315
Gothabyrig (mint), 9275, 9291
Gourdon, paten of, 11714
Gowran, co. Kilkenny, 9706–07
Graffoe, Lincs., deanery, 3809
Grange-over-Sands, Lancs., 9027
Grantham, Lincs., 6567
Gravesend, Kent, 1785–87 : (coins), 8897
Greatham, co. Durham, 10361
Greek, 6978, 7004, 7033–34, 7046, 10177
Greenhill, co. Cork, 9625, 9638, 9643
Greenloaning, Perthshire, 9883
Greenstead, Essex, 3873, 4327, 10179, 10191, 10199
Greenwich, Surrey, 6612–13, 8453, 11467
Gregory I, St. and pope, 3526a, 3533, 3547, 3948, 3950–51, 3960, 4126, 4343, 4868
Gregory VII, pope [Hildebrand], 3546, 3549–51
Gregory, of Tours, (Bede and), 4242
Grellan, St., 4823
Grendel, 7629, 7632–34, 7639–42 : (in A.–S. place-names), 6330, 6470
Grentmesnil, Hugh de, 1356
Gresford, Denbigh, 2254
Greymoor hill, Cumberland, 9417–18
Grimbald, of St. Bertin's, St. Omer, 6968
Grimketel, bp. of Selsey, 4059
Grimsby, Lincs., 1838, 10257
Grims ditch, 919, 7831–33, 7835, 7837, 7840–41, 7844–45, 7847
Grimthorpe, Yorks., 8353
Groundsel, 7394
Gruffydd, ap Cynan, 1608, 1611
Gruffydd, ap Llywelyn, king of Gwynedd, 1604
Guaire, king of Aidhne, 1161, 1165
Guarantee, law of, 2503, 2575
Guénolé, 1st abbot of Landévennec. See Winwalloc
Guildown, Surrey, 8452
Guildford, Surrey, 10449
Guillaume, de Jumièges, de Poitiers. See William
Guinnion, Castellum [?=Binchester], 5957
Gulval, Cornwall, 9566–67, 9578
Gundrada, countess of Warenne, 485–501, 8772
Gundulf, bp. of Rochester, 4052, 4054, 4072, 5677, 10138, 10151, 10163

Gunilda, *sister to Harold II*, **1342**

Gunwallo, *St.*, **5029**

Gur, Lough, co. Limerick, **7989**

Guriat, *9th c. Welsh prince*, **1183**

Guriat [crux], Isle of Man, **9811**

Gurness, broch of, Orkney, **8037**

Gurrane, co. Kerry, **9674**

Gurranes, co. Cork, **9624**

Gussage [place-name], **6347**

Guthlac, *St.*, **4336–46**

Guthred-Cnut, *king of York* (coins), **9065–66, 9072**

Guthrie, Forfar (bell), **11750**

Gwalchmei, **520**

Gwent, **2240, 2257**

Gwinear, *St.*, **5089**

Gwladys, *sister of Tydvil*, **1035**

Gwynedd, **3429** : (geneology of princes), **518** : (saints), **5035**

Gytha, *countess of Wessex* [wife of Godwin], **1347, 3872**

Habit, Benedictine, **3606**

Haceombe [place-name], **6786**

Hackness, Yorks., **9544** : (monastery of), **3732**

Hadrian, *abbot of St. Peter and St. Paul at Canterbury*, **4394, 6110**

Hadstock, Essex, **740–41**

Hæselersc (Hazelhurst), Sussex (charter, 1018), **419**

Hæsten, [Viking chief v. Alfred] (c. 840–c. 910), **1195, 7916**

Haiae [Domesday], **2786**

Hale [place-name], **6414**

Hales, Norfolk, **10188**

Halesworth, Suffolk, **10631**

Halifax, Yorks., **2996, 6642**

Haliwer-folk, **4303**

Halley's comet, **7404**

Halnaker, Sussex, **6683**

Halton, Lancs., **10606**

Halton, West, Lincs., **4405, 10881**

-ham [place-names], **6402**

Hamble creek, Hants. (Viking ship in), **2289**

Hamilton, Lanark, **11337**

Hampnett, West, Sussex, **10395**

Hampshire, **2030, 2088** : (architecture, ecclesiastical), **10435–36, 10440, 10447** : (barrows), **345** : (beacon system in), **2305** : (boroughs), **2749**: (cemeteries), **8412–25** : (charters), **353** : (churches), **3895** : (Domes-

day), *see* Domesday (Hants.) : (ecclesiastical history), **3811** : (field names), **353** : (forests), **3037, 3040**, *see also* New Forest : (inscriptions), **10976** : (Jutes in), **2094** : (Meon-waras), **2074, 2109, 11636** : (mills), **2707** : (place-names), **353, 6710, 6719, 6721** : (roads), **6188, 6201** : (sculpture), **10435, 10976, 10979–80** : (West Saxon conquest of), **884, 981** : (William I in, 1066), **1523.** *See also* Alverstoke, Arreton (I.o.W.), Barton Stacey, Basingstoke, Boarhunt, Bonchurch (I. o.W.), Botley, Bowcombe down (I.o.W.), Breamore, Calbourne (I.o.W.), Chessell down (I.o.W.), Clausentum, Corhampton, Crondall, Droxford, Farley Chamberlayne, Finkley, Gosport, Hamble creek, Hayling (South), Kingsclere, Meon valley, Micheldever, New Forest, Nursling, Oakley, Odiham, Oliver's battery, Preshaw, Preston Candover, Romsey, Shalfleet (I.o.W.), Southampton, Stockbridge down, Wellow, Wherwell, Whitchurch, *Wihtgaraburh* (I.o.W.), Winchester, Wonston

Hampstead, Middsx., **1924** : (charters), **356**

-hampton [place-names], **6383**

Hampton, Little, Glos., **8707, 11502**

Hamstead Marshall, Berks., **7975**

Hamworthy, Dorset, **8701**

Hanging bowls, **8564, 8567, 8575, 8579–83, 8586, 8599, 8602, 8609, 8612–14, 11576, 11582** : (chronology of), **8583**

Hanley Castle, Worcs., **10738**

Hanna [Danish chief] (in Axe valley), **1708**

Harberton, Devon, **11032**

Hardham, Sussex, **10401**

Hardown hill, Dorset, **8433**

Harkirke find (coins), **8888, 8904**

Harlinde and Relinde, *SS.*, **11816a**

Harlowbury, Essex, **1354**

Harnham, East, Wilts., **11611**

Harnham hill, Wilts., **8460, 8462, 8475**

Harold I, *Harefoot, king* (alleged son of), **1379** : (coins), **9167, 9268**

Harold II, *king*, **1337–38, 1361, 1363, 1410, 1433, 1465, 1851, 1863, 4049** : (coins), **8956, 9174–84** *passim*, **9285** : (posterity of), **1366**

Harp (Sutton Hoo), 8094. *See also under* Music

Harpingden (Piddinghoe), Sussex, 6685

Harringay, Middlesex, 1870

Harrington, Cumb., 10837, 10861

Harrogate, Yorks., 8500, 8728, 9497

Harston, Leics., 8306

Harthacnut, *king* (coins), 9166, 9168, 9256

Harting, Sussex (coins), 9147

Hartland, Devon, 1695, 3692

Hartlebury, Worcs., 3255

Hartlepool, Durham, 3882, 8348, 9485, 9488, 9515, 10864

Hasting [Viking chief]. *See* Hæsten

Hastings, Sussex, 2001–02, 6690

Hastings, *battle* (1066), 1400–30, 2821

Hatfield Chase, Yorks., *battle* (633), 1126, 1132, 1965

Haughley, Suffolk, 1760

Hauxton, Cambs., 8124

Havelok, *the Dane*, 1292, 1330

Hawick, Roxburghshire, 4319

Hawkeswell (Hauxwell), Yorks., 9475

Hawkshill, Surrey, 8457

Hawnby, Yorks., 10937

-*hay* [place-names], 6790

Hayling, South, Hants., 10980

Hazel-Gill, Cumberland, 9478

Hazelhurst (Ticehurst), Sussex (charter, 1018), 419

Heaberht, king of Kent (coin), 8954

Heathen burials defining boundaries, 268, 307

Heathen deities [place-names], 6293

Heathen place-names, 6325, 6386

Heathfield, *battle*. *See* Hatfield Chase

Heavens, seven, 7601

Heavitree, Devon, 6783

Hebrides, 7524, 11650 : (bishops), 3860: (brochs), 8064 : (Norsemen in), 728, 2208–09, 2221, 6915

Hedda, *abbot of Peterborough* (ring), 11620

Heddon-on-the-Wall, Nhd., 10367

Hedges, 2723

Heiu, *St.*, *abbess of Hartlepool*, 3706

Hell [place-name], 6399

Hellebore, 7457

Hemistona [Domesday manor, Devon], 6044

Hempston, Little, Devon, 6044

Hemyock, Devon, 6771

Henbury, Glos. (charter, 883), 1865

Hending, proverbs of, 7666–68

Hen Gapel, Carmarthen, 11364

Hengist (and Horsa), 169, 868, 896, 915, 932, 940, 962, 974–75, 977, 988, 995–97

Henry, *of Huntingdon*, 65, 1755

Hepworth, Suffolk, 3264

Heraldry, 1452, 1735, 2106, 10048, 11956

Herbals, 7407–08, 7410, 7451, 7474

Herbert, *St.*, *of Derwentwater*, 4418

Herebert, *earldorman of Lindesay*, 9004

Hereford (cathedral library : A.–S. mss. and archives), 367, 372 : (Gospels), 5683 : (Saxon ditches), 7842 : (see of), 3836

Herefordshire, 1816, 1833, 1841, 1902 : (churches), 5038 : (dedications), 5038 : (Domesday) *see* Domesday (Herefordshire): (earthworks) 7935, 7938: (historical geography), 5876a: (place-names), 6507–09, 6525. *See also* Arrow valley, Bosbury, Ewias Harold, Golden valley, Hereford, Holme Lacy, Llanveynoe, Pipe, Richard's Castle, Stanford Bishop, Sutton Walls

Hereward, *the Wake*, 1587–93

Hermits, 4097, 4100

Hernia, 7478

Heronden, Kent (charter, 968), 1795, 6118

Hertford (Synod of, 673), 3293

Hertfordshire, 1918, 5892 : (archaeological survey of), 7743, 8329 : (Domesday) *see* Domesday (Herts.) : (ecclesiastical history of), 3832 : (place-names), 6597–98, 6600–01, 6605–06 : (towns and villages, origin and forms), 5883. *See also* Danesfield (Watton), Hitchin, Letchworth, Oxhey, Pirton, Reed, Rodenhanger (manor), St. Albans, Stevenage, Walden (King's), Wheathampstead, Wymondley

Hescombe, Somerset, 2940

Hesse, 5236, 5239, 5260, 5304, 5307, 5311, 5322–23

Hessett, Suffolk, 1741

Hessilgil Crags, Cumberland, 9501

Heversham, Westm., 10820, 10843

Hexham, Northumberland, 3880, 10349–52, 10354, 10357, 10905, 10908, 10912–13 : (bishops of), 3827, 3829, 3831, 3849, 10913

Heysham, Lancs., 1984, 4680, 10378, 10606, 10882–83, 10890, 10892, 10894

Hibaldstow, Lincs., 8573
Hibernensis [canons], 5602, 5615, 5625
Hickes (George), biography of, 37
Hickling, Leic., 10692
Hidation, 22, 3053–3133
Higham, Kent (charter, 774), 364
Highdown, Sussex, 8374, 8377, 8379, 8388, 8574, 11589
Hilbre, Cheshire, 10651
Hilcombe, Somerset, 1135
Hilda, *St., abbess of Whitby*, 3706, 3725, 3882, 4393, 4395, 4417, 4430
Hildebrand. *See* Gregory VII, *pope*
Hildeburg, 940
Hildersham, Cambs., 8586
Hillswick, Shetland, 8630
Hionne [Æthelberht's laws, 36], 2449
Hippocampus [motif], 11968
Historical Manuscripts Commission (A.–S. documents), 55
Hitchin, Herts., 1863, 9005, 11582
-*ho, hoe* [place-names], 6380
Hob hill, Saltburn, Yorks., 8347
Hoddom, Dumfriesshire, 2230, 11255
Hog-backs, 10579, 10606, 10616–17, 10833, 10855, 10882, 10890, 10892, 10894, 11309, 11319, 11333
Hogstetter, Whalsay, Shetland, 8010
Hoke-day, 2440
Holcombe, Devon, 1719
Holdenby, Northants., 8246, 8248
Holme Lacy, Salop (grant, 1085), 337
Holme Pierrepoint, Notts., 11563
Holy Island. *See* Lindisfarne
Holyrood, *Chronicle of*, 223
Holywood stone, co. Wicklow, 11112, 11155
Homola [law], 2447
Hone, 8642
Honedon, near Clare, Suffolk (coins), 9133
Hoo, Kent, *nunnery*, 3735
Honau, *Irish abbey*, 5242, 5250, 5252
Hook Point, co. Wexford, 9706, 9770
-*hope* [place-names], 6382
Hope, Derbs., 10673
Hoprig (Cockburnspath), Berwickshire, 8544
Hordwell, Berwickshire, 11690
Horn (for drinking), 8650, 11448, 11450: (tenure), 3233–42, 11450, 11453
Horn, *Childe*, 1294
Hornby, Westm., 10841
Horncastle, Lincs., 8700
Hornsea, Yorks., 8356, 8358, 8363–64

Hornsey, Middlesex, 1870, 6609
Horsa, 895. *See also* Hengist (and Horsa)
Horseflesh, 7466
Horse-shoes, 8649, 8658
Horsley, West, Surrey, 10442
Horton Kirby, Kent, 8173–74
Houghton, Hunts., 8305
Household of king, 2331–32, 2335, 2344
Hove, Sussex, 6697
Hovingham, Yorks., 10937
Howdenshire, Yorks., 1959, 1979–80, 3124
Howe hill, Yorks., 8351
Howel, *the Good. See* Hywel Dda, *king of Dyfed*
Howick, Northumberland, 8350
Howletts, Kent, 11469, 11490, 11638–39
Howth, *Garland of* [Gospels], 7260, 11941–42
Hoxne, Suffolk, 8686, 11533
Hruringaham [=Wrangham], 6082
Hubba [Viking], 1256
Huddersfield, Yorks., 1937
Hugh, *de Grentmesnil*, 1356
Hugh, Fitz Grip (Domesday manors of his wife), 2027
Hugh Lupus, *earl of Chester*, 1517, 1532
Hugh, *St., of Rahue*, 4863
Huish Episcopi, Somerset, 8427
Hulham, Devon, 1718
Hull, Yorks., 2000, 8605, 11609–10
Humber, river, 6440
Hundred-pennies, 2620–22
Hundreds, 3150–98
Hunstanton, Norfolk, 8125, 8143, 11530
Hunston, Suffolk, 10631
Hunterston brooch, 11726–27, 11733
Hunting, 2646–48, 7685
Huntingdon, 2741 : (mint), 9269
Huntingdon, Henry of. *See* Henry, *of Huntingdon*
Huntingdonshire (archaeology of), 8330: (Domesday) *see* Domesday (Hunts.): (earthworks), 7941 : (place-names), 6602, 6607 : (pottery), 8572 : woodland), 3024. *See also* Godmanchester, Houghton, Huntingdon, Paxton (Great), Ramsey, St. Neot's, Somersham, Stanton, Weald
Hurley, Berks. (foundation of monastery and charter of William I), 427
Huth, Huath, *king of Northumbria* (coins), 9035, 9048, 9052, 9059, 9063

Hwicce, **1875** : (boundaries of), **5939** : (monasteries, Benedictine revival), **3612**

Hyde abbey. *See* Winchester

Hyning, Westmorland, **8761**

Hythe, Kent, **8762, 8769, 8778, 8784**

Hywel Dda, *king of Dyfed*, **803, 2586–2609** *passim*, **2683** : (coins), **9242** : (historical setting), **1318**

Ibar, *St.*, **4783, 4819**

Icklingham, Suffolk, **11584**

Icknield Way, **928, 6199**

Idunet, *St.*, **4769**

Ilam, Staffs., **10723, 10732**

Ilchester, Somerset (mint), **9281**

Ilfracombe, Devon, **1678**

Ilkley, Yorks., **6649, 10925, 10962**

Illtud, *St.*, **4451, 5090, 6223, 7010, 7024**

Illuminations, **7130, 7319, 10064, 10175–76, 10925, 11828–11946**. *See also* Manuscripts

Ilminster, Somerset (charter from Ine, 725), **2080**

Imbolc [pagan festival, Feb. 1], **3511**

Imokilly, co. Cork, **2162, 4478**

Inch, Inverness (bell), **11742**

Inchagoill (Lough Corrib), co. Galway, **2132, 9648–49, 9651**

Inchbrayock, Forfar, **11298**

Inchcombe, Fife, **3764**

Inchiquin, co. Clare, **3769**

Indract, *St.*, **5091, 5109**

Ine, *king of Wessex*, **1116** : (charter to Ilminster, 725), **2080** : (charters of), **324** : (compensation paid to for Mul), **2476** : (grant of Brent to Glastonbury, 663), **342** : (in Somerset), **1107** : (laws of), **2417, 2437, 2487**

-ing [suffix] (in personal names), **588** : (in place-names), **2872, 6363, 6369–70, 6373, 6378–79, 6384, 6388, 6390, 6392, 6394, 6482**

Ingelri sword, **8735**

Ingelric, *priest*, **1573**

Ingetlingum, Yorks., **6649**

Ingimund, **1332**

-ingham [place-names], **6568**

-ingja [place-names], **6393**

Ingleby, Derbs., **6549, 6556, 8219, 8221**

Ingulf, *abbot of Croyland*, **394, 3650**

Inheritance, **2463, 2500**

Inis bó finne, co. Westmeath, **11118**

Iniscaltra (Lough Derg), co. Galway, **2149, 9650**

Inisclothran [in Lough Ree], **10489**

Inisfallen, *Annals of*, **190–91, 205, 460**

Inishkea North, co. Mayo, **8533, 10127–29, 11138**

Inishkeel, co. Donegal, **11173**

Inishmurray, co. Sligo, **2177–78**

Inishowen, co. Donegal, **11119, 11131**

Inismacsaint, co. Fermanagh, **4826**

Inis-Mahee, co. Down, **4768**

Inis-mocht, co. Meath, *monastery*, **3799**

Inisvickillane, co. Kerry, **9705**

Inquisitio Comitatus Cantabrigiensis, **2840, 2843, 3084**

Insects, **7375, 7377**

-intune [place-names], **6367–68, 6687**

Invasions, *Book of*. *See* Leabhar Gabala

Inver- [place-names], **6847, 6855**

Inverness (Macbeth's castle at), **6127**

Inverness-shire (place-names), **6880**. *See also* Barra (island of), Castle Tioram, Dores, Dun Telve (broch), Dun Voradale (Raasay, Skye), Eigg (island of), Eriskay (island of), Inch, Inverness, Kilbar (Barra), Kildonan (Eigg), Lochaber, Mains of Croy, Raasay (Skye), Skye (island of), Strathardle, Strathdearn

Inverurie, Aberdeenshire, **8540**

Iona, Argyllshire (coin-hoard), **9191a, 9211–12** : (monuments), **11242, 11244, 11246, 11248–49** : (place-names), **6851, 6895**. *See also* Columba, *passim*

Ipswich, Suffolk, **8127–31, 11572** : (coins), **9144–46, 9155**

Iraland, **6150, 6158, 6174**

Irchester, Northants., **8554**

Ireland (architecture, ecclesiastical), **10462–10505** : (genealogies), **506–09, 512–13, 515–16, 521** : (inscriptions), **9590–9795** : (name), **6806, 6819, 6824, 6826** : (Norse geography of), **5894, 5902** : (place-names), **6805–33** : (river names), **6435** : (roads), **6198** : (sculpture), **11055–11175**. *See also* each county

Ireland's Eye, co. Dublin, **10497**

Isell, Cumb., **10819, 10821, 10823–24**

Isis, river (in A.–S. charters), **301**

Island-bridge, co. Dublin, **8490, 11674**

Islay (Argyllshire, **8482, 8498, 8791, 9132, 11243, 11247, 11250** : (place-names), **6916**

Isle of Saints, Argyllshire, 5908
Isleworth, Middlesex (coins), 9149
Islip, Northants., 8237, 8254, 11528
Ita, *St.*, 4457
Italy (cult of St. Brigid in), 5133 : (cult of St. Columbanus in), 5459, 5462 : (cult of St., i.e. king, Oswald in north), 4347, 4354, 4358, 4360–61, 4366, 4369–71 : (cult of St. Patrick in), 4707, 4712 : (Irish saints in), 5406–98, 7000. *See also* Rome
Iutae [Bede], 941, 8837
Iver, Bucks., 10308 10323
Ivo, *de Tail-Bois*, 1527, 1544, 1552
Ivory, 11419–57
Iwerne valley, Dorset, 3265
Ixworth, Suffolk, 8155, 11514, 11553, 11585

Jænberht, *abp. of Canterbury* (coins), 8969 : (grant to, 774), 364
Jamnes and Mambres [apocrypha], 5824
Jarlath, *St., 1st bp. of Tuam*, 4811
Jarlshof, Shetland, 716, 2215, 8026, 10120–22
Jarrow, Durham (church), 10329–48 *passim* : (inscription), 9474–75, 9499 : (monastery), 3704, 7133, 10329, 10345a, 10346 : (sculpture), 10875
Jedburgh, Roxburghshire, 10917, 10923
Jervaulx, Yorks., 6640, 6650
Jewellery, 3140, 6955, 11458–11737. *See also* in Cemeteries section, *passim*
Johannes, *Irish bp.* (*d.* 1066), 5233
John, *St., of Beverley*, 4033a, 4076
John Scotus Erigena. *See* Erigena
Jonas, *of Bobbio*, 5441
Joseph, *St.* (O.E. legend of his bones), 7557
Judith, *queen to Æthelwulf*, 1187
Judith, *wife of Tostig, earl of Northumbria*, 7130
Jumièges, *abbey* (A.–S. mss.), 7147
Junius Psalter, 5700
Jurby, Isle of Man, 9815
Jury, 2345, 2480, 2492, 2494
Justus, *St., 4th abp. of Canterbury*, 4079
Jutes, Jutland, 854a, 855a, 880, 978, 987, 990, 1000, 1782, 2094, 7830, 8197–98, 8753, 8763, 8766, 8808, 8810b, 8835, 8848, 11490 : (jewellery), 11634–39 : (pedigrees, royal), 474 : (pottery), 8616

Kaltraeth, *battle. See* Catraeth
Karl, *Hundason, ' king of Scots '*, 1630
Kea, *St.*, 5085
Kedington, Suffolk, 10630, 10633
Keeils [Manx chapels], 3411–12, 3422
Keighley, Yorks., 6637
Keills, Argyll, 11245
Kells, co. Meath (sculpture), 11065, 11090
Kells, *Book of*, 5679, 5691, 11849, 11864, 11910–23, 11927, 11939, 11941–42 : (Irish charters in), 378
Kemble (John Mitchell), biography of, 36
Kemble, Wilts., 8461
Kemerton, Glos., 1872
Kempston, Beds., 8206, 8209–10, 8608, 11532
Kendal, Westm., 10826
Kenelm, *St.*, 4410
Kenfig, Glam. (brooch), 11703 : (inscription), 9934, 9947
Kent, 1774–96 : (archaeological survey of), 7749, 7762 : (architecture, ecclesiastical), 10204–36 : (cemeteries), 8164–8200 : (charters), 258, 279, 281, 426, 1781, 6118, 6498, 6502 : (Domesday) *see* Domesday (Kent) : (ecclesiastical history), 3826 : (economic history), 2659 : (foreign relations), 1637 : (hidation), 3071 : (hundreds), 1782, 3170, 3197 : (insciptions), 9516 : (jewellery, polychrome), 11513, 11578 : (kingdom of, to 859), 1781 : (place-names), 6376, 6402, 6498–6503 : (pottery), 1780, 8597, 8616 : (social history), 2659 : (tenures), 3247, 3253, 3257–58 : (tribal complexity), 8810b. *See also* Aylesford, Barham downs, Bexley, Biffrons, Breach down, Bridge, Boley hill, Bourne park, Broadstairs, Burmarsh, Canterbury, Chilham, Crundale down, Darenth, Dartford, Deal, Dover, Eastry, Faversham, Finglesham, Folkestone, Fordwich, Gravesend, Heronden, Higham, Hoo, Horton Kirby, Hythe, Kingston, Lullingstone, Lydd, Lyminge, Milton Regis, Minster, Northfleet, Otford, Ozingell, Ramsgate, Reculver, Richborough, Ringwold, Rochester, Romney, Ruckinge, Sampton-in-West-Hythe, Sandwich, Sarr,

Kent (*continued*)
Sittingbourne, Stodmarsh, Stonar, Stone-juxta-Faversham, Stowting, Surrenden, Swanscombe, Tenterden, Teynham, Thanet, Thurnham, Wantsum (channel), Westbere, Westenhanger, Westwell, Whitfield, Whitstable, Wickham, Wickhambreux, Wilmington, Wingham, Worth, Wye down
Kentigern, *St.*, 3391, 5009, 5016, 5025, 7609, 11254, 11337
Kenwith castle, Devon, 1727
Kerry, *county* (inscriptions), 9652–85 : (place-names), 6818 : (round towers), 10557, 10565. *See also* Aghadoe, Aglish, Ballintaggart, Ballinvoher, Ballymorereigh, Balliwiheen, Cahirciveen, Church Island, Cloghanecarhan, Drung Hill, Dunloe, Emlagh, Glenferis, Gortatlea, Inisvickillane, Kilbonane, Kilcolman, Kilfontain, Kilkeshagh, Killarney, Killorglin, Kilmalkedar, Lachareigh, Maumanorig, Rathduff, Reask, Skellig Michael (island of), Temple Monaghan, Tinnahally, Waterville
Kerswell (Abbot's and King's), Devon, 6774
Kertch, Crimea, 11496, 11555, 11560
Kessog, *St.*, 5003, 5011
Kesteven, Lincs. (place-name), 6569
Keswick, Cumb., 6662
Ketill (name), 638
Kettering, Northants., 8240, 8244–45, 8247, 8352–53
Kevin, *St.*, *of Glendalough*, 4807
Keyne, *St.*, 5041, 11738
Kieran, *St. See* Ciaran
Kil, Kill [place-names], 8539
Kilbannon, co. Galway, 10567
Kilbar, isle of Barra, Inverness, 11335
Kilbonane, co. Kerry, 9663, 9680
Kilbride, Argyllshire, 11339
Kilbride, Perthshire, 11270
Kilbunny, co. Waterford, 10499
Kilcolman, co. Kerry, 9670
Kilcoo, co. Leitrim, 9791
Kilcullen, co. Cork, 9622
Kilcullen, co. Kildare, 11170
Kildalton, Islay, Argyllshire, 11243
Kildare, 4508, 4510
Kildare, *county*, 2135 : (grave, 7th c.?), 8521 : (inscriptions), 9686–9705 : (round towers), 10563. *See also*

Allen (Almain) (hill of), Castledermot, Clane, Curragh (the), Donaghmore (Maynooth), Kilcullen, Killeen Cormac, Kilteel, Knockaulin, Maynooth, Moone
Kildonan, Eigg, Inverness, 11820
Kildonan, Sutherland, 8013
Kildonan bay, Kintyre, 8008
Kildwick-in-Craven, Yorks., 10932
Kilfenora, co. Clare, 3854
Kilfontain, co. Kerry, 9679
Kilian, *St.*, *apostle of Franconia*, 5346, 5399–5405
Kilkenny brooch, 11697
Kilkenny, *county* (inscriptions), 9706–15. *See also* Ballyboodan, Brittas, Dunbel, Dunmore cave, Gowran, Kilkieran, Killamory, Kilree, Lamogue, Legan, Tullaherin, Tybroughney, Ullard
Kilkeshagh, co. Kerry, 9774
Kilkieran, co. Kilkenny, 1120, 11158
Kilklispeen, co. Tipperary : *now* Ahenny, *q.v.*
Killadeas, co. Fermanagh, 11148
Killaine, co. Louth, 4813, 4843
Killaloe, co. Clare, 2186, 3854, 4829, 9773, 9776
Killamory, co. Kilkenny, 11158, 11169
Killarney, co. Kerry, 9684
Killeavy, co. Louth, 10484
Killeen Cormac, co. Kildare, 9686–9701
Killian, [Chillien], *St.*, *of Aubigny*, 5154, 5158–59
Killincoole, co. Louth (coins), 9128, 9138
Killineer, co. Louth, *battle* (868), 2155
Killiney, co. Dublin, 10497
Killorglin, co. Kerry, 9672
Killoughternane, co. Carlow, 10491
Killua, co. Westmeath, 8520, 11681, 11791
Killucan, co. Westmeath, 11670
Kilmacduagh, co. Galway, 3854, 10555
Kilmainham, co. Dublin, 8490
Kilmal Kedar, co. Kerry, 3908, 9660, 9683, 10488
Kilmannin, co. Mayo, 9725
Kilmaronock, Dumbartonshire, 11318
Kilmartin, Argyllshire, 11270
Kilnasaggart, co. Louth, 9720–22, 11162
Kiloran bay, Colonsay, Argyllshire, 8480, 8511, 11641
Kilpeacon, co. Limerick, 9769, 11127
Kilree, co. Kilkenny, 10553

Kilrush, co. Waterford, 9745
Kilslattery, co. Louth, 4790
Kilslieve [Cill-Sleibe-Cuillin], co. Armagh, 3790
Kiltarlity, Inverness, 6882
Kiltearn, Ross-shire, 6896
Kilteel, co. Kildare, 11144
Kiltera, co. Waterford, 9731, 9736
Kiltiernan, co. Galway, 8526
Kiltire, co. Waterford, 9739
Kilvington (place-name), 6348
Kin, 2468
Kincardine (forts and camps), 8004 : (place-name), 6912. *See also* Aquhollie, Fetteresso, Fortoun, Kinneff
King- [place-names], 6702
Kingham, Oxon, 1845
King's County [Offaly]. *See* Clonmacnoise, Drumcullin, Durrow, Ferbane (Gallen priory), Kinnitty, Lemanaghan, Ridgemount
Kingsclere, Hants, 2091
Kingscross, co. Bute, 8487
Kingston, Kent (brooch), 11637
Kingston, Surrey, 2309, 2317, 3878, 8443, 10433–34, 10981
Kingston, Lewes, Sussex, 8382
Kingstown, co. Dublin. *See* Dún Laoghaire
Kingswinford, Staffs., 10726
Kinneff, Kincardine, 11311
Kinneigh, co. Cork, 10551–52, 10556, 10561
Kinnitty, King's County, 11140
Kinross-shire (place-names), 6875–76. *See also* Tullibole
Kintbury, Berks., 8783, 9194
Kintradwell, Sutherland, 8059
Kintyre, Argyllshire, 4961
Kinwardstone, Wilts., 6761
Kippax, Yorks., 10949
Kirby, West, Cheshire, 3896, 10325, 10643
Kirby hill, Boroughbridge, Yorks., 10380
Kirk Andreas, Kirk Michael, etc. [Isle of Man]. *See* Andreas, Michael., etc.
Kirkburn, Yorks., 10960
Kirkby, Lancs., 10896
Kirkby Stephen, Westm., 8339, 10827–28, 10845–46, 10859
Kirkconnel, Dumfriesshire, 11251
Kircudbright (motes, forts and doons), 8006–07. *See also* Dalbeattie, Drumcoltran, Mote of Mark, Talnotrie, Trusty's Hill

Kirkdale, Yorks. (inscribed sundial), 547, 9472, 9512, 10376a, 10379, 10380b
Kirk Hammerton, Yorks., 10375a, 10380a
Kirkheaton, Yorks., 9484, 10940
Kirklevington, Yorks., 10975
Kirkmadrine, Wigtown, 2231, 9835–42, 11289, 11292
Kirkmichael, Banffshire, 11312
Kirknewton, Midlothian, 11333
Kirton-in-Lindsay, Lincs., 10161
Knickeen, co. Wicklow, 9750
Knoc y Doonee, Isle of Man (tumulus), 8534
Knockalafalla, co. Waterford, 9784
Knockaulin, co. Kildare (dun of Aillinn), 2168
Knockfierna stone, co. Limerick, 9795
Knockmaon, co. Wateford (coins), 9245
Knockshanawee, co. Cork, 9628, 9633, 9774
Kyneburh, *queen of Northumbria*, 1134

Lackareigh, co. Kerry, 9675
Lackford, Suffolk, 8136, 8555
Lacnunga, 7410–11, 7413, 7422, 7434, 7504
Lacy, *Roger de*, 337
Laoghaire, *king of Ireland* (*temp. St. Patrick*), 1022, 1026, 6140, 6197
Laeghaire Mac Crimhthainn, 7591
Lagore crannog, 8532, 8545
Lahman, 2493
Laidgen. *See* Lathren
Laisrén, *abbot of Lethglenn, co. Carlow*, 7651
Lake District (mountain names), 6656 : (Vikings in), 1939
Laluwy, *St.*; 5118
Lambeth Psalter, 5710, 5715
Lamborne, Berks., 2051
Lamel hill, Yorks., 8368
Lamlash, co. Bute, 8486
Lammas field, Somerset, 2117
Lamogue, co. Kilkenny, 9706, 9710
Lampeter, Cardigan, 10035
Lanalet Pontifical, 5765
Lanarkshire (forts, camps and motes), 8003 : (place-names), 6894. *See also* Cambusnethan, Clydesdale, Glasgow, Hamilton
Lancashire, 1885, 1943, 1964, 1993, 3126, 8344 : (ancient monuments, north, inventory of), 10042 : (churches), 3879, 3898 : (conquest of, ? date),

Lancashire (*continued*)
1113 : (dedications), 4128 : (Domesday), *see* Domesday (Lancs.) : (ecclesiastical history), 3843 : (ethnology), 8814 : (Lancashire and king Arthur), 1046, 1073 : (place-names), 6386, 6409, 6658, 6661, 6666, 6671, 6676, 6678–80, 6682 : (sculpture), 10640, 10880–10900 : (settlement of), 959, 994. *See also* Aldingham-in-Furness, Aughton, Burnley, Cartmel, Claughton hall, Cuerdale, Culcheth, Furness, Fylde (Foreland of the), Grange-over-Sands, Halton, Heysham, Kirkby, Lancaster, Liddell, Liverpool, Manchester, Meols (North), Mersey valley, Pennington, Penwortham, Rampside, Urswick, Whalley, Winwick
Lancaster, 8341, 9050, 9492, 9496, 9498, 10884, 10887, 10889
Lancelot du Lake, 5957 : (name), 621
Lanchester, co. Durham, 8629
Lancing, Sussex, 8373, 8770
Land, 3097–3133 : (female ownership), 6326 : (land law), 2490, 2502a, 2509, 2511 : (measurement of), 531–32, 539, 542, 548, *see also* under Domesday : (transfer of), 3133
Landelech [Domesday site], 6013
Landnamabok, 1945 : (Gaelic names in), 640
Lanfranc, *abp. of Canterbury*, 3295, 3545, 3602, 3611, 3978–97, 5677 : (monastic constitutions), 3602 : (Penenden heath), 2451–55
Langandene, Wilts., 6069–70
Langdale, Little, Westmorland, 2363
Langford, Oxon., 10743
Langford, Hanging, Wilts., 11008
Langton, East, Mid-Lothian, 8709
Lanhadron, Cornwall, 9568
Lanhill, Wilts. (barrow), 1272
Langteglos-by-Camelford, Cornwall, 9564, 9569
Lapidary, 7344–45
Largo bay, Fife, 8538, 11732
Lastingham, Yorks., 3710, 10379, 10381, 10973
Latheron, Caithness, 11301
Lathren, 183, 5778
Latin learning and writing, 7005–07, 7012, 7028, 7047
Laughton-en-le-Morthen, Yorks., 7949, 10375, 10377

Launceston, Cornwall, 1701, 11053 : (mint), 8918
Laws, 2356–2609
Lay of the Beach, 1564
Lea, river, 1217, 1230–31
Leabhar Bretnach [Irish Nennius], 159, 165
Leabhar Gabála [Book of Invasions], 187, 193, 211
Leabhar na gCeart [Book of Rights], 198, 2180, 2183, 2688
Leabhar na-Huidhre [Book of the Dun-Cow], 179, 219, 5862, 7272–73, 7582, 7595, 7650
Leades, co. Cork, 9624
Leagrave, Beds., 8213
Leathley, Yorks., 10364
Lebor. *See* Leabhar
Leckhampton, Glos., 8674
Leeds, Yorks., 6630, 10933, 10939, 10946a
Leek, Staffs., 10724, 10729–30, 10733
Legal procedure, 2357–58, 2362, 2483
Legalis homo, 2499
Legan, co. Kilkenny, 9706, 9710
Leicester, 11451: (burh), 7939: (earldom, 1066–), 1545 : (mint), 9270, 9320, 9336
Leicestershire, 1837, 1861–62 : (archaeology of), 8331 : (Domesday), *see* Domesday (Leicester) : (origin of earldom), 1545 : (place-names), 6527–28, 6533, 6541, 6554 : (sculpture), 10691–95. *See also* Barrow, Belvoir, Breedon-on-the-hill, Glen Parva, *Godmundeslaech* (= Gumley), Harston, Hickling, Leicester, Lowesby, Melton Mowbray, Rothley, Saxby, Sharnford, Sproxton, Stoke Golding, Twyford, Westcotes
Leigh, Essex, 8117
Leigh, North, Oxon., 8265
Leighton Buzzard, Beds., 8207–08
Leinster (' Graves of Leinster men '), 2129 : (hagiology of), 4481, 4493 : (kings of), 2140, 2182 : (Scandinavian), 2144
Leitrim, *county*. *See* Cloonmorris, Kilcoo
Leix, *county*. *See* Queen's County
Lemanaghan, King's County, 4835, 11124, 11801, 11803
Lemon [river-name], 6467
Lencten-ádl, 7468a
Lennox, 2207
Leofric, *abbot of Peterborough*, 3676

Leofric, *bp. of Crediton and Exeter*, 4035, 4067, 4069, 6111, 7125, 7150, 7219
Leofric Collectar (Collectaneum), 5768–69
Leofric, *earl of Mercia* [vision of], 7652, 7658
Leofric Missal, 3224, 3231, 5751, 5784, 7246
Leofwine, huntsman to Æthelred II., (charter for, 987), 396
Leonaford, royal vill (887), 6078
Leprosy, 7429, 7451, 7461, 7469, 7473
Lérins, isle of (St. Patrick at), 4671
Letchworth, Herts., 11614
Lethnott, Forfarshire, 11327
Leudard, *bp.*, 8982
Leutherius, *bp. of Winchester* (grant to Malmesbury, 675), 317
Levenwick, Shetland, 8031
Lewannick, Cornwall, 9565, 9581–83
Lewes, Sussex, 8698, 8772, 10402, 10406, 11608
Lewinna, *St.*, 4388, 4424
Lewis, Ross-shire (place-names), 6887
Lewisham, Surrey, 2110, 6619. ——, *priory*, 3717
Leyden, lorica of, 5779
Leys [place-names], 6389
Lezayre parish, Isle of Man, 6841, 8522, 8537
Lia tail [coronation stone at Tara], 2316
Liathmor-Mochoemog, co. Tipperary, 3792, 10492–93
Liber Landavensis. *See* Llandaff, *Book of*
Liberalis stone, Yarrow, 9871–72, 9891
Libraries, 7123–87a : (dispersal of), 41 : (St. Gallen), 5566 : (Waltham abbey), 75
Liddell, Cumb., 7960
Liddesdale, 3441 : (stone), 9884
Lide- [place-names], 6421
Liebermann (Felix), biography of, 40
Liffey valley (forts), 7986
Lifton, Devon, 1679
Limerick, *county* (Aenach sites), 6073 : (castles), 7996 : (churches), 3910 : (Northmen of), 1314 : (Patrick's itinerary through), 4668–69. *See also* Ardpatrick, Ballingarry, Caherelly, Donaghmore, Dysert, Gur (Lough), Kilpeacon, Knockfierna stone, Mountrussell, Mungret abbey
Lincoln, 1856–57, 6563, 8318, 8606, 10258–59, 10265, 11459 : (charter of

William I), 3830 : (inscription at St. Mary-le-Wigford), 9441 : (mint), 9301 : (St. Mary-le-Wigford), 3875, 9441, 9451, 10266 : (St. Peter at Gowts), 10266 : (see of), 3830 : (sculpture), 10696, 10711
Lincolnshire, 1852a, 1854, 1905, 1909, 1912 : (archaeology in), 1889, 7765, 8308, 8315, 8700 : (architecture, ecclesiastical), 10256–68 : (conversion), 3535–37 : (dedications), 4150: (Domesday), *see* Domesday (Lincs.) : (ecclesiastical history), 3806 : (ethnology), 8847 : (Peterborough estates in), 3675 : (place-names), 6343, 6560–77 : (pottery), 8589–90 : (sculpture), 10696–10711 : (see), 3830 : (sheriffs), 3165 : (sokemen), 3220 : (woodland), 3025. *See also* Alkborough, Aveland, Axeholm (isle of), Bain (river), Bardney, Barholme, Barkwith (East and West), Barnetby-le-Wold, Barrow, Barton-on-Humber, Baston, Bennington (Long), Benniworth, Brigg, Caenby, Caistor, Cammeringham, Coleby, Conisholme, Crowland, Crowle, Digby, Elkington (South), Epworth, Ferriby (South), Gedney, Glentworth, Graffoe (deanery of), Grimsby, Halton (West), Hibbaldstow, Horncastle, Howletts, Kirton-in-Lindsay, Lincoln, Lindis (river), Loveden hill, Miningsby, Riseley, Ruskington, Scothorn, Scotter, Scunthorpe, Searby, Sleaford, Stamford, Stow, Tetney, Threckingham, Till (river), Torksey, Willoughton, Winterton, Witham (river), Woolsthorpe.
Lindfield, Sussex, 2009 : (charter, 765), 376
Lindis (river), Lincs., 6441, 6448
Lindisfarne (Gospels), 5691–92, 5695, 7140, 7226, 7229, 10038, 11849, 11851, 11927, 11936, 11938–39 : (history of), 1941, 1951, 1994, 3687 : (inscriptions), 9504, 9507, 10919 : (place-name), 6653 : (see of), 3813, 3820, 3829 : (sculpture), 10919–20
Lindsey, 1901, 6568, 6570–72 : (bishopric of), 1869, 6116
Lingfield, Surrey, 6705, 6718
Linlathen, Forfarshire, 8542
Linton, Cambs., 8146

Lismore, co. Waterford, 2137–38, 2141, 3863, 7008, 11137, 11151 : (Book of), 4476, 4496

Lisnaskea, co. Fermanagh, 11146

Liverpool, Lancs., 1974, 6666

Livinus, *St.*, 5506–07

Llanarth, Cardigan, 10005

Llanarthney, Carmarthenshire, 11359, 11362

Llanbadarn Fawr, Cards., 11404

Llanbadarn Fynydd, Radnor, 5975

Llanboidy, Carmarthenshire, 10004

Llancarfan (charters), 417

Llandaff, Glam. (bishops of and Teilo churches), 3866 : (charters), 290

Llandaff, *Book of*, 233, 236, 1671

Llandanwg, Merioneth, 10018

Llanddetty stone, Brecknock, 9932

Llanddewibrefi, Cardigan, 10035

Llandecwyn, Merioneth, 9950, 9952

Llandevaelog, Brecknock, 11418

Llandilo, Carmarthenshire, 9988, 11360, 11365–66, 11368

Llandough, Glam., 11382, 11386

Llandrinio, Montgom., 11414

Llandyssil, Cards., 11685

Llan Elltyd stone, Merioneth, 9953

Llanerfyl, Montgomeryshire, 10015

Llanfachreth, Anglesey, 11356

Llanfallteg, Carmarthenshire, 9980, 9990

Llanfechan, Cardigan, 10016

Llanfeigan, Brecknock, 11412

Llanfihangel, Merioneth, 9951

Llanfwrog, Denbighshire, 10017

Llangefelach, Glam., 11384

Llangollen, Denbigh, 991, 10008, 10030, 10034

Llangors, Brecknock, 9929–30

Llangwyllog, Anglesey, 10032

Llangwyryfon, Cardigan, 10014

Llanrhaiadr, Montgom., 11406

Llanrhidian, Glam., 11385

Llanrudian, Pembrokeshire, 9987

Llansadyrnin, Carmarthenshire, 9978

Llantrisant, Glam., 11394

Llantwit Major, Glamorgan, 2243, 5049, 7010, 9933, 9937, 9946, 10518, 11375–81

Llanveynoe, Herefordshire, 9442, 10756

Llanwinio, Carmarthenshire, 9961, 9979

Llanwnda, Pembrokeshire, 10001

Llanwnws, Cardigan, 10009, 10019

Llowes, Radnor, 11405, 11410

Llwyfenydd [home of Urien of Reged : site], 6129

Llystyn Gwyn, Carnarvonshire, 10013

Llywarch the Aged, 7593

Llywarch Hen, 1028–29, 1038, 8528

Llywel stone, Brecknock, 9923, 9925

Llywelyn ab Seisyllt, 1317

Lochaber, Inverness, 6877

Lochlee, Angus, 11312

Lockridge, Berks., 8397

Loding. *See* Lathren

Logierait, Perthshire, 11272

Loidis, Yorks. *See* Elmet

Lombards (relation to Angles), 1648

London, 1797–1812a, 7754, 7847, 10748 : (Alfred rebuilds, 886) 696 : (All Hallows, Barking), 10747 : (All Hallows, Staining), 6124, 10270–72 : (archaeology), 7771, 8332, 10044 : (architecture, ecclesiastical), 10269–75 : (churches), 3890, 5885 : (Domesday), *see* Domesday : (early riverside settlements), 1805 : (Essex, capital of), 1801 : (ethnology), 8841 : (Fetter lane), 8650 : (guilds), 3049, 3051 : (place-names), 6609–19, 6711 : (St. Alphege church, London Wall), 3870 : (St. Martin's-le-Grand, charter, 1068), 405, 412 : (*ditto*, sanctuary), 3459 : (Saxon invasion), 904, 938 : (Saxon settlement), 979 : (topography), 5877

Long-bow (origin of), 2299

Longbridge, Warw., 8290–91, 11481

Longcastle, Wigtown, 11294

Long hundred (120), 541, 545

Longevity [Irish saints'], 4454

Loom, loom weights, 7686, 8632, 8636

Lorica, 4148a, 5778–92 *passim*, 7518 : (Gildas), 5785, 5788, 5791–92 : (Lathren, Loding), 183, 5778 : (Leyden), 5779 : (St. Patrick's breastplate), 4543, 4554, 4560–61

Lorrha, co. Tipperary, 11125

Lorsch, 7185

Lost literature, 49, 74

Lot, *king of Orkney*, 1090

Lothian, 1953 : (acquisition of, by Edwin), 971 : (ceded to Malcolm II, 1018), 1602

Lots, 3495

Lough Lyn, co. Westmeath (coins,) 8900

Loughor, Glam., 9936

Louth, co. Louth, 2145, 10131

Louth, *county* (Columba in), 4944 : (Feighin in), 4791 : (inscriptions), 9716–22 : (monasteries), 2158, 2174 :

Louth, *county* (*continued*)
(motes), **7985, 7991, 7995** : (Patrick and), **4684** : (place-names), **6830** : (wells), **4497**. *See also* Barnafeadog, Castle Bellingham, Drogheda, Dromiskin, Dunleer, Funshog, Killaine, Killeavy, Killincoole, Killineer, Kilnasaggart, Kilslattery, Louth, Omeath, Smarmore (Ardee), Termonfechin

Loveden hill, Lincs., **8307**
Lowesby, Leics., **8710**
Lowick, Northumberland, **8343**
Lowther, Westm., **10816, 10833**
Lowthorpe, Yorks., **10956**
Lozinga, *Herbert de, bp. of Norwich*, **4034, 4070**
Luce, Old, Wigtown, **11287, 11312**
Lucky, unlucky, days, **7499**
Luffenham, North, Rutland, **8273, 8278–79, 8284–85**
Lugaid MacMaenaich, *St.* (Munster), **4818**
Lugle and Luglien, *SS.*, **5162**
Lull, *abp. of Mainz*, **5271, 5346**
Lullingstone, Kent, **8569**
Lumphanan, Aberdeen, **8711**
Lundr [sanctuary], **3476, 3510**
Lunnasting, Shetland, **9870**
Luppitt, Devon, **11015, 11017**
Luss, Dumbartonshire, **11319**
Lustleigh, Devon, **9586–87**
Luton, Beds., **8201–03, 8780**
Luxeuil, **5446–57** : (script of), **7309**
Lydd, Kent, **1794, 10207, 10225**
Lyddington, Rutland, **1843**
Lyde- [place-names], **6421**
Lydford, Devon, **1717, 1731, 7967**
Lyminge, Kent, **3884–85, 3903, 8178, 10221, 10235**
Lyminster, Sussex, **10398**
Lynchets, **7757**
Lynton, Devon, **1694**
Lypiatt, Glos., **10684–85**

Mabinogion, **232, 239, 642, 2592, 7035, 7586, 7588, 7621**
Mabon vab Modron, **7588**
Macbeth, *king of Scotland*, **1601, 1603, 1617, 1625, 1628–29, 6127**
Macclesfield, Cheshire, **10653**
MacCreiche, *St.*, **4854**
MacCuilinn, *St., of Lusk*, **4529**
Macduff's cross, Fife, **9876**
Machar, *St.*, **5006**

Machars, Wigtown, **11288**
Mackney, Berks. (charter), **333**
MacRegol of Birr, *Gospels of*, **11934**
Mægcynren, **2644**
Mael Duin, **6228a, 6231–32, 6234**
Maelruain, *founder of Tallaght monastery*, **3771**
Maelsuthain, **4767**
Maen Achwyfan, Flint, **11369–74**
Maes-how, Orkney, **7755, 9843–51, 11265**
Magesætas, **5868, 6300**
Magh Adhair, co. Clare, **2328**
Magh Rath, *battle* [site], **6128**
Maghera, co. Down, **9780**
Magic, **7451, 7475–76, 7480, 7482–7552**
Magnenn, *St., of Kilmainham*, **4485**
Magnus, *St., earl of Orkney*, **1619**
Mahee, Inis, co. Down, **4768**
Maiden [place-names], **6410**
Maiden stone, Aberdeenshire, **9892**
Maildun, **6228a, 6231–32, 6234**
Mainistrech (Flann), **2152**
Mains of Croy, Inverness, **8883, 11552, 11695**
Mainz, **5232, 5239, 5243, 5345, 7186**
Malaria, **7468a**
Malcolm I, *king of Scots*, **8527, 8541**
Malcolm II, *Canmore, king of Scots*, **1601–02, 1617** : (estate, Corby, Northants.), **292, 3097** : (grant by, to Macduff's descendents), **314**
Maldon, Essex (*burh*), **7897** : (mint), **9293**
Maldon, *battle* (991/3), **1285–87, 1302, 1306, 1312–13, 1316, 6098** : (personal names in poem), **613**
Malmesbury, Wilts., **3270, 10988** : (mint), **9229, 9257**
Malmesbury, *abbey*, **3667–71** : (charters), **317, 385, 8461**
Malmesbury, William of. *See* William, *of Malmesbury*
Malo, *St.*, **5166, 5188**
Malton, Yorks., **6343, 11632**
Malvern, Worcs., **3737**
Mamwys [Welsh law], **2593**
Man, *Isle of*, **1019, 2190–2200** : (architecture, ecclesiastical), **10520–21** : (bishops), **3860** : (conditions in 5th c.), **1019**: (connection with Cumberland and Westmorland), **5899** : (*ditto* with Ireland), **1653–54** : (*ditto* with Scotland), **2228** : (inscriptions), **9796–9826, 9868, 11196** : (land tenure), **3103** : (name of),

Man, *Isle of* (*continued*)
  6835, 6837 : (Norse mythology in),
  3494 : (Northmen in), 2199 : (Norwegian conquest of), 1175, 2192,
  2196 : (personal names), 624, 635–
  37, 640 : (place-names), 635, 637,
  6834–45 : (schools and scholarship),
  7003 : (sculpture), 11176–11225 :
  (ship-burial in), 8502, 8535 : (treens
  and keeils), 3411–12, 3422 : (weapons), 8733 : ('Wonders of the '),
  7587. *See also* [n.b. prefix Kirk-
  omitted from place-names], Alkest,
  Andreas, Arbory, Balladoyne, Balla-
  queeney, Ballavarkish, Braddan,
  Bride, Calf of Man, Cronk Conoly,
  Cronk Kecillane, Cronk yn How,
  Douglas,Fort St.Mary,Guriat(Crux),
  Jurby, Knoc yn Doonee, Lezayre,
  Maughold, Michael, Onchan, Ram-
  say, Ronaldsway, Santon, Sodor,
  Woodbourne
Manannan Mac Lir, 7584
Manaw, Mano, 5972
Manchan, *St., abbot of Mendroichet, Leix*
  4835, 4860, 11801, 11803
Manchester, 3100, 10895
Mancus (the word), 8928–29
Maningford Bruce, Wilts., 10427
Mann [personal name], 6636
Manning [moneyer], 9315
Manningham, Yorks., 6636
Manor, 3259–90
Manor Water stone, Peebles, 9884
Manshead hundred, Beds., 6065
Manumissions, 280, 3199, 3204, 3208,
  3213, 3224, 3229, 3231
Manuscripts, 7123–7317 *passim*, 10925,
  11947, 11955, 11960–61
  Individual mss., which contain pub-
  lished A.-S. material, here cited :
  Phillips MS. 9194 (Life of St.
  Fechin of Fore), 4526
By city or place :
      A.   British Isles
Aberystwyth :
  National   Library   of   Wales :
  Llanstephan MSS. 116 (Laws of
  Hywel Dda—Dimetian code), 2601 :
  201 (Arthur), 7610
  Peniarth MSS. 20 (Brut y Tywyso-
  gion), 234–35 : 29 (Black Book of
  Chirk), 2600 : 386 (Life of St.
  Wulfstan), 4027

Cambridge :
Corpus Christi College
  MSS. C.C.C.C. 12 (Letter of Alfred
  to bps.), 6979–80 : 41 (Homily),
  5685, 7554 : 140 (manumissions),
  3204 : 173 (A.-S. C., A text), *see*
  Anglo-Saxon Chronicle : 183 (list
  of 70 disciples *and* Bede's Life of St.
  Cuthbert), 7564 : 4219, 11933 :
  201 (Laws of Cnut), 2434 : 265
  (Worcester eccles. collns.), 7216 :
  286 (Canterbury Gospels), 7241,
  11945 : 308 (Passio S. Ethelberti),
  4413 : 367 (vision of earl Leofric),
  7652 : 383 (*Geréfa*), 2411 : 391
  (charms *and* Wulfstan's Prayer
  Book), 7551 : 5807
Fitzwilliam Museum
  MS. McClean 187 (Brendan), 6246
University Library
  MSS. Ec.3.59 (Life of Edward the
  Confessor), 1388 : Ff. 1, 23 (Psal-
  ter), 5702 : Ii. 1. 33 (Genesis),
  5671 : Ii. 2. 4 (letter of Alfred to
  bps.), 6979–80 : Kk. 5. 16 (Moore
  memoranda), 1930 : Kk. 5. 32
  (Byrhtferth fragment), 7364 : Ll.
  1. 10 (Book of Cerne), *see* Cerne,
  Book of
Canterbury :
Cathedral Library
  ' Charta antiqua ' (Fonthill, Wilts.),
  313 : Gospel fragment, 5698
Dublin :
Abp. Marsh's Library
  MS. Z3. I. 5 (Life of St. Canice *and*
  Life of St. Fin Barre), 4771 : 4528
Franciscan Library
  MS. A2 (Book of Hymns), 7259
Royal Irish Academy
  MS. 3B. 23 (teaching of Maelruain,
  Tallaght), 3771 : MS. 23 P. 3 (Mon-
  astic Rules), 5622a
Trinity College
  MSS. B. 2 (St. Ragener), 4428 : E.
  4. 2 (Book of Hymns), 7259 : H. 2.
  7 (Irish genealogies), 507 : H. 2. 15
  (Senchus Mór), 2543 : H. 3. 17
  (canonical hours), 5840a
Durham :
Cathedral Library
  MS. B iii (A.-S. miniatures), 11946

H

Manuscripts (*continued*)
Edinburgh :
National Library
MS. XL (Life of Columba *and* Penance of Adam), **4889** : **5839**

Exeter :
Chapter Library
MS. 3815 (Exeter Martyrology), **4131**

Holkham Hall :
MSS. 708–09 (Winchester school), **11926**

London, Lambeth Palace :
MS. 427 (Lambeth Psalter *and* St. Mildred), **5710, 5715, 4412**

London, British Museum :
MSS. Additional 9381 (Bodmin Gospels), *q.v.* : 11205 (forged charter of William I to Coventry), **359, 414** : 24199 (Prudentius), **7242** : 37517 (Bosworth Psalter), **5714, 7222** : 39943 (Bede's Prose Life of Cuthbert), **4216** : 40165a (Mercian Martyrology), **4148** : 47967 (Tollemache Orosius), **7216a**

MSS. Arundel 60 (Litany *and* Psalter), **4152** : **5699a, 5717** : 65 (Penitential), **5586** : 155 (Liturgies), **5825**

MSS. Cotton Augustus II 42 (will of Badanoð Beotting), **2460** : II 91 (charter, Sandtun, Kent), **422** : II 99 (charter, Higham, Kent), **364** : II 102 (charter, Sandtun, Kent), **422**

MSS. Cotton Tiberius A III (De consuetudine monachorum), **3599, 5631, 11946** : (charms), **7498, 7500** : (lapidary), **7344–45** : A XIII (Worcester charters), **395** : B IV (A.–S. C., D Text) *q.v.* : B V (Bede, De natura rerum), **7406** : (calendar, 10th c.), **528** : B XIII (cosmology), **7493** : C II (Bede, Eccl. Hist. [glosses]), **4169** : C VI (armour : 10th c. Psalter), **8688** : C IX. 7 (charter, Waltham), **75**

MSS. Cotton Caligula A VII (Heliand), **7235** : A XIV (runes), **9435** : A XV (magic), **7498.**

MSS. Cotton Claudius B IV (Genesis), **5671** : (armour), **8688** : (building of Babel), **10176** : C VII [formerly] (Utrecht Psalter) *q.v.*

MSS. Cotton Nero B II (Offa I), **7553a** : (foundation charter of St. Albans), **3739** : D IV (Lindisfarne Gospels), **5693, 11873, 11936** : E I (anon. life of St. [abp.] Oswald), **4042**

MSS. Cotton Otho B XI (burnt fragments of A.–S. C., MS. G), **92** : C I (vision of monk of Wenlock), **7647** : C V (Northumbrian runes), **7497** : E XIII (Irish law of distress), **2535**

MSS. Cotton Vitellius A XV (Flores of Augustine), **5658** : (Beowulf), **7224, 7237, 7250** : C III (A.–S. Herbal), **7220, 7407, 7414** : E XVIII (Kalendarium [Psalter]), **462**

MSS. Cotton Vespasian A I (Vespasian Psalter), **7227** : A XIV (Welsh hagiology), **5055** : (Wulfstan, re Ordination), **3543** : B VI (list of 70 disciples), **7564** : (genealogy), **471** : D VI (Kentish hymn), **5831** : D XIV ['Farrago multarum rerum Saxonice'] (A.–S. Life of St. Neot), **1228, 4422, 4445** : (Last Judgement), **7543** : (homilies), **5815, 5818** : (Gospel of Nicodemus), **5685** : (charms, etc.), **7484–85.**

MSS. Cotton Titus A XXV (Irish Annals) *q.v.* : D XXVI and XXVII (prognostics), **46**

MSS. Cotton Domitian I. 6 (library of Athelstan), **7131** : VIII (A.–S. C., MS. F) *q.v.*

MSS. Cotton Cleopatra A II (Vita S. Monennae), **4775** : B V (Book of Basingwerk), **238**

MSS. Cotton Faustina A X (Rule of St. Benet, postscript), **3586** ; B IX (Chronicle of Melrose), **226**

Cottonian rolls ii. 11 (Crediton indulgences), **3327**

MSS. Egerton 745 (Vie de s. Édouard, roi), **1393** : 1782 (Irish taboos), **7583**

MSS. Harley 24 (King Arthur, M.E.), **1049** : 53 (genealogy), **466** : 408 (grant of Wrottesley to Evesham abbey), **332** : 436 (grant from Athelstan to Wilton abbey, 937),

Manuscripts (*continued*)
MSS. Harley (*continued*)

357: 491. 2 (de obitu Willelmi regis), 1502: 863. 20 (Athanasian creed), 5827: 2892 (Canterbury Benedictional), 5762: 2904 (Psalter), 11937: 2961 (Leofric Collectar), 5768: 3271 (place-names), 6283: 3763 (Evesham Chartulary), 548: 3776 (Vita Haroldi), 1363: 3859 (Old-Welsh genealogies), 502, 517: 4353 (Laws of Hywel Dda), 2608: 4843 (miracles of St. Cuthbert), 4295: 6258 (περὶ διδάξεων), 7418

Harleian charters 83 A 1 (Weald, 814), 320: 83 A 2 (Wulfgeat's will), 2462

Harley roll Y 6 (Guthlac roll), 4342

MS. Lansdowne 436 (St. Cuthburga), 4402

MSS. Royal 1 B. VII (Gospel Book of St. Cuthbert), 5693: 2 B. V (Psalter), 5701: 4 A. XIV, f. 106b (charm against wens), 7552

MS. Stowe 38 (*Hæselersc* charter, 1018), 419

Oxford:
Balliol College
MS. 350 (Herefordshire Domesday), 2886

Bodleian Library
Archiv. Seld. D 52 (Rule of St. Fulgentius), 3590
Ashmole MSS. 43 (St. Brendan), 6241: 328 (Byrhtforth), 64, 7361–69
Auct. MS. D II. 19 (Gospels of MacRegol of Birr), 11934: F III. 6 (charms), 7534
Crawford charters 1–4, 7, 10, 13 (Crediton), 321
Digby MS. 112 (St. Indract), 5091, 5109
Hatton MSS. 114 (Worcester 'trembling hand'), 7301: 115 (magic), 7498: 116 [formerly Junius 24] (Life of Chad), 4077
Junius MSS. 11 (Caedmon), 7243, 11928, 11930: 24 [now Hatton 116] (Life of Chad), 4077: 27 (Psalter), 5700

Laud MSS. 610 (Bede, E.H., Irish), 4175 *and* (Irish genealogies), 512–13 *and* (Irish prayer for long life), 5787 *and* (Psalter of Mac-Richard Butler), 213: 636 (A.–S. C., E text, Peterborough), *q.v.*: Greek 39 (Acts, Codex E), 7217, 7234: Latin Liturg. MS. F. 5 (Gospel Book of St. Margaret), 7263, 11935

Misc. MSS. 340 and 342 (Ælfric, Homilies), 7239: 343 (O. E. Homily), 4345

Rawlinson MSS. B484 (list of Irish saints), 4470: B 845 *and* B 505 (Irish saints, Columba), 4490, 4894: B 488 (Tigernach) *q.v.*: B 502 (Ambra Choluimb Chille), 202, 4901: B 503 (Annals of Inisfallen), 191: B 514 (Betha Colaim Chille), 4896

Corpus Christi College
MS. 197 (survey of Bury and history of Edmund the Martyr), 328

St. John's College
MS. 17 (Byrhtferth's diagram), 7368

Salisbury:
Cathedral Library
MS. 38 (Aldhelm glosses), 3931

Stonyhurst College:
MS. lxix (Bede's death-song), 4211

Welbeck abbey:
(Vie de s. Édouard), 1393

Worcester:
Cathedral Library
MS. 173 (Liturgy), 5833: 4° MS. 5 (charms), 7534

B. Foreign

Anger:
MS. 14 (St. Patrick), 5601

Bern:
Stadt-Bibliothek
MSS. 207 (Bede), 4214, 9532: 671 (A.–S. gilds, tithes, etc.), 2029, 2642

Brussels:
Bibliothèque Royale
MSS. 1650 (Aldhelm, De laudibus virginitatis), 3924, 3932: 2324 (Betha Fursa), 5218, 5223: 4190–

Manuscripts (*continued*)
Bibliothèque Royale (*continued*)
    4200 (Betha Adamnáin), **4881**:
    5100–04 (Martyrology of Tallaght),
    4498, 7603: 5301–20 (Irish Annals)
    q.v.: 6131 (Eachra Conaill Gulban),
    1020: 8957–58 (Life of St. Secun-
    dinus), **4796**: 9565–66 (runes),
    9379: 18644–72 (Vita Bonifatii),
    5284, 5287

Cambrai:
    MS. 619 (Canones Hibernici), **196**

Cracow:
Chapter Library
    MS. 43 (monastic conferences), **7261**

Florence:
Laurentian Library
    (Codex Amiatinus), *q.v.*

Freiburg-im-Breisgau:
University Library
    MS. 702 (St. Luke, Irish and A.-S.),
    7262

Karlsruhe:
    MS. Reichenau 167 (Bede), **4189**

Melk (Austria):
Library of Benedictine monastery
    MS. 370 (Bede, De temporum
    ratione), **4189**

Milan:
Ambrosian Library
    MSS. C 301 (Columbanus, psalms),
    5417, 5427: S 17. sup. (Alcuin),
    7057

Munich:
Stadtsbibliothek
    MS. Latin 13067 (runic inscription),
    9434

Paris:
Bibliothèque Nationale
    Celtic MSS. 1 (Brendan: Columba),
    6250: **4903**

    Latin MSS. 4126 (Pictish history),
    808: 8824 (Paris Psalter) *q.v.*: 9389
    (Northumbrian illumination), **79,
    118**: 10837 (Bobbio Missal: Calen-
    dar of St. Willibrord), **5726–30,
    5518**

Rome:
Vatican Library
    MSS. Regina 12 (Bury Psalter),
    5724: 338 (charm for fever: runes),
    7508, 9407

Rouen:
Public Library
    MSS. A 27 (Lanalet Pontifical),
    5765: Y34/22 bis (A.-S. calendar),
    5773

St. Gallen:
    MSS. 270 (runes), **9379**: 878 (runes),
    7995: 1395 (Vulgate), **5697**

Tours:
Municipal Library
    MS. 1008 (Brendan), **6238, 6253**

Turin:
    MS. F. iv. 1 (Irish liturgical frag-
    ment), **5850, 5863**

Valenciennes:
Municipal Library
    MS. N 4 (Dicuil), **7400**

Vercelli:
    MS. CXVII (Homilies), **5816, 5820–
    21**

Vienna:
Imperial Library
    MS. 16 (Irish glosses), **7276**

Manwood hundred, Sussex, **381**
Maolrubha, *St.*, **5002, 5018, 5022**
Maplestead, Great, Essex, **10632**
Mar, Aberdeenshire, **2234**
Margam, Glam., **9938, 9947, 11390,
    11392, 11395**
Margam Mountain, Glamorgan, **2681**
Margaret, *St.*, *queen of Scotland*, **1353,
    4967–73, 5016**: (Gospel Book of),
    7263, 11935
Marianus, *of Ratisbon*, **7265**
Marianus Scotus, **4799, 5258, 5261, 5398**
Marilles, Brabant (A.-S. brooch), **11464**
Marinus, *St.*, **5251**
Mark, *king of Cornwall*, **1083, 5974, 9585**
Marlborough, Wilts., (mint), **9273**
Marriage by purchase, **2495**
Marriage law, **2471, 2479**
Marston St. Lawrence, Northants., **8241–
    42**
Martham, Norfolk, **3273–74**

Martinus, *of Laon*, **7049**
Marton, Warw., **8287, 8289**
Marylebone, St., **3261**
Maserfield, *battle* (642), **872, 1111, 1118, 1148, 6093–94**
Masham, Yorks., **10957**
Mass-books (9th c.), **5758**
Matilda, *queen of William I*, **485**. *See also* under Gundrada (her daughter)
Matriarchy (Picts), **813, 842**
Mattesdune, Glos., **1820**
Maughold (St.), Isle of Man, **3780, 9808, 11212, 11216–17, 11219, 11221, 11223–24**
Maumanorig, co. Kerry, **9678**
Mawgan (Meneage) cross, Cornwall, **9570**
Maynooth, co. Kildare, **9702–05**
Mayo, *abbey*, **3765, 4789**
Mayo, *county* (inscriptions), **9723–27** : (round towers), **10560**. *See also* Aghagower, Aghaleague, Belladooan, Bracklaghboy, Breastagh, Caher island, Doonfeany stone, Doughmaksone, Inishkea North, Kilmannin, Mayo, Meelick, Tullaghane
Meath, *county*, **2183, 2688** : (crosses), **11123** : (diocese), **3852** : (place-names), **6833**. *See also* Cairon, Duleek, Inis-mocht, Kells, Mooretown, Painestown, St. Cairan, Tara, Trim
Meath, *kingdom*, **2175, 2184**
Meaux abbey, Yorks., **11629**
Medan, *St.*, (bell), **11781**
Medeshamstede, *abbey*. *See* Peterborough
Medicine, **5767, 7407–7552, 9416–17, 11742, 11745**
Medmerry farm, Selsey, Sussex, **8659**
Meelick, co. Mayo, **11126**
Meiford, Montgomeryshire, **2263, 11407, 11415**
Meigle, Perthshire, **11269, 11274**
Melbourne, Derbs., **10306, 10326**
Melhus, Norway (reliquary), **11810**
Melling, Westm., **10841**
Melor, *St.*, **5117**
Melrose, *Chronicle of*, **226**
Melton Mowbray, Leics., **8320**
Menscryfa stone (Madron), Cornwall, **9571, 9576**
Menston, Yorks., **6636**
Mentmore, Bucks., **8322–23, 9011**

Menvendanus stone, Carmarthenshire, **10004**
Meols, North, Lancs., **4287**
Meon valley, Hants., **2109, 6726, 11634**
Meonwaras, **2074, 2109, 11636**
Mercia, **1108–09, 1125, 1140, 1273, 1869, 1797–1927** : (Alfred in), **1271** : (boundary, with East Saxons), **5932** : (*ditto*, western), **5924, 5935** : (coins), **8987–9016**, and *see also* under individual kings : (conquest of, by Ceawlin), **900** : (conversion of), **3529** : (crisis of c. 700), **1108–09** : (in 871–924), **1273** : (making of), **872** : (origin of shires), **3191**
Mercian Register (chronology of), **459**
Mercredsburn, *battle* (485), **968, 6107**
Meretune, *battle* (871), **6109**
Merioneth (inscriptions), **9950–59**. *See also* Dolgelly, Llandanwg, Llandecwyn, Llan Elltyd, Llanfihangel, Towyn
Merlin and Vita Merlini, **1071, 3489, 7613, 7620, 7624, 7626**
Mersea, Essex, **1237**
Mersete hundred, Salop, **1834**
Mersey valley, **1928**
Merstham, Surrey, **6126** : (grant of land by Eadred, 947), **2698**
Merthyr Mawr, Glam., **11391**
Mestesforde [Domesday : ? = Matlock], **6017**
Metals (precious), **10040, 10077, 10925, 11550, 11715**. *See also* Gold
Metz, **5243**
Michael (Kirk), Isle of Man, **9820, 11194, 11197, 11202, 11225**
Micheldever, Hants., **2092**
Middlesex, **1808, 1892, 1899, 1900, 3085, 3288** : (archaeology of), **7771** : (Domesday), *see* Domesday (Middlesex) : (earthworks), **7832, 7845** : (forest of), **3039** : (hidation), **3065** : (place-names), **6609–18** *passim*. *See also* London. *See also* Edgware, Edmonton, Hampstead, Harringay, Hornsey, Isleworth, Pinner, Ruislip, Send, Shepperton, Sunbury, Syon, Twickenham
Midlothian (place-names), **6906**. *See also* Bow, Cramond, Dalmahoy, Edinburgh, Kirknewton, Langton (East)
Milborne Port, Somerset, **10456**
Milburga, *St.*, *abbess of Wenlock*, **4398**

Mildenhall, Suffolk [? = Clovesho], 6100, 6105, 11821 : (graves), 8138, 8152, 8609
Mildenhall, Wilts., 8477 : (jewellery), 11542
Mildred, *St.*, 3886, 4412
Millport, Bute, 11338
Mills, 2690, 2692, 2694, 2701, 2704, 2707–08, 2712 : (click mill), 2719 : (hand mill), 7687
Milred, *of Worcester*, 52
Milton, Dorset, *abbey*, 3723, 4114, 5086
Milton, East Lothian, 8536
Milton (Clevedon), Somerset, 2937
Milton Bryan, Beds., 10753
Milton Regis, Kent, 8182, 11470
Minehead, Somerset, 6799
Minety, Wilts., 11003
Miningsby, Lincs., 10708
Minster [place-names], 3292, 6404
Minster-in-Sheppey, Kent, 3871, 10209
Minster, Thanet, 3886
Minster Lovel (jewel), 11598
Minsters, 3292, 3354
Mitcham, Surrey, 8434–36, 8455, 8458, 8757
Mochaoi, *St.*, *of Nendrum*, 3777, 4768
Mochonna, *St.* (shrine), 11787, 11804
Mochrum, Wigtownshire, 10510
Mochta, *St.*, 1st *bp. of Louth*, 4825, 10131
Mochuda, *St.*, *of Lismore* [St. Carthage], 4787, 4817, 4856, 7008, (Rule of), 5609, 5855
Mochulla, *St.*, *of Tulla*, 4870
Modan, *St.*, *abbot of Mailros*, 5008
Modena (Arthurian sculptures at), 1056, 1068–69, 1077, 1085, 1087
Modenna, *St.*, 4782
Modwen, *St.*, 4414, 4427
Moedoc, *St.* [Mogue], 4858, 4869, 10108, 11753, 11756
Moengal, *St.*, *abbot of Bangor*, 4871
Mogue, *St. See* Moedoc
Moiun, *barony of*, 2783
Molaise, *St.*, *abbot of Devenish*, 4485, 4847, 4861, 5001, 5836, 9873, 10134 : (Gospel of), 10108
Mold, Flint, 8708
Moling, *St.*, 802, 2134, 4536–40
Molio, *St.*, 4861
Molmen and *molland*, 3223, 3228, 3230, 3465
Molton, South, Devon, 1730
Molua, *St.*, 4848
Moluag, *St.*, 5023–24

Monaghan, *county*. *See* Clones
Monasterboice, co. Louth, 11065, 1088–99
Monasterium Salicis [near Luxeuil], 5466
Monataggart, co. Cork, 9611–15
Monenna, *St.*, 4775, 4785, 4842
Monetville [Domesday : Staffs.], 6021
Monifieth, Forfarshire, 11330
Moninne, *St.*, 3790
Monkton, West, Somerset (charters), 351 : (granted to Glastonbury, 682), 326
Monkwearmouth, Durham (church), 3690, 10144, 10328–47 *passim* : (inscriptions), 9474–75 : (monastery), 3690, 3704, 10333 : (sculpture), 10867, 10878
Monmouth, 2259
Monmouth, Geoffrey of. *See* Geoffrey, *of Monmouth*
Monmouthshire, 1878, 6928, 6944–45. *See also* Caerleon, Caerwent, Chepstow, Monmouth
Mons Agned, Mons Badonicus. *See* Agned, Badon
Montague coin collection, 8870
Montbray (Geoffrey of), *bp. of Coutances*, 1370, 2113, 2940
Montgomery, Roger de, *earl of Shrewsbury*, 1408, 1411–12, 1554–57
Montgomeryshire (geography of its Shropshire border), 5873 : (saints), 5044. *See also* Buttington, Carno, Llandrinio, Llanerfyl, Llanrhaiadr, Meifod, Newtown, Rhyd y Groes, Welshpool
Months, 528, 544, 7350, 7354, 7356, 7358
Montrose, Kincardine, *museum*, 11298
Monymusk, Aberdeenshire, 11334 : (reliquary), 11334, 11789, 11793, 11799, 11806
Moon, ages of the, 7498
Moone, co. Kildare (abbey), 3766 : (cross), 3766, 11133, 11168–69
Mooretown, co. Meath, 8801
Moot sites, 6059–73
Mor [sister of St. David], 5108
Moray, Celtic province of, 2202
Morayshire (ecclesiastical history), 5004 : (place-names), 6901. *See also* Brodie, Burghead
Morham, East Lothian, 11305
Mortimer, Berks., 2032, 9523–24
Mote of Mark, Rockcliffe, Kircudbright, 8007
Mount Music, co. Cork, 9623

Mountrussell, co. Limerick, 9757
Mousa, Shetland (broch), 8027, 8029, 8034
Moylough, co. Sligo (reliquary), 11797
Muadhnat, *St.*, 4777
Mucel, 1266
Mudgeley, Somerset, 10136
Mugginton, Derbs., 10305
Muirchertach mac Erca, 1031
Muirchertach na gCochall gCroiceann, 5906, 5910
Muirchú's Life of St. Patrick, 4567–97 *passim*
Muiredach, *abbot of Monasterboice*, 11088–99 *passim*
Muirtheimhne (N. Louth), 2146
Mul [brother of Cædwalla], 2476
Mulholland [surname], 508
Mullagh, co. Cavan, 9760, 9778
Mulling, *Book of*, 5688–90
Munchin, *St.*, 4764
Mungo, *St. See* Kentigern
Mungret, co. Limerick, *abbey*, 3782
Munster (Eóghanachta: rulers from 5th c.), 516: (history of, 450–800), 2161: (kings of, 484–737), 7596: (mss. of), 180: (Mór of), 7596: (St. Patrick in), 4681
Mura, *St.*, 3768, 4859, 4862, 11745, 11755
Murtly, Perthshire, 11275
Music, 2596, 2648, 7318–41
Mynydd Carn, *battle* (1081), 6130
Myton, Warw., 11587

Naal, *St.*, *of Inver-naile*, 4827
Naile, *St.*, 4855
Nar (river), Norfolk, 6474
Nash, Herefordshire, 2887
Nassington, Northants., 8249–51
Navestock, Essex, 1752
Nechells, Warw., 6519
Nechtanesmere, Forfar, *battle* (685), 1143
Nectan, *St.*, *of Hartland*, 3692, 5041, 5081, 5098
Nendrum, co. Antrim, 3777
Nennius, 139, 154–78
Neorx(e)nawang (paradise), 7648–49, 7653
Neot, *St.*, 1201–02, 4116, 4121, 4422, 4445, 5118
Nerthus, 3508
Ness, valley of (saints associated with), 5010
Nestown, Cheshire, 10656

Netheravon, Wilts., 8467
Nevern, Pembrokeshire, 9993, 10025, 11344, 11397, 11399, 11402
New Forest, 1522, 2121, 2821, 3018, 3033, 3037
Newark, Notts., 8604
Newbald, North, Yorks., 8361, 8363
Newbury, Berks., 2052, 2076, 10445a
Newdigate, Surrey, 6030
Newent, Glos., 10683, 10686–87
Newnton, North, Wilts., 8468, 8751: (charter, 892), 366: (charter, 933), 366, 388
Newport Pagnell, Bucks., 8611
Newton Abbot, Devon, 1705
Newton, King's, Derbs., 8218, 8224, 8226
Newton St. Cyres, Devon, 1720
Newton stone, Garioch, Aberdeenshire, 9833, 9852–63, 9874, 9895
Newtown, Montgomery, 6947
Nicknames, 587, 601, 619
Nico ditch, 7836
Nicodemus, *Gospel of*, 5682, 5685
Nicras, 7631
Nigg, Ross, 11284
Nine Maidens (cult of in Scotland), 5015
Nine magic herbs, Lay of, 7492, 7504, 7509, 7511, 7530, 7534a
Ninian, *St.*, *bp. of Galloway*, 807, 3434–35, 4106, 4452, 4974–99, 5016, 11293
Niridanum, monasterium, 6110
Nith Bridge, Dumfriesshire, 11253
Nithsdale, Dumfriesshire, 11252, 11256: (place-names), 6910
Niwetone [Domesday: ? = Draycott-in-the Moors, Staffs.], 6018
Noë, *king of Powys*, 1157
Norbury, Derbs., 10661, 10670
Norfolk, 1737–38, 8159: (architecture, ecclesiastical), 10178–10203 *passim*: (Domesday), *see* Domesday (Norfolk): (Norse settlements), 1769: (place-names), 6478–79, 6491: (pottery), 8591–92: (round towers), 10178, 10195: (sculpture), 10618: (sheriffs), 3171. *See also* Burgh, Castle Acre, Castle Rising, Cringleford, Elmham (North), Evesham (near Bungay), Gimingham, Hales, Hunstanton, Martham, Nar (river), Norwich, Santon, Stibbard, Testerton, Thetford, Toftrees, Whissonsett, Wissey (river)
Norham, Nhd., 10924

Normandy (and Sussex), 2013 : (under William I), 1551
Normanton, Rutland, 10742
Northampton, 1898, 8631, 10719–20 : (mint), 9356
Northamptonshire (architecture ecclesiastical), 10276–92 : (cemeteries), 8237–56 : (Domesday), see Domesday (Northants.) : (geld-roll, 1066–75), 1377 : (hidation), 3054, 3056, 3076 : (hundreds), 3160 : (invasion of), 899 : (place-names), 6530, 6538: (sculpture), 10712–20. See also Badby, Barnack, Brackley, Brigstock, Brixworth, Bulwick, Castor, Corby, Daventry, Desborough, Duston, Earl's Barton, Holdenby, Irchester, Islip, Kettering, Marston St. Lawrence, Nassington, Northampton, Peakirk, Peterborough, Ravensthorpe, Stow-Nine-Churches, Sudborough
Northfleet, Kent, 8190, 8561
Northumberland, 1957 : (architecture, ecclesiastical), 10370 : (place-names), 6652, 6654, 6664, 6667, 6673–75 : (river names), 6460 : (sculpture), 10901–24. See also Alnmouth, Alnwick, Bamborough, Benwell, Birtley, Burradon, Bywell, Capheaton, Carham, Corbridge, Edlingham, Falstone, Galewood, Gosforth, Heddon-on-the-Wall, Hexham, Howick, Lindisfarne, Lowick, Norham, Nunnykirk, Ovingham, Rothbury, Simondsburn, Tynemouth, Warden, Warkworth, Whitehill Point, Whittingham, Winston, Yevering (Old)
Northumbria, 930, 973, 1133, 1138, 1383, 1928–2000, 6672 : (acquires Lothian, under Edwin), 971 : (architecture, ecclesiastical), 10369 : (boundary), 5923, 5925–26, 5940 : (Charlemagne in its annals), 1181 : (coins), 9017–80 : (inscriptions), 9452–9515 : (institutions), 2274 : (libraries), 7132 : (monasticism), 3613 : (origins of), 878 : (royal genealogy), 479 : (Scandinavian kingdom of), 1177, 1293 : (sculpture), 10758–10975
Northumbrian priests, laws of, 2444
Northworthy, Derbs., 1910
Norton, Devon, 1720

Norton, co. Durham, 10374
Norway, 1644
Norwegian saints (cult in England and Scotland), 4084
Norwich, 1773, 2740, 4741a, 10184 : (mint), 9305, 9315
Norwick, Shetland, 8510
Nothelm, king of Sussex (charter to Selsey, c. 682–85), 420
Nottingham, 1849, 1879–80, 1904, 1920, 6547, 6557, 7945 : (mint), 9272, 9346
Nottinghamshire, 1925 : (archaeology of), 8333 : (churches), 3897 : (Domesday), see Domesday (Notts.) : (place-names), 6539, 6545: (sculpture), 10746. See also Aslockton, Bawtry, Bridgford (East and West), Chilwell (East), Coates, Flawford, Holme Pierrepoint, Newark, Nottingham, Plumtree, Rolleston, Shelford, Sneinton, Southwell, Sutton Bonington, Tuxford
Nud Hael, king of Strathclyde, 9871–72, 9891
Numbers, 7359
Nunburnholme, Yorks., 10927
Nunnaminster, Book of, 5790
Nunnykirk, Nhd., 10921–22
Nursling, Hants., 2036, 5344, 6725
-ny, -ney [suffix], 6387
Nymet, Devon, 387, 1691
Nympton, Devon, 6787, 6789

Oadh, king of Picts, 8540
Oakley, Hants. [? = Aclea], 6081, 6084
Oaksey, Wilts., 10596, 11007
Oath, 2465
Obligations, law of, 2358, 2515
Obthrust, 7630
Occaney, Yorks., 8369
Ocha, battle (?482), 1021
Ockford, Dorset, 6752
Ockley, battle (852). See Aclea
Octa and Ebissa, 988
Odiham, Hants., 2089
Odilo [moneyer], 9263
Odin, 3500. See also Woden
Odo, bp. of Bayeux, 1582 : (deed for Trendley, Wickhambreux, Kent), 383 : (Penenden heath), 2451–55
Óengus, the Culdee. See Ængus
'Offa I' and Offa—Constance legend, 671, 1184, 7553a, 7561, 7565, 7571–72

Offa, *king of Mercia*, 1128 : (charter of Higham, 774), 364 : (charter to Lindfield, 765), 376 : (charter to St. Albans, 795), 3739 : (charter to S. Denis, 790), 375 : (coins), 8987–88, 8991, 8994–99, 9002, 9006–08, 9010–14 : (grant of land in Bixlea, 772), 408 : (grant of land in Westbury, 791–96), 377 : (letter to, from Alcuin), 7078

Offa's dyke, 2247, 7786–7815, 7837

Offaly, *county*. *See* King's County

Offchurch, Warw., 8290–91

Ogams, 7505, 9525–10035

Ogmore, Glam., 9939, 9949

O'Gorman, *Martyrology of*, 4480

Ohthere, (voyage of), 6146–85

Okehampton, Devon, 1733

Olaf Haraldsson, *St.*, *king of Norway*, 4401

Olaf Kuaran (Quaran), *king of Norway*. *See* Olaf II, Sihtricson

Olaf Peacock, 5921

Olaf II, Sihtricson (Quaran), *king of York and Dublin*, 1330, 9071, 9111–12, 9114

Olaf Tryggvason, *king of Norway*, 1292, 1306, 1335

Olaf, the White [Amhlaeibh], 1168

Olave, *St*. *See* Olaf Haraldsson

Old Lands, Sussex [place-name], 6691

Oliver's battery, Hants., 8413, 8550–51, 8612

Omeath, co. Louth, 2159, 6820

Onchan, Isle of Man, 11205

Ongar, Essex, 1768, 7898

Onibury, Salop (grant, 1085), 337

Open field system, 2717, 3278, 3287, 3290

Ophthalmology, 7415

Oran, *St.*, 4908, 4917

Oran, co. Roscommon, 10558

Orc, orcnéas, 7636–38

Orcoit, *kingdom*, 1826

Ordeal, 2473, 2487, 2489, 2553

Ordination of bishop, 3543

Orkney, 2204, 2217–18, 2227, 2236–37, 9215 : (architecture, ecclesiastical), 10508 : (bishops), 3860 : (brochs), 8018, 8022, 8025–41 *passim* : (Celtic Church in), 3435 : (early Christian remains in), 2236 : (ethnology), 8827 : (inscriptions), 9887–88 : (Norwegian colonisation of), 700 : (Oðal law in), 2584 : (place-names), 2224, 2226, 6870–71, 6898, 6900 : (raid on Wales), 1604 : (sculpture),

11260–66 : (settlement of, 8th c.), 1158 : (tings), 2583 : (Viking burials), 8489, 8494, 8507 : (Viking house-burning), 1610. *See also* Ayre (broch), Birsay, Burray (island of), Burrian (broch), Caldale, Egilsay (island of), Evie, Firth, Gurness (broch), Maes-how, Papa Westray (island of), Rennibister, Ronaldsay (North, island of), Rousay (island of), Sandwick, Skaill, Stronsay (island of)

Orkneyinga Saga, 224, 227–28, 1570, 1606

Ormside, Great, bowl, 8553

Oronsay, isle of, Argyllshire, 2213, 8495, 8499, 8505, 11641

Orthanach, *bp. of Kildare*, 4834

Orton Scar brooch, 11640

Orwell, Cambs., 11483

Os-, 566, 585, 593

Osberht, *king of Northumbria*, 1172 : (coins), 9033, 9079

Oslac (charter of), 297

Osmund, *St.* (rite of), 5771

Osric, *king of Northumbria*, 4438

Ossory (holy wells), 4472 : (kings of), 2172

Osti, 6152–53, 6173–74

Oswald, *St.*, *king of Northumbria*, 1111, 1118, 1129, 1136, 1148, 3536, 4134, 4347–72, 6113 : (relics), 4122, 4304

Oswald, *St.*, *bp. of Worcester*, *abp. of York*, 52, 4042–43, 4058, 4065 : (anonymous Life of), 71

Oswestry, Salop, 1136, 1834, 1911, 6113

Oswin, *king of Kent*, 1145

Oswy, *king of Northumbria*, 1131, 4395

Osyth, *St.*, 4382, 4384, 4439–40

Otforth, Kent, 1775

Oðal law, 2584

Ottery St. Mary, Devon, (charter), 399

Oudoceus, *St.*, 5092

Ousdale, Caithness, 8056

Ouse, river (Danish camp on, 921), 1305

Outlawry, 2486

Overchurch, Cheshire, 9444–45

Overton, Market, Rutland, 8274–75, 8281, 11488, 11527

Ovingham, Nhd., 10910

Oxen (Irish), 7606

Oxford, 1850, 1882–84, 1895, 3867, 10309–12, 10749, 11630 : (mint), 9091, 9265, 9276, 9319, 9345 : (place-name), 6590, 6592

Oxfordshire (archaeological survey of), **7756** : (cemeteries), **8257–71** : (charters), **355** : (Domesday), *see* Domesday (Oxon.) : (ethnology), **8810** : (hidation), **3064** : (hundreds), **3159**, **3164a** : (insurgents of 1065 in), **1339** : (place-names), **6578**, **6586**, **6590** : (pottery), **8560** : (roads), **355**. *See also* Asthall, Aston, Bampton, Bensington (Benson), Brighthampton, Broughton Poggs, Burford, Cassington, Chadlington, Chislehampton, Cropredy, Deddington, Dorchester, Ducklington, Ewelme, Filkins, Kingham, Langford, Leigh (North), Oxford, Standlake, Stanton Harcourt, Stoke (North), Wheatley, Yelford

Oxhey, Herts. (charter, 790), **287**

Oxna, isle of, Shetland, **11651**

Ozingell, Kent, **8188**

Padstow, Cornwall, **11052**

Paganism, **3473–3516, 7451**

Paignton, Devon, **6788**

Painestown, co. Meath, **9754**

Palgrave, Suffolk, **11534**

Palladius, **4686, 4692, 4696, 4698, 4700–03, 4722**

Palnatoki [Dane], **1321**

Pandal Wood, Essex, **7907**

Papa Westray, Orkney, **2224**

Papacy (relations with), **3543–59** : (St. Patrick and), **4752**

Papil, Shetland, **11267**

Paris Psalter, **5703–06, 5708–09, 5718**

Parish, **1981, 3462–63, 3465, 3467–68, 3471**

Parker (Matthew) (as A.-S. student), **38, 39, 41**

Parrett, Somerset, **5878**

Pascal controversy, **522, 3408, 3560–78, 4467, 5421**

Patrick, *St.*, **4541–4760** : *see* under the various sub-divisions, *also* : **3370, 3417, 6200, 11101, 11130** : (bell), **508, 11765, 11767, 11807** : (churches), **10479** : (Malmesbury's Life), **1677** : (penitential), **5601** : (Rule), **5621** : (travels), **2125, 2175, 5907, 6131–32**

Patrington, Yorks., **6638, 10967**

Patrishow, Brecknock, **9928**

Patronage, Church, **3457**

Patromynics, **586, 588, 6369, 6379, 6388**

Patton, Salop (exchange of land, 901), **310**

Paul, *St.* (Irish versions of vision of), **7600**

Paul Aurelian, *St.*, *1st bp. of Léon*, **5176, 5200–01, 11739**

Paulinus, *St.*, *of Wales*, **5127, 5165**

Pavia, **3995, 7002**

Paxton, Great, Hunts., **8585, 10304**

Paynell (Ralph), *founder of secular canons, York*, **3345**

Peakirk, Northants., **1886, 3646**

Pega, *St.*, **1886**

Pelegrinus, *St.*, **5412**

Pellitus, magician, **1647**

Pembrokeshire (earthworks), **8073–74** : (ethnology), **8832** : (inscriptions), **9960–10004** : (place-names), **6948, 6951** : (sculpture), **11396–11403**. *See also* Bridell, Caldy island, Carew, Castell Villia, Clydai, Cwm Glöyne, Llanrudian, Llanwnda, Nevern, Penally, St. David's, St. Edren's, Spittal, Stackpole-Elidyr, Steynton, Trefgarne (Little), Trehowel, Whitesand Bay

Penally, Pemb., **11403**

Penbryn, Cardigan, **10016**

Penda, *king of Mercia*, **872, 1104, 1126, 1144** : (genealogy), **872** : (name), **551**

Penenden heath trial, **2451–55**

Penge, Surrey [in Kent, since 1888], **6700**

Penhawger, Cornwall, **6031**

Penitentials, **5576–5626,** *passim.* For that of Columbanus, *see* under Columbanus, *St.*

Penletheru, *battle* (1087), **6133**

Penmachno, Carnarvonshire, **10027, 10029**

Penmon, Anglesey, **11351–52, 11354, 11357**

Pennington, Lancs., **7959**

Penrhos Llugwy, Anglesey, **10010–11**

Penrith, Cumb., **10830–31, 10854**

Pentre Poeth [Brecknock] stone [British Museum], **9927, 10028**

Penwortham, Lancs., **1989**

Pen-y-Mynnid stone, Brecknock, **11417**

Peonna, *battle of* (658), **1135**

Percy (William de), (parentage of), **481**

Perham down, Wilts., **8478**

Peri Didaxeon, **7410, 7418**

Péronne (Irish colony at), **5153, 5161**

Perranporth or Perranzabuloe, Cornwall, (St. Piran's oratory), **3904, 3906, 10517, 10519**

Pershore, Worcs., **3686, 10751.** ——, *abbey*, **3740** : (granted to Westminster by Edward the Confessor), **3731**

Perthshire (forts and camps), **8004** : (place-names), **6918–19** : (sculpture), **1269–76.** *See also* Abernethy, Breadalbane, Coldoch, Dunblane, Dunfallandy, Dunkeld (Little), Forteviot, Fortingall, Fowlis Wester, Gellyburn, Gleneagles, Glenlyon, Greenloaning, Kilbride, Logierait, Meigle, Murtly, St. Madoes, Scone, Weem

Peterborough, Northants. (brooch), **11672** : (burials), **8256** : (mint), **9357** : (sculpture near), **10716**

Peterborough, *abbey*, **3672–79, 7139, 7148, 10282–84, 11743**

Petersfinger, Wilts. (cemetery), **8476**

Peter's pence (origin of), **1658, 3553, 3555**

Petrock, *St.*, **5075–76, 5122**

Phillack stone, Cornwall, **9571**

Physiologus, **7370–74**

Pickering, Yorks., **11659**

Picts, **761, 807–42, 1191, 2160, 2202, 2213, 2220, 2234, 2324, 5000, 5002, 5019, 6143, 7027, 8540, 8825, 8838, 9855, 9892** : (art), **10074–75, 11240, 11273, 11295, 11308** : (Columba's relations with), **4955, 5018, 5022** : (diocese of), **3859** : (inscriptions), **832, 9828–31, 9852–63, 9874–75, 9897** : (invade Argyllshire, 736, 741), **1163** : (kings, list of), **757, 819, 833** : (Ninian and), **4982, 4991–92** : (place-names), **6846, 6856–57, 6922**

Pig [place-names], **6413**

Pigments, **11850–52, 11884**

Pignoris capio, **2537**

Pigs (Domesday), **2700, 3042**

Pilgrimages, 500–800, **6208–17**

-pill [in place-names], **6409**

Pillow-stone, **8343, 10920**

Pillsápe, **7433**

Pilton, Devon, **1681**

Pinhoe, Devon, **1376, 3110**

Pinner, Middlesex, **1915, 7845**

Pinnosa, *St.*, **5120**

Pins, **8640, 8653, 11459, 11486, 11646, 11660, 11663, 11673, 11701, 11705, 11728, 11730**

Pipe, Herefordshire, *battle* (1054), **6087**

Piran, *St.*, **5046** : (oratory of), **3904, 3906, 10517, 10519**

Pirminius, *St., of Reichenau*, **5248, 5558**

Pirton, Herts., **7924**

Pit [place-names], **6419**

Pitney, Somerset, **11574**

Pittington, co. Durham, **8699**

Place-names, **6283–6953**

Plants, **306, 346, 7388–99, 7470**

Plegmund, *St., abp. of Canterbury*, **4386** : (coins), **8967, 9129**

Pleshy, Essex, **7911–12**

Pliny (Bede's citations from), **4191**

Plough, plough team, **2699, 2710, 2714–15, 2720, 2722, 2724, 7674**

Plumbland, Cumb., **10816, 10819**

Plumstead, Surrey, **2042**

Plumtree, Notts., **10314**

Plympton, Devon, **1729**

Poitou (relations with Ireland), **1634**

Pontefract, Yorks., **1380**

Population, **2757, 2800, 3019**

Porius stone, near Dolgelly, Merioneth, **9956**

Port-, **6341**

Portglenone, Antrim, **8628**

Porth-Kerdin [site], **6144**

Portland, Dorset, **2056**

Portreeve, **2728, 2744, 2746**

Portslade, Sussex, **6686, 8371–72, 8380**

Portsmouth, *battle* (779), **1106**

Port Talbot, Glam., **9942, 11388**

Pottern, Wilts., **2066**

Potters, **8594**

Pottery, **8547–8620** : (dating of), **8567a, 8585** : (Kentish), **1780** : (styles of decoration), **8566, 8596.** *See also* under Cemeteries, *passim*

Powys, **2248, 2260**

Praying in water, **4096, 4099**

Preshaw, Hants., **11636**

Prestbury, Cheshire, **10644–45**

Prestbury, Glos., **1832**

Presteigne, Radnor, **2930**

Preston Candover, Hants., **8685**

Priesttown, co. Tipperary, **9781**

Primate (claims for precedence, York v. Canterbury), **3344, 3817**

Priscian glosses [St. Gallen], **7268, 10012**

Prittlewell, Essex, **8113, 8150**

Procedure, legal, **2483, 2501**

Prognostics, 7484, 7500–01
Property [law], 2475, 2500 : (married woman's), 2469
Proverbs, 7662–70
Punpeius Carantorius stone, Glam., 9941, 9943, 11392
Purbeck, Dorset (Domesday manors), 2027
Purley, Surrey, 8442
Purton, Wilts., 2043, 8470
Pusey horn, 3233, 3240–42

Quadripartitus, 2416
Quantocks, Somerset, 6028, 6743, 7576
Queen's County [Leix]. See Timahoe
Quern-stone, 8651
Quethiock cross, Cornwall, 11042
Quigrich [crozier of St. Fillan], 11773, 11776, 11779–81, 11783–85

Raasay, Skye, Inverness, 11314
Radnor (name), 6925, 6953
Radnorshire, 2247 : (Domesday), see Domesday (Radnor) : (place-names), 6926. See also Diserth, Llowes, Presteigne
Rædwulf, king of Northumbria, 9018–19, 9033
Rægnald, king of York, 1293 : (coins), 9017, 9046, 9068
Raft, 7349, 7770
Ragener, St., 4428
Ragley park, Warw., 8295, 11509
Ragnall Ivarson, 1311
Ragnar Lothbrok (and his sons), 1174, 1176, 1186
Raith, battle (596), 1023
Rammesleah, Sussex, 2006, 2012
Rampside, Lancs. (sword), 8725
Ramsbury, Wilts., 11010 : (bishopric), 3802, 3804, 3834
Ramsey, Hunts., abbey, 3689 : (scriptorium), 11937
Ramsey, Isle of Man (sculpture), 11218
Ramsey bay, Isle of Man (fort), 8066
Ramsgate, Kent, 8166, 8192
Ransom by weight, 7586
Raoilinn, St., 4778
Raoul, de Gael, earl of Norfolk, 1568
Rathcanning, co. Cork, 9617–18
Rathcobane, co. Cork, 9619
Rathcroghan, co. Roscommon, 9788–89
Rathdown, Dublin, half-barony, 11154, 11165
Rathduff, co. Kerry, 9677

Rathgall, co. Wicklow, 7994
Rathgormuck, co. Waterford, 9728
Rathmoley, co. Tipperary, 11666
Rathmore, Ulster, 7981
Raven-banners, 736
Ravensthorpe, Northants., 10290
Ravenna Annals, 4179
Rayleigh, Essex, 7894, 7903, 7905, 7914
Rea [river name], 6455
Reading, Berks., 8404–05, 8410–11, 8672
Reask, co. Kerry, 11175
Reay, Caithness, 8495, 8497, 8789
Recruitment of sailors (c. 1000), 2292
Rectitudines singularum personarum, 3215, 3277, 6305
Reculver, Kent, 1776, 3736, 3877, 10223, 10228, 10638a : (coins), 8940
Redbournstoke hundred, Beds., 6064
Redulf. See Rædwulf
Reed, Herts., 7923, 10322
Regius Psalter, 5701
Regnald. See Rægnald
Regularis Concordia (c. 970), 3580a, 3608, 3610, 3615
Reichenau, 5227, 7184, 11831, 11879, 11907
Reigate, Surrey, 10977
Relics, 1111, 3408, 4103–23, 4331–32, 4334, 4349, 4357, 4399, 4420, 4424, 4968, 5086, 5173, 5496, 7451, 11775, 11781 : (of St. Cuthbert), 4281, 4302, 4304, 4314, 4320–21, 4323, 7134
Reliquaries, 7680, 11786–11815
Rendlesham, Suffolk, 1736
Renfewshire. See Arthurlee
Rennibister, Orkney, 8788
Repton, Derbs., 1822, 1858–59, 1873, 1910, 3705, 6540, 6556, 6558, 8220, 8743, 10293–99
Restenneth, Forfar, priory, 3797
Rheinau, 5559
Rhinns of Galloway, Wigtown, 11286
Rhuddlan, Denbigh, 11409
Rhyd y Groes, Montgomery, battle (1039), 1623
Rhynie, Aberdeenshire, 11321
Rian Bo Phadraig [Decies], 6200
Ricemarch, Psalter of, 11940–42
Richard's Castle, Herefordshire, 1817, 7933
Richborough, Kent, 3958, 5887, 10636 : (coins), 8941
Rickling, Essex, 7901
Riddles, 4148a, 5280, 7671–7726

Ridgemount, King's County, 11734
Ridgeway, Berks., 6199
-rige [suffix], 639
Rihthamscyld [law], 2445
Ringmer, Sussex, 8376
Ringmere, battle (1010), 6115
Rings, 4300, 8112, 11615-33 : (inscriptions), 9412-23
Ringwould, Kent, 8750
Ripon, Yorks., 1968a, 3728a, 3881, 4115, 10352-53, 10355-56
Risborough, Bucks. (charter, 903), 6589 : (place-name), 6589
Riseley, Kent, 11490
Risinghoe, Beds., 7942
River names, 6308, 6423, 6431-72
Roads, 6186-6203, 6334, 6345, 7775
Robert, bp. of Hereford, 337
Robert Curthose, duke of Normandy, 1512-13, 1534, 1575
Robert, de Todeni [Tosny], 1528
Robert, fitz Wimarch, 1352
Robert of Jumièges, abp. of Canterbury (Missal of), 5751-53, 5759
Roche Court down, Wilts., 8479, 8786
Rocheford hundred, Essex, 1763-64, 6488
Rochester, Kent, 1783, 1790, 8180, 8182-83, 10210, 10213-14, 10224, 10226 : (castle), 10226 : (early community), 3837
Rocliffe, Cumb., 10813, 10840
Rodd, Herefordshire, 2887
Rodenhanger, Herts., manor, 287
Roeburgh hundred, Berks., 5884
Roger, de Montgomery, earl of Shrewsbury, 1408, 1411-12, 1554-57
Rognvaldr, 1606
Rolleston, Notts., 10755
Rolleston, Staffs., 10721-22
Roman traditionist influence, 2266
Rombaut, St., 4852
Rome (Anglo-Saxons at), 1655, 1657-58, 6214 : (journeys and routes to), 5539, 6207, 6211-12, 6214-15
Rom-feoh, 3553
Romney, Kent, 1792
Romsey, Hants., 8738, 10461
Ronaldsay, North, Orkney, 6900
Ronaldsway, Isle of Man, 7759, 8647, 8655, 11193
Roos Carr, Yorks. (boat model and figures from), 7740, 7744, 7753, 7767 : (pendant), 11609 : (pin heads), 11486

Ros [place-names], 6935
Roscam, co. Galway, 10569
Roscommon brooch, 11676
Roscommon, county. See Carns (hill of), Drummin, Oran, Rathcroghan
Rosneath, Dumbarton, 11336
Rosscarbery, co. Cork, 5914
Ross, co. Cork (diocese), 3865 : (monastic school), 3773
Ross Hill, co. Galway, 9647
Ross-shire (place-names), 6920 : (sculpture), 11331. See also Edderton, Kiltearn, Lewis (isle of), Nigg, Tarbat, Valtos (isle of Lewis)
Rothbury, Nhbd., 10901, 10904, 10906, 10911
Rotherham, Yorks., 8881
Rothesay, Bute, 11317
Rothley, Leics., 8338, 10695
Rothwell, Yorks., 10931, 10952
Round towers, 2124-25, 2149, 2173, 8798, 10462-63, 10465, 10476, 10502-03, 10525-70, 11126 : (in East Anglia), 10178, 10195
Roundway hill, Wilts., 8472
Rous Lench, Worcs., 10303, 10740
Rousay, Orkney, 2225, 8504
Rowe ditch, 7805, 7814
Rowsley, Derbs., 10677
Roxburghshire. See Borthwick Mains, Ednam, Gattonside, Hawick, Jedburgh, Kelso, Liddesdale
Royal Irish Academy (bell in), 11769 : (catalogue of antiquities), 11642 : (linulae in museum), 11696 : (ogam inscribed stones at), 9787
Ruckinge, Kent, 5888
Rugby, Warw., 8288, 10741
Ruislip, Middlesex, 1825
Rumbald, St., 4383
Rumold, St., bp. of Mechlin, 5502, 5508
Rumon, St., of Tavistock, 5071, 5085, 5098
Runes, 9378 et seq. See also Hunterston brooch
Rus-Glass, co. Cork, 9626
Ruskington, Lincs., 8311
Ruthin, Denbigh, 10031
Ruthwell, Dumfriess. (cross, inscription), 9452-70 : (cross, sculpture), 10038, 10762, 10764-97 : (place-name), 6655 : (7th-9th c. cross), 11258
Rutland 1837, 1860, 1896-97 : (cemeteries), 8273-85, 8764 : (Domesday) see Domesday (Rutland) : (jewellery), 11488-89 : (place-names),

Rutland (*continued*)
  6546 : (settlement of), **972**. *See also*
    Cottesmore, Glaston, Luffenham
    (North), Lyddington, Normanton,
    Overton (Market), Stretton
Ruyton, Salop, **3276**
Rynagh, *St.*, **4824**

Sacramentarium Gelasianum, **5745**
Sadberge, co. Durham, **1967**
Saddlescombe, Sussex, **8384, 9177, 9179,
  9188, 9293**
Saffron Walden, Essex, **8156–57, 10623**
Sagas (A.-S.), **32, 57** : (Scottish and
  Irish local names in the), **5912,
  6913–14**
Sailors (recruitment of, c. 1000), **2292**
St. Albans, Herts., **10302**
——, *abbey*, **3720, 3739, 4028, 4419** :
  (charters, 793, 795), **3739**
St. Allen crosses, Cornwall, **11054**
St. Andrews, Fife, **3440, 9423, 10105,
  10142, 10514, 11277–84**
St. Asaph, Flint, **6933**
St. Bees, Cumb., **10850–51**
St. Blane, Bute, **11300**
St. Buryan, Cornwall, **1696** : (charters),
  286, 322 : (spurious charter, 943),
  403
St. Cadvan stone, Towyn, Merioneth,
  9954–55, 9957–59
St. Cairan, co. Meath, **9754, 9783**
St. Calais, William of, *bp. of Durham*, **4057**
St. Cleer, Cornwall (king Doniert's
  stone), **11036–37**
St. David's, Pembrokeshire, **9966, 10000,
  10003, 11396, 11401**
St. Denis, *abbey of* (charters), **375, 411**
St. Edren's Pembrokeshire, **9965–66**
St. Gall, **5563, 5565–66, 5571, 7040,
  7050** : (library), **7040, 7175, 7180,
  11900, 11909** : (mss.), **7177–79,
  7313, 11830–31, 11900–09** : (scrip-
  torium), **7176, 11905**
St. Helen's, Scilly Isles, **3788**
St. Hilary, Cornwall, **9567**
St. Kew, Cornwall, **9564**
St. Madoes, Perthshire, **11271**
St. Marychurch, Devon, **2616, 11022**
St. Michael's Mount, Cornwall, **1724**
St. Mullins, co. Carlow, **2134**
St. Neot stone, Cornwall, **11041**
St. Neots, Hunts., **3700, 10133**
St. Riquier, *abbey* (English lands), **6019**

St. Vigeans, Forfar (inscriptions), **9854,
  9864–67** : (sculpture), **11309–10,
  11320, 11324**
Salcombe Regis, Devon, **1713–14**
Sale [law], **2510**
Saltair na Rann, **210, 5848, 7598, 7656**
Salterbridge, co. Waterford, **9742**
Saltways, **5874, 6195, 6203, 6334**
Salzcraggie, Helmsdale, Sutherland, **8060**
Sampton (in West Hythe), Kent (charter,
  732), **422**
Samson, *St.*, *bp. of Dol.*, **5202–14, 6220,
  7010**
Sanctain, *St.*, (hymn of), **5859**
Sancton, Yorks., **8345, 8363, 8407, 8605**
Sanctuary, **3459–60, 3510**
Sandall, Yorks., **7964**
Sandbach, Cheshire, **10642, 10646–50,
  10654, 10657, 10659**
Sandwich, Kent, **11554**
Sandwick, Orkney, **8030, 8041**
Sandwick, Shetland, **8510**
Sandy, Beds., **8214–15**
Santon, Isle of Man, **9807**
Santon, Norfolk, **11652**
Sarr, Kent, **8170**
Sarum, Old, Wilts., **2060, 7971, 7974** :
  (bishopric), **3823**
Sativola, *St. See* Sidwell
Saul, co. Down, **4647, 5907**
Sawdon, Yorks., **11673**
Sawyl Benisel, *king of the Britons*, **8519**
Saxby, Leics., **8272, 8283, 11535**
Saxony (missionaries in), **5231, 5234,
  5264, 5305**
Scandinavian settlement (geography of),
  5896
Scarborough, Yorks., **6626, 8792**
Scarriff, co. Clare, **8723**
Scattery island, co. Clare, **4831, 8727**
Sceorstan, *battle* (1016) [? = Sarson,
  near Andover], **6074**
Scilly isles, **3788, 7747, 11539** (place-
  names), **6946**
Scone, Perthshire, **2323**
Scop, **7330**
Scotby, Cumb. (coins), **9104**
Scothin, *St.*, **4837**
Scothorn, Lincs., **6571**
Scotland, **2201–39** : (architecture, eccle-
  siastical), **10506–15** : (charters), **371**:
  (ethnology), **8806, 8818–19, 8834,
  8838, 8846, 8849–50** : (inscriptions),
  9827–99 : (kings, list of), **757** :
  (map, northern sheet, 450–850),

Scotland (*continued*)
 5903 : (place-names), 6846–6923 :
 (sculpture), 11226–11339. *See also*
 under each county
Scotter, Lincs., 5897, 6572
Scraba mountain, co. Down (coins),
 9243, 9247
Script, 7291–7317. *See also* Scriptoria
Scriptoria (Bobbio), 7172, 7302, 7314 :
 (Breton), 7303 : (Canterbury), 7235:
 (Lorsch), 7185 : (Mainz), 7186 :
 (Ramsey), 11937 : (St. Gallen),
 7176, 11905 : (South German),
 7181 : (Tours), 7182 : (Würzburg),
 5399. *See also* Script
Scunthorpe, Lincs., 8582
Seaford, Sussex, 1268, 4388
Seaham, co. Durham, 10359–60
Seals, 375, 9362–77
Seamer, Yorks., 11591
Searby, Lincs., 8314
Seaton, Devon, 1699
Sechnall, *St., bp. of Domnach-Sechnaill,*
 4562–63, 4734, 4744, 4766, 4796,
 5853
Seckington, Warw., 7932
Secundinus, *St. See* Sechnall
Seddlescombe. *See* Saddlescombe
Sedulius, *Scotus,* 7113–17
Seemochuda, co. Waterford, 9738
Segnescome [Domesday site], 6014
Seisdon hundred, Staffs., 1871
Seiwold, *abbot of Bath,* 7129
Selby, Yorks., 8354
Selkirkshire. *See* Torwoodlee, Yarrow
Selsey, Sussex (jewellery), 11567–68 :
 (see), 3838–39, 3848, 4050
Selsey, *monastery,* 4016a : (charter from
 Cædwalla), 382 : (charter from
 Nothelm (c. 682–85), 420
Selworthy, Somerset, 6738, 6745
Senan, *St.,* 4822, 4831, 5096, 5110, 5121,
 11814
Senchas Sil hIr, 2128
Senchus mór, 2276, 2519, 2524–80 *passim*
Send, Middsx. (charter, 962), 369
Senlac, *battle* (1066). *See* Hastings
Sepulture, modes of, 8082–83, 8091, 8546
Serf, *St.,* 5007
Serfs, 3199–3232 *passim,* 3287
Sescenn Uarbeoil, 6816
Seskinan, co. Waterford, 9732
-*sett* [place-names], 6385
Setting adrift, 2505
Seven Sleepers of Ephesus, 7490, 7508

Severn (river) [place-name], 6446
Severn valley (West Saxon invasion of,
 577), 861, 909
Sevington, Wilts., 9202
Shaftesbury, Dorset, 2024, 2081.
——, *abbey,* 1274
Shalfleet, Isle of Wight, Hants., 2103
Shankill, co. Waterford, 9740
Shannon (shrine), 11798, 11812
Sharnford, Leic., 6531
Sharpening-stones, 8622
She [place-names], 6416
Sheela-na-gigs, 10596, 10608, 10749,
 11007, 11062, 11064, 11068, 11085,
 11102–03, 11141, 11342
Sheepwalk hill, Toddington, Beds., 8204
Sheffield, Yorks., 1934, 7949, 7953, 7961,
 10950–51
Shefford, East, Berks., 8400, 8403
Shefford, West, Berks., 8389
Shefford Woodlands, Berks., 10978
Shelagh, dau. of Olaf Cuaran, 1325
Shelford, Notts., 10754
Shenchy dyke, Fife, 7848
Shepperton, Middlesex, 8327
Sherborne, Dorset, 2046, 2048, 2118 :
 (diocese), 3818, 3828, 3834. *See
 also* Aldhelm
Sheriffs, 3165, 3171, 3174–77
Shermanbury, Sussex, 7920
Shetland, 2210, 2217–18, 2236, 7580 :
 (architecture, ecclesiastical), 10508 :
 (brochs), 8025–41 *passim* : (early
 Christian remains in), 2236 : (eth-
 nology), 8827, 8836, 8839 : (in-
 scriptions), 9879–82 : (Norwegian
 colonisation of), 700 : (Oðal law
 in), 2584 : (place-names), 6858,
 6867–68 : (sculpture), 11259–68 :
 (tings) 2583. *See also* Bressay (island
 of), Burra, Clibberswick (Unst),
 Clickhimin, Copister (broch), Cunningsburgh, Fair Isle, Hillswick,
 Hogstetter (Whelsay), Jarlshof
 (Sumburgh), Lunnasting, Mousa
 (broch), Norwick, Oxna (island of),
 Papil, Sandwick, Whiteness
Ship burial, 8502, 8511, 8535, 11641
Shipbuilding, 7352
Ships, 2285–87, 2289, 2291, 2293–96,
 2300, 2302–04, 11210, 11216
Shires, 22, 3150–98
Shoebury, Essex, 5980, 7906, 7916–17,
 8113
-*shot* [place-names], 6375

Shotwick (Wirral), Cheshire, 10319
Shrewsbury, Salop (mint), 9294, 9307,
    9326 : (Norman earls of), 1569
Shrines, 4140, 4314, 5733a, 11750, 11765,
    11786–11815
Shropshire, 6025 : (charters), 409 :
    (Domesday), see Domesday (Shrop-
    shire) : (forts), 7943 : (geography
    of its Montgomery border), 5873 :
    (place-names), 6505, 6510, 6515 :
    (ploughman), 2720. See also Al-
    caston moat, Bridgnorth, Cressage,
    Easthope, Felton, Onibury, Os-
    westry, Patton, Ruyton, Stanton
    Lacy, Stanton (Long), Titterstone
    Clee, Wenlock, Whittington, Wikey
Shudy camps, Cambs., 8137, 8147a
Sidbury, Devon, 1714, 10428–29
Sidmouth, Devon, 1714
Sidnacester [site], 6116
Sidwell, St., 4373–81 : (name), 576–77,
    590
Siefred, king of York (coins), 9068–70
Sigeric, abp. of Canterbury, 6211–12,
    6215
Sigurd [sculpture], 10598–99, 10606,
    11195, 11218
Sigurd Silkbeard, king of Dublin, 7525
Sihtric, 4th abbot of Tavistock, 3680
Sihtric, king of York (coins), 9129
Silchester, Berks., 2035, 9557, 11541 :
    (Arthurian associations), 5966 : (re-
    gion of, 5th–6th c.), 956
Silk, 7343
Sillan, St., of Imbliuch, 4814
Silver [place-names], 6406
Simondsburn, Nhd., 10915
Sitha, St., 4439
Sittingbourne, Kent, 8181–82, 8186–87,
    8199, 8682
Situlæ. See Buckets
Silward Digri, 1373
Skaill, Orkney, 11649, 11678
Skates, 8648
Skellig Michael (island of), co. Kerry,
    11139
Skelton, Yorks., 9479, 9483
Skin (of Viking), 714, 740–41
Skip [place-names], 6381
Skitten, Caithness, 8043
Sky-god (Celtic), 3484
Skye, (island of), Inverness., 6861, 8503
Slanore, co. Cavan, 3767
Slaves, 2482, 3199–3232 passim
Slave trade, 3201

Sleaford, Lincs., 8336
Slebhine, abbot of Iona, 1008
Slighe Cualann [road], 6197
Sligo, county. See Drumcliff, Irishmurray,
    Moylough
Smarmore, Ardee, co. Louth (coins),
    9199
-snade [place-names], 6377
Snakes (in Nennius), 7616 : (Patrick
    and), 4730, 4748 : (wounds from),
    7531
Snape, Suffolk, 8112, 8115
Snedgus and MacRiagla (voyage of),
    6235–36
Sneinton, Notts., 6547–48, 6557
Sockburn, co. Durham, 10873
Sodor, 9818
Soham, Cambs., 1762, 8133, 11461
Sokemen, 3206, 3214, 3220
Solway, 2229
Somerford Keynes, Wilts., 10425, 10451
Somerset, 2026, 2075, 2105, 2113–14 :
    (Alfred in), 1202, 2026 : (archaeo-
    logy of), 7739, 8426–30 : (Arthur
    in), 1050, 2026 : (Boniface and),
    5312 : (boundary), 5928, 5930 :
    (charters), 350–51 : (conquest, by
    Saxons), 906, 998 : (conquest by
    Normans), 1525, 1549 : (Domes-
    day), see Domesday (Somerset) :
    (Dunstan in), 3973–75 : (early
    Christianity in), 3531 : (ecclesiasti-
    cal history of), 3821 : (geography of
    lower Parrett), 5878 : (hagiology
    of), 4136 : (hidation), 3057 : (Ine
    in), 1107 : (mints), 9281–82 : (name
    of), 6731–32, 6736 : (Patrick in),
    4679 : (place-names), 6409, 6731–
    33, 6736, 6746, 6756–59, 6798–99,
    6802 : (religious houses), 3714 :
    (river names), 6452 : (roads), 6192–
    93 : (sculpture), 10987–11009 passim :
    (shire), 3166 : (Welsh princes in,
    6th–7th c.), 5937. See also Athelney,
    Banwell, Bath, Bath (hundreds),
    Bedminster, Buckland Denham,
    Burnett, Cadbury, Camel (West),
    Camerton, Cannington, Cantuckton,
    Charlcombe, Chew Stoke, Comb-
    wich, Cruc(t)an, Evercreech, Far-
    leigh Hungerford, Fiddington,
    Glastonbury, Hescombe, Hilcombe,
    Huish Episcopi, Ilchester, Ilmin-
    ster, Lammas' Field, Milborne Port,
    Milton (Clevedon), Minehead,

Somerset (*continued*)
  Monkton (West), Mudgeley, Pitney, Quantocks, Selworthy, Taunton, Watchet, Wedmore, Wellington, Wells, Westwood, Witham, Wraxall, Yeovil
Somersham, Hunts., 8135
Sompting, Sussex, 4006, 6698, 10382, 10389, 10391
Sotwell, Berks. (charter), 333
Southampton, Hants., 6717, 7979, 8418a, 8419, 8421, 8879 : (mint), 9356
Southend, Essex, 1763–64, 8113, 8149, 8151, 8767, 11547
South Hams, Devon (charter, 962), 402
South Hill, Cornwall, 9567, 9573, 9588
Southwark, Surrey, 8737, 11446
Sowerbyshire, forest of, Yorks., 3030
Spades, 2705
Spain (in British chronicles), 1647
Speenhamland, Berks., 8781
Spike Island, co. Cork, 3787
Spittal, Pembrokeshire, 10016
Spoons, 1156, 8110, 8654
Sproxton, Leic., 10695
Stackpole-Elidyr, Pembrokeshire, 10016
Stafford, *Robert de* (grants Wrottesley to Evesham abbey, 1072), 332
Staffordshire, 1874, 1917, 1926, 6016 : (carucate in), 3059 : (charters), 308, 332 : (Domesday), *see* Domesday (Staffs.) : (forest tenures), 3044 : (hidation), 3059–62 : (place-names), 6513, 6526 : (religious houses), 3713 : (saints of), 4130 : (sculpture), 10721–34. *See also* Barlaston, Beeston Tor, Bristlingcote, Burton, Checkley, Drayton-in-the-Moors, Enville, Fotherley, Ilam, Kingswinford, Leek, Rolleston, Seisdon hundred, Stone, Tamworth, Tettenhall, Wichnor, Wolverhampton, Worsfield, Wrottesley
Stainmore, Yorks., *battle* (c. 950), 1294, 1298.
—— (Reycross on), 1299, 1315
Stake, burning at, 2504
Stamford, Lincs., 1877, 8606, 9094 : (mint), 9332, 9335, 9338–39, 9357
Stamford Bridge, Yorks., *battle* (1066), 1369, 1380, 1965
Stammering, 7453–54
Standlake, Oxon., 8266, 8268–69, 8271
Stane Street, 6187

Stanford Bishop, Herefordshire, 3944, 3956, 3959
Stanton, Hunts. (charter, 1012), 384
Stanton Harcourt, Oxon., 4416, 8271
Stanton Lacy, Salop, 10316, 10321
Stanton, Long, Salop (exchange of land, 901), 310
Stantun (of Magosaetae) (grant of land to Ealhstan, 958), 299
Stanwix, Cumb., 10847
Stapenhill, Derbs., 8223
Stapleford, Cambs., 10620
Stapleford, Derbs., 10679
Staveley, Derbs., 6534
Stevenage, Herts., 1814
Steyning, Sussex, 2010, 10635 : (mint), 9309
Steynton, Pembrokeshire, 9989, 9992, 10002
Stibbard, Norfolk, 6495
Sticklepath, Devon, 11014
Stigand, *bp. of Selsey, Chichester*, 4050, 4068
Stirlingshire (place-names), 6874. *See also* Tapock (broch), Torwood
Stirrup, 8738
Stockbridge down, Hants., 8416 : (mint), 9260
Stockholm, *Cabinet of Medals* (A.-S. coins in), 8867
Stockholm farm, Berks., 8684
Stockton, Wilts. (charter, 901), 365
Stodden hundred, Beds., 6064
Stodmarsh, Kent, 8164
Stoke Canon, Devon, 6780
Stoke d'Abernon, Surrey, 10443
Stoke Golding, Leics., 8599
Stoke, North, Oxon., 10757
Stonar, Kent, 1780, 3947
Stone, Bucks., 8316–17
Stone, Staffs., 1836
Stone-juxta-Faversham, Kent, 10220
Stoneykirk, Wigtownshire, 6908
Stow, Lincs., 3876, 6116, 10261
Stow Heath, Suffolk, 11581, 11584
Stow-Nine-Churches, Northants., 10715
Stow, West, Suffolk, 8153, 8161, 11520
Stowe Missal, 5731–44, 5756, 5837, 5849
Stowting, Kent, 8168–69, 8193
Stradelei, [Domesday :   ? = Golden Valley], 6015
Stranraer, Wigtown, 11296
Strasburg (Irish bps. of), 5240
Stratford-on-Avon, Warw., 11612
Strathardle, Inverness., 2206

I

Strathbogie, Aberdeenshire, **6883**

Strathclyde, **2219, 2233** : (Arthur's battles in), **1071** : (Celtic numerals of), **537** : (charters), **390–91** : (Church in), **3391** : (fall of), *see* Catraeth : (royal genealogy), **511**

Strathdearn, Inverness. (place-names), **6921**

Stratton, Glos., **8231**

Streoneshal [?=Strensall], **6104**: (name), **6631, 6646**

Stretton, Rutland, **10737**

Strines, Derbs., **6550**

Stronsay, Orkney, **2226**

Stroud, Glos., **6593**

Studland, Dorset, **10437, 10444**

Studley, Warw., **8716**

Sturm, 1*st abbot of Fulda*, **5283, 5364, 5368, 5393**

Stylus, **11455, 11600**

Succession, laws of (A.-S.), **2472, 2475** : (Irish), **2562** : (Scottish), **2585**

Sudborough, Northants., **10718**

Sudreys, **2198, 2223**

Suffolk (architecture, ecclesiastical), **10178–10203** *passim* : (cemeteries), **8160** : (churches), **3889** : (Domesday), *see* Domesday (Suffolk) : (ecclesiastical history of), **3812** : (medical archaeology), **7463** : (Norsemen in), **1750** : (place-names), **6497** : (river names), **7472** : (round towers), **10178, 10195**. *See also* Ashfield (Great), Bealings (Little), Beccles, Brandon, Burgh castle, Bury St. Edmunds, Cavenham, Cornard (Little), Dunwich, Elmham (South), Eye, Freckenham, Frostenden, Halesworth, Haughley, Hepworth, Hessett, Honedon (near Clare), Hoxne, Hunston, Icklingham, Ipswich, Ixworth, Kedington, Lackford, Mildenhall, Palgrave, Rendlesham, Snape, Stow heath, Stow (West), Sutton Hoo, Thorndon

Suibhne Geilt, *king in Ulster*, **7592, 7594**

Suidbercht, *St.*, **5237**

Sulian, *St.*, **5093**

Sulung [plough-land], **3083, 3123**

Sunbury, Middsx. (charter, 962), **369, 415–16**

Sunderland, Durham, **4235, 6657**

Sundials, **525, 529–30, 533, 535, 538, 547, 10379**

Sunecastre, Asheldham, Essex, **7908**

Sunning-hill, Berks., **9520**

Sunt, Sussex, **6698**

Surety system, **2512**

Surgery, **7451, 7479**

Surius (Laurentius), (his lives of saints), **4088**

Surnames, **552–54, 572, 578, 587, 598, 600–01** : (Devon), **602** : (Dorset), **571** : (genesis of), **573** : (Irish), **631, 645** : (Manx), **635–37**

Surrenden, Kent (charters), **370** : (conveyance of lands, c. 1020), **309**

Surrey (archaeology of), **7772, 8434–59** : (architecture, ecclesiastical), **10440** : (conquest and settlement by West Saxons), **937–39** : (Domesday), *see* Domesday (Surrey) : (mints), **9358** : (place-names), **6701, 6703, 6707–09, 6711, 6716, 6727–28** : (river names), **6448** : (sculpture), **10977, 10981**. *See also* Abinger, Anstie Bury, Banstead, Battersea, Beddington, Bermondsey, Betchworth, Blackheath, Carshalton, Cheam, Chertsey, Cobham, Compton, Coulsdon, Croydon, Dorking, Eashing, Esher, Ewell, Farthing down, Fetcham, Godalming, Greenwich, Guildford, Guildown, Hawkshill, Horsley (West), Kingston, Lewisham, Lingfield, Merstham, Mitcham, Newdigate, Penge, Plumstead, Purley, Reigate, Stoke d'Abernon, Southwark, Thursley, Walton-on-Thames, Wandsworth, Weybridge, Wimbledon, Witley

Sussex, **2001–18, 3203** : (architecture, ecclesiastical), **10382–10409** : (Arthur in), **5961–62** : (cemeteries), **8370–88** : (charters), **293, 300, 304, 404** : (Danes in), **2017** : (Domesday), *see* Domesday (Sussex) : (forest and woodland), **3031** : (hidation), **3077–80** : (hundreds), **3154, 3162, 3168, 3186** : (migration from, temp. Ine), **1139** : (mints), **9327** : (place-names), **6683–98** : (roads), **6196** : (sculpture), **10634–38** : (settlement of S. Saxons), **944, 969–70, 1001** : (*ditto* in E. Sussex downs), **2008**. *See also* Aldingbourne, Alfriston, Anderida (forest), Arundel, Battle, Bexhill, Bishopstone, Bolney, Bosham, Brighton, Broyle, Buncton,

Sussex (continued)
Chancton farm, Chichester, Chithurst, Clayton, Devil's dyke, Eastbourne, Ferring, Ford, Framfield, Funtington, Glynde, Goring, Halnaker, Hardham, Harpingden (Piddinghoe), Harting, Hastings, Hazlehurst (Ticehurst), Highdown, Hove, Kingston, Lancing, Lewes, Lindfield, Lyminster, Manwood (hundred), Medmerry farm (Selsey), Portslade, Rammesleah, Ringmer, Saddlescombe, Seaford, Selsey, Shermanbury, Sompting, Stane St., Steyning, Sund, Swanborough (hundred), Thakeham, Toddington, Waldron, Washington, Weald, Willingdon, Worth, Worthing
Sutherland, 2212 : (brochs), 8051 : (brooches from), 11725 : (place-names), 6865–66, 6886, 6911. See also Dornoch, Dunrobin, Durness, Golspie, Kildonan, Kintradwell, Salzcraggie (Helmsdale)
Sutton Bonington, Notts., 8598
Sutton Courtenay, Berks., 3621, 8643
Sutton-Hoo, Suffolk : ship-burial, 663, 1150–56, 1736, 6982, 7318a, 7742, 8092–8110, 8641, 8692–93, 11515–17, 11519 : (coins), 8101, 8108, 8880, 8889, 8895, 8899
Sutton-on-Derwent, Yorks., 10938
Sutton Waldron, Dorset, 2726
Sutton Walls, Herefordshire, 4385
Swæbheard, king of Kent, 1147
Swallowfield, Berks., 2085
Swanborough hundred, Sussex, 3186
Swanscombe, Kent, 1577
Swastika, 10823–24, 10849, 11063, 11205
Swein, earl, 1362
Swein Forkbeard, king of Denmark, and England, 9169
Swinbeorh, Wilts. [= Swanborough Tump], 6069, 6071–72
Swine. See Pigs
Swithun, St., bp. of Winchester, 3998–4004
Switzerland (libraries, mss., in), 7173–80, 7298, 7311, 11903 : (missionaries in), 5553–75
Symeon, of Durham (History of the kings : sources), 47 : (history for 10th c. in), 1280
Synchronisms, 445–46, 455
Syon, Middlesex, 8703

Taboo, 7519, 7583
Taliessin, Book of, 231, 242, 1030
Tailltiu (sanctuary of), 3513
Tallaght, co. Dublin (Martyrology of), 4466, 4475, 4498 : (monastery of), 3771 : (Rule of), 5623
Talnotrie, Kirkudbright, 11709
Tamworth, Staffs., 1881, 9228
Tanistry, 2581, 2585
Taplow, Bucks., 8312, 8325, 8335, 8481
Tapock broch, Torwood, Stirlingshire, 8048, 8050, 8063
Tara, co. Meath, and kingdom of Tara, 2142, 2151, 2147, 2169, 2316, 4605, 7764 : (brooch), 11711, 11729, 11735
Tarbat, Ross, 11323, 11332, 11710
Taunton, Somerset, 2072, 2075, 2107, 9213
Tavistock, Devon, 1680, 1683, 1688, 1732, 9584 : (abbey), 3680–85 : (its foundation charter, 981), 3683–84
Tawton, Bishops, Devon (mythical see), 3800, 3808
Tawton, North, Devon (hundred of), 3179
Tawton, South, Devon, 1712
Te Deum, 5763
Teesdale (place-names), 6660
Teffont Magna, Wilts., 10990, 11008
Teilo, St., abbot-bp. of Llandaff, 5105
Templeanvach, co. Waterford, 9729
Temple Managhan, co. Kerry, 9659–60
Tenterden, Kent, 1778, 1795
Tenures, 2689, 3012, 3103, 3120, 3124–25, 3233–58 : (burgage tenure), 2735 : (forest tenure), 3044
Teon [law], 2446
Termonfechin, co. Louth, 11169
Teroy fort, Wigtownshire (broch), 8045, 8054
Test valley, Hants., 2120, 6725a
Testerton, Norfolk, 6495
Tethba, cos. Longford and Westmeath, 2130
Tetney, Lincs. (coins), 9136
Tettenhall, Staffs., 6522
Tewkesbury, Glos., abbey, 3698, 3728
Textiles, 7343, 8623, 11816–27 : (Cuthbert), 4281, 11816–17, 11819, 11822, 11826–27. See also Bayeux tapestry
Textus Roffensis, 43, 66, 384, 3836, 3900
Teynham, Kent, 11545
Thakeham, Sussex, 8565

Thames (river name), **6449, 6458, 6469**
Thames valley (conquest of), **904, 926–
27, 935** : (topography of upper),
5866
Thanes, **3218, 3222**
Thanet, Kent, **3697** : (Vikings in), **1796**
Theale, Berks., **8593**
Theft, **2466, 2536, 7523**
Theodore, *abp. of Canterbury*, **3300, 4041,
4062** : (coins), **8979** : (Penitential),
5581, 5583, 5585
Theodulf, *Capitula of*, **5589**
Thetford, Norfolk, **1739, 1746, 1753a,
7891, 8126** : (mint), **9279**
Thirnby, Lancs. [Domesday manor],
6022
Thomas I, *abp. of York* (rights in York),
373, 374
Thor (hammer on York coins), **9058** :
(in Ireland), **3499**
Thorfinn, *earl of Orkney*, **1618**
-*thorn* [place-names], **6398**
Thorndon, Suffolk, **1751**
Thorney, Cambs., *abbey*, **3699** : (Liber
Vitae), **610**
Thorney island, (Danes at, 893), **1265**
Thornhill, Yorks., **1172, 9513, 10970**
Thorold (spurious charter to Crowland,
1051), **394**
-*thorpe* [place-names], **6382**
Thorpe Salvin, Yorks., **10942, 10948**
Threckingham, Lincs., **6566**
' Three fragments ' (of Irish annals). *See*
Annals (Irish)
Thrybergh, Yorks., **10959**
Thunder, **7485**
Thunor, **3697, 6499**
Thurible, **11460**
Thurleston, as boundary term, **277**
Thurnham, Kent, **8165**
Thursley, Surrey, **8576, 10445**
Thurstan, *son of Wine*, **1354**
Thyle [sage], **3483**
Thyra, *wife of Gorm the Old* (? daughter
of Æthelred the Unready), **1375**
Thyrs, **7635**
Tickford, Bucks., **11619**
Tides, **1236, 1609**
Tideslow, Tideswell, Derbs., **6532**
Tidfirth, *bp. of Hexham*, **10913**
Tigernach, *Annals of*, **194, 197, 212, 217**
Tighearnain, *St.* (shrine), **11815**
Tilehurst, Berks., **7980**
Till (river), Lincs., **6442**
Tillage, **2693**

Timahoe, Queen's County, **10560**
Time-reckoning, **7354**
Tin trade, **3146**
Tings, **2363, 2583**
Tinnahally, co. Kerry, **9664**
Tintagel, Cornwall, *monastery*, **3789,
10522**
Tioram, Moidart, Inverness, **8583**
Tipperary, *county* (A.-S. coins in), **8901.**
See also Ahenny, Aherlow glen,
Carrick-on-Suir : Clonmel, Liath-
mor-Mochoemog, Lorrha, Priest-
town, Rathmoley
Tírechán's memoir of St. Patrick, **4567–
97** *passim*
Tiree, island of, Argyllshire, **4952, 11705**
Tisbury, Wilts. (charters), **340**
Tissington, Derbs., **8225**
Tithe, **2642, 3404, 3469**
Titterstone Clee, Salop, **8695**
Tiverton, Devon, **1722**
Toddington, Beds., **8204, 8212**
Toddington, Sussex, **6692**
Toftrees, Norfolk, **10619**
Tollemache Orosius, **7216a**
Toller Fratrum, Dorset, **11012, 11035**
Tonsure, **3373, 3378**
Tools, **3134, 11260**
Toothache, **7547**
Topped mountain, co. Fermanagh, **9793**
Torbay, Devon, **6767**
Torbeckhill, Dumfries, **8722**
Torhtulf [moneyer], **9310**
Torksey, Lincs., **1835, 6573**
Torquay, Devon, **1734**
Torr [place-names], **6403**
Torwoodlee, Selkirkshire, **8047, 8061**
Tory island, co. Donegal, **2139**
Tot [place-names], **6412**
Totemism, **7569**
Totnes, Devon (mint), **9265, 9361**
Totnore hundred, Sussex, **6059**
Tours, **7067, 7187a, 11848a**
Towns. *See* Boroughs
Towyn, Merioneth, **9954–55, 9957–59**
Trade, **2510, 3134–49, 11737** : (Irish with
West Gaul), **3149** : (place-names),
6291, 6334 : (tin), **3146** : (wool),
3144–45
Trallong, Brecknock, **9926, 10016**
Traps, otter, **8661–69, 11083**
Travel, **3138, 6204–82**
Treason, **2484**
Trefgarne, Little, Pembrokeshire, **9968**
Treflys, Carnarvonshire, **10006**

Tregaron, Cardigan, **10033**
Tregoney, Cornwall, **9563**
Trehowel, Pembrokeshire, **9993**
Tremadoc, Carnarvonshire, **10026**
Trent [river], **6432, 6443–44, 6457**
Trevena, Cornwall, **9574**
Trewhiddle, Cornwall, **11551, 11571** (coins), **8908–10**
Tribal hidage, **3085–96**
Trim, co. Meath, **3758, 3853**
Trinoda necessitas, **2350–54**
Tristan (combat with dragon), **7612** : (historical), **1102** : (native land of), **6135**
Trog, **8633**
Trolls, **7628, 7641**
Trowbridge, Wilts., **2055, 2064**
Trumwine, *bp. of the Picts*, **3859**
Trusty's Hill, Kircudbrightshire, **11295**
Tuckamine, co. Carlow, **9779**
Tudual, *St., 1st abbot and bp. of Tréguer*, **5180**
Tullaghane, co. Mayo, **9727**
Tullaherin, co. Kilkenny, **9706, 9714**
Tullibole, Kinross, **11316**
Tullylease, co. Cork, **2148, 9634**
-*tun* [place-names], **6763**
Tuxford, Notts., **11499**
Tweed [river], **6450, 6462**
Twickenham, Middlesex, **8324**
Twínihte, **7397**
-*twistle* [place-names], **6381**
Twitchen [place-names], **6407**
Twrch Trwyth, **7621**
Twyford, Leic., **2613**
Tybroughney, co. Kilkenny, **11121, 11159**
Tynan, co. Armagh, **11163**
Tynemouth, Nhd., **10902–03**
Typography. *See* Script
Tyrone, *county* (inscriptions), **9777.** *See also* Ardhoe, Ardstraw, Aughas-cribbagh, Clogher
Tysilio, *Chronicle of*, **238, 245–46, 251–52.**
—, *St.*, **5093**

Ua Briain kingship, **2143**
Ua Maelechlainn kings of Meath, **2184**
Uhtred, *under-king of Hwicce* (charters of), **302, 7245**
Uí Bruicc, *king of the Déssi*, **515**
Ui Cruinn, kings of Aithir, **2165**
Uí Fearmaic, co. Clare, **11152**
Uí Liatháin, Munster (genealogies of kings of), **516**

Uí Maccaille. *See* Imokilly, co. Cork.
Ulf, *the seneschal, of Lincs.* (Domesday holdings, and his wife's), **2909**
Ulidia [sub-kingdom of Ulster], **7984**
Ullard, co. Kilkenny, **11134, 11171**
Ulleskelf, Yorks. (coins), **9040**
Ulphus, horn of, **3235–39, 11450, 11453**
Ulster (ancient territories of), **5913** : (Annals of), **207** : (archaeology of), **7738, 10094** : (bells), **11759, 11761** : (earthworks), **7981** : (round towers), **10564**
Ultain, *St.*, **5217**
Uncleby, Yorks., **8367**
Unecungga [Tribal Hidage], **3086**
Ungus, *king of the Picts* (invades Argyllshire, 736, 741), **1163**
Uppsala, *University* : coin collection, **8868**
Upton (Wirral), Cheshire, **9443**
Upton Snodsbury, Worcs., **8298–99**
Ure [river], Yorks., **6640, 6650**
Urien, *of Reged*, **6129**
Urith, *St., of Chittlehampton*, **5080, 5119**
Urse, *d'Abetot, sheriff of Worcester*, **1583**
Urswick, Lancs., **9503, 10885–86, 10888**
Utrecht, *bishops of*, **5526**
Urecht Psalter, **5713, 7203–15, 11832, 11876**

Vagrancy, **2655**
Valtos, isle of Lewis, Ross, **11661**
Vask [place-names], **6423**
Vercelli Book, **62, 7221**
Vespasian Psalter, **7227**
Veterinary medicine, **7451**
Viano [Fian], *St.*, **5406**
Vigmund. *See* Wigmund
Vikings, **693–735** : *also* (antiquities), **7769** : (art), **10046, 10052–53** : (burial customs), **8482** : (cemeteries), **8480–8518, 8788–94** : (Christian), **3306** : (geography of their times), **5893–5902** : (in Ireland), **693, 695, 702, 704, 708–09, 715, 717, 729, 734, 737–38, 751, 755, 5749, 5894, 5899, 5902** : (in Man), **735** : (in Scotland), **698–700, 718, 3396, 5901**: (in Wales), **720** : (jewellery), **11640–74** : (religion), **3324** : (seafaring and shipping), **705, 734, 5893** : (weapons), **8712–44** : (western influence on), **6993, 7015**
Village Communities, **1004, 2672, 3259–90**

Village types (nucleated settlements, etc.), **5882**

Villeinage, **2672, 3202, 3207, 3212, 3225–26, 3232**

Vine [river name], **6465**

Vine-scroll [ornament], **8566, 11230, 11966**

Vineyards, **2716, 2721**

Virgates, **2789**

Virgilius, *St., bp. of Salzburg*, **5225, 5253, 5291, 5295, 7118–22**

Vis [place-names], **6423**

Visions, **367, 4944, 7600, 7643–61**

Vita Æduuardi regis, **1391**

Vita Gadelica Cantabrigiensi, **6246**

Vita Merlini. *See* Merlin

Vitalianus stone, Cwm Glöyne, Pembrokeshire, **9998**

Vortigern, **246, 251–52, 885, 922, 932, 961, 991**

Vortimer, **992**

Vortiporis, *prince of Demetia*, **9980, 9990**

Vulgate, **5668–77**

Wadard, of Bayeux [retainer of bp. Odo], **1445, 1475, 1524**

Wakefield, Yorks., **10974**

Walberthwaite, Cumb., **10811, 10842**

Walburga, *sister of St. Willibald*, **5229, 6213**

Walden, King's, Herts., **8212**

Waldron, Sussex, **10403**

Wales 2240–63 : (architecture, ecclesiastical), **10516, 10518, 10523–24** : (bishops consecrated by archbishop of Canterbury), **3861a** : (boundaries), **5931, 5937** : (coinage), **9242** : (dykes), **7851–52** : (ethnology), **8828–30, 8854–55** : (forts), **8065–75** : (genealogies), **502–04, 517–19** : (geography, political), **5909** : (inscriptions), **9900–10035** : (maps), **5917** : (monastic libraries), **7144** : (place-names), **6924–53** *passim* : (sculpture), **11340–11418** : (stone monuments, inventory), **11347**. *See also* under each county

Walintune, S. Lancs. [Domesday], **6035**

Wallach, *St., 1st bp. of Aberdeen*, **3416**

Wallingford, Berks., **7966, 7969, 8399, 8691, 8724, 9371, 10161, 10437a, 10457**

Wallop [? site], **6089**

Wallop [river name], **6456**

Waltham, Essex (place-name), **6343**

Waltham, *abbey*, **3695, 3702, 3729, 3734, 10186** : (charter), **75, 3729** : (library of), **75** : (mill), **2701**

Waltheof, *earl of Northumbria*, **1594–1600**

Walton, Cumb., **10848**

Walton, Yorks., **10971**

Walton-on-Thames, Surrey, **8588**

Wanborough, Wilts., **8469**.

——, *battle* (591), **881**

Wandsworth, Surrey, **8736**

Wanley (Humphrey), biography of, **37**

Wansdyke, **892, 7816–30, 7840**

Wantage, Berks., **2038, 10983–84, 11002**

Wanten dyke, **7801**

Wantsum channel, Kent, **1780, 1793, 5887**

Wapentake, **3173, 3192**

War Ditches, Cherryhinton, Cambs., **8141**

Warden, Nhd., **10367**

Wareham, Dorset, **2025, 2033, 3902, 8713, 9519, 9994, 10020**

Warenne (family of), **1562** : (Gundrada, *countess of*), *see* Gundrada

Warkworth, Nhb., **10365**

Warwick, **1839, 7929**

Warwickshire, **1830, 1867** : (antiquities of), **7733, 7735** : (cemeteries), **8287–97, 8300** : (Domesday), *see* Domesday (Warwick) : (ethnology), **8826** : (geography, forest of Arden), **5952** : (hundreds), **3194–95** : (place-names), **6504, 6516, 6520**. *See also* Arden (forest of), Aston, Aston Cantlow, Baginton, Bidford-on-Avon, Birmingham, Compton Verney, Coventry, Edgbaston, Emscote, Longbridge, Marton, Myton, Nechells, Offchurch, Ragley Park, Rugby, Seckington, Stratford-on-Avon, Studley, Warwick

Washburn [river], Yorks., **6628**

Washington, Sussex (coins), **9174**

Watchett, Somerset (mint), **9355**

Water mills. *See* Mills

Waterbeach, Cambs., **8644, 10133**

Waterford, **10485**

Waterford, *county* (inscriptions), **9728–46** : (place-names), **6809, 6827**. *See also* Ardmore, Clonea, Decies, Drumloghan, Dunhill, Fox's Castle, Garranmillion, Garraun, Kilbunny, Kilrush, Kiltera, Kiltire, Knockalafella, Knockmaon, Lismore, Rath-

Waterford, *county* (*continued*)
gormuck, Salterbridge, Seemochuda, Seskinan, Shankill, Templeanvach, Waterford

Watergrasshill, co. Cork, **9642**

Waterpit down, Cornwall, **11044**

Waterville, co. Kerry, **11122**, **11139**

Watt's dyke, **7785**, **7794–95**, **7799–7800**, **7809**

Waulsort, *abbey*, **5510**

Wayland, *the smith* (and his smithy), **6090**, **7577–78**, **11424**, **11438**

Wealcynne [in Alfred's will], **5918**

Weald, Hunts., **8319**

Weald, Sussex, **3031**

Wealh, Weall, Weala [place-names], **1007**

Wealhpeow (name), **582**

Weardbyrig (mint), **9292**

Weargincel [? = butcher-bird], **7380**

Wearmouth, Durham. *See* Monkwearmouth

Wedmore, Somerset, **1219**, **9170**, **10136** : (peace of), **1215**

Weem, Perthshire, **4311**

Weights, **524**, **534**, **543**, **3143**

Weland, *the smith*. *See* Wayland

Welford, Berks., **2050**

Wellington, Somerset, **2059**

Wellow, Hants., **2093**

Wells, cult of, **3485**, **4472**, **4497**

Wells, Somerset, **3883**, **4064**, **10995** : (bishopric), **3834**, **4066**

Welshpool, Montgomeryshire, **2253**

Wenlock, *abbey*, **3701**, **3703** : (grant of land to, 901), **310**

Wens, **7552**

Wensley, Yorks., **8714**, **9487**

Wéofod, **3507**

Weorthig [A.-S. C., 931, site], **6123**

Werburga, *St.*, **1910**, **4386a**

Werefrith, *of Worcester*, **52**

Wergeld, **2390**, **2468**, **2514**, **3210**

Wergi [Domesday manor], **6034**, **6042**

Werrington, Devon, **1684**, **1702**, **5933**

Werstan, *St.*, **3737**

Wessex, **2019–2123** : (beginnings of), **876–77**, **917**, **964**, **982**, **1006** : (bishoprics), **3805**, **3818** : (conquest of, 6th c.), **885a** : (conversion of), **3525**, **3530**

West Lothian (place-names), **6881**, **6906**. *See also* Abercorn, Dalmeny

Westbere, Kent, **8179**

Westbury, Glos., **1234**, **2881**, **3730** : (grant of land, 791–96), **377**

Westcotes, Leics., **8303**

Westenhanger, Kent (charter, 1035), **424**

Westmeath, *county* (crosses), **11123**. *See also* Athlone, Ballinderry Lough, Bealin, Inis bó Finne, Killua, Killucan, Lough Lyn

Westminster, *abbey*, **1386**, **3731**, **3740**, **10273–75** : (charters), **339** : (Saxon palace), **10132** : (situation and extent), **1806** : (title-deed, 962), **369**

Westmorland, **1948**, **1983**, **1987**, **3126** : (ancient monuments, inventory of), **10042** : (archaeological survey of), **7745** : (Domesday), *see* Domesday (Westmorland) : (place-names), **6386**, **6677** : (sculpture), **10809–59** : (Teutonic settlements), **887**. *See also* Appleby (Old), Brough, Heversham, Hornby, Hyning, Kendal, Kirkby Stephen, Langdale (Little), Lowther, Melling

Westphalia (missionaries in), **5257**

Westwell, Kent, **11558**

Westwood, Somerset (charter, 987), **396**

Wetwang, Yorks., **6623**

Wexford, *county*. *See* Baginbun, Beg-Eive, Cotts (The), Ferns, Fethard, Hook Point

Weybridge, Surrey, **8448**

Whaddon chase, Bucks. (coins), **9160**

Whale, **7376**

Whale-hunting, **6185**

Whalley, Lancs., **1119**, **10899**

Wharram-le-Street, Yorks., **10142**

Wheat, **2711**

Wheathampstead, Herts., **8601**

Wheatley, Oxon., **8261–62**

Wherwell, Hants., *abbey*, **3694**

Whissonsett, Norfolk, **10626**

Whitbeck, Cumb., **10852**

Whitby, Yorks., **8646**, **8656** : (abbey), **3721**, **3732**, **3742**, **4430**, **11506** : (crosses), **3721**

Whitchurch, Hants., **2090**, **8412**, **10446**

Whitchurch Canonicorum, Dorset, **10453**

Whitcombe, Dorset, **11018**, **11026**

Whitehill Point, Nhd., **11613**

Whiteness, Shetland, **11268**

White Island (Lower Lough Erne), co Fermanagh, **11100–07**

White Notley, Essex, **10193**

Whitesand bay, Pembrokeshire, **10516**

Whitfield, Kent, **10204**, **10227**

Whithorn, Wigtown, **2231, 9838, 9877, 10511–12, 11290**. For Candida Casa, see **4974–99**, passim
Whitstable, Kent, **1791**
Whitsun, names for, **23**
Whittingham, Nhb., **10368**
Whittington, Salop, **1834**
Whittlesey meer, Cambs., **5875**
Wiccii. See Hwicce
Wicganbeorg, battle (851), **399**
-wich, wick [place-names], **6372**
Wichnor, Staffs., **8321**
Wick, Caithness, **11654**
Wicken Bonhunt, Essex, **10189**
Wickham, Kent, **8697**
Wickhambreux, Kent, **8167** : (deed, Odo, bp. of Bayeux), **383**
Wicklow, county (inscriptions), **9747–51** : (place-names), **6828–29**. See also Aghowle, Baltinglass, Bray, Castletimon, Delgany, Donard, Dunbolg, Glendalough, Holywood stone, Knickeen, Rathgall
Widsith (historical side of), **866**
Widworthy, Devon, **7977**
Wigesta [Tribal Hidege], **3087**
Wight, Isle of, **2086, 3895, 8420, 9517** : (place-names), **6714–16** : (sea-fight off, 897), **1236**
Wiglaf, king of Mercia (spurious charter to Crowland, 833), **394**
Wigmund, abp. of York (coins), **9018–19, 9027, 9033, 9076**
Wigtownshire (sculpture), **11285–96**. See also Glasserton (St. Ninian's cave), Glenluce, Kirkmadrine, Longcastle, Luce (Old), Machars, Mochrum, Rhinns of Galloway, Stoney kirk, Stranraer, Teroy fort (broch), Whithorn
Wihtgaraburh, Hants., **6715**
Wihtred, king of Kent (charter, 699), **421** : (laws), **2422**
Wikey, Salop, **3276**
Wilbraham, Little, Cambs., **8116, 8138–39, 8147**
Wilfrid, St., bp. of York, **3300, 3849, 4005–25** : (Cædwalla's charter to, for Selsey), **832**
Wilgils [father of Wilbrord], **4390**
William I, king, **68, 1482–1586, 7927** : (charters, general), **259** : (charter to Battle abbey), **305** : (charter to Bury), **327** : (charter to Coventry abbey, spurious), **359, 414** : (charter

to Hurley monastery, Berks.), **427** : (charter to Lincoln), **3830** : (charter to St. Martin's-le-Grand, London), **405, 412** : (coins), **8963, 9067, 9217–38, 9242** : (Gregory VII demands fealty from), **3546** : (landing-place), **1413, 1415, 1424** : (laws), **2405, 2409, 2419, 2425** : (medical history of), **7464** : (muster roll), **1430** : (seals), **9362, 9370, 9374** : (sword of), **1516**
William, fitz Osbern, **1537**
William, of Jumièges, **51, 68**
William, of Malmesbury, **45, 1676–77, 3661, 3664, 3666, 6971**
William, of Poitiers, **51, 68**
William, the wanderer, **7555**
Willibald, St., bp. of Eichstadt, **4392, 5230, 6105, 6208, 6213, 6217, 6217a**
Willibrord, St., **5328, 5514–52** : (Calendar of), **549, 5518, 5531, 5534**
Willingdon, Sussex, **6059, 8645**
Willoughton, Lincs., **8579, 8602**
Wills, **280, 2456–62, 6705** : (Alfred), **431, 2053, 2456–58, 5918, 6069–72** : (Badanoð Beotting), **2460** : (Deodred, bp. of London), **3825** : (Wulfgeat of Donnington, 1005), **1852, 2462** : (Wulfric Spot), **330, 2459**
Wilmington, Kent (charter, 700), **425**
Wilne, Derbs., **9474, 10666, 10674**
Wilton, Wilts. (bowl), **8614** : (cross), **11514** : (mint), **9285**
Wilton, Wilts., abbey, **3719, 9366** : (chartulary, 892–1045), **361** : (deed of gift of North Newenton to, 933), **366, 388** : (grant from Athelstan, 937), **357** : (seal), **9366**
Wiltshire, **2073, 2122** : (archaeology of), **7737, 8460–79** : (bishopric), **3824** : (charters), **306–07, 346, 354** : (conquest of), **892** : (Domesday), see Domesday (Wilts.) : (dykes in), **7840** : (ethnology), **8805, 8843** : (hundreds), **3157, 3196** : (mints), **9304, 9341–43** : (place-names), **6730, 6734, 6737, 6740, 6744, 6747–51, 8843** : (roads), **6188** : (sculpture), **10986–11010** passim : (woodland), **3028, 3035**. See also Abury, All Cannings, Amesbury, Basset down, Bedwyn, Braden (forest of), Bradford-on-Avon, Britford, Britwell, Broadchalke, Broughton Gifford, Burbage, Chippenham,

Wiltshire (*continued*)
Codford, Cricklade, Devizes, Downton, Ebbesbourne Wake, Edington, Ellendune, Fonthill, Harnham (East), Harnham hill, Kemble, Kinwardstone, Langandene, Langford (Hanging), Lanhill, Malmesbury, Maningford Bruce, Mildenhall, Minety, Netheravon, Newnton, (North), Oaksey, Perham down, Petersfinger, Potterne, Purton, Ramsbury, Roche Court down, Roundway hill, Sarum (Old), Sevington, Somerford Keynes, Stockton, *Swinbeorh*, Teffont Magna, Tisbury, Trowbridge, Wanborough, Westbury, Wilton, Wylye valley
Wimbledon, *battle* (568), **949**
Wimborne, Dorset, **1171, 4402, 4404**
Winchcombe, Glos. (abbey), **3691, 3707** : (mint), **9278**
Winchester, Hants., **2077, 5833, 10431, 10979, 11449, 11634, 11669** : (Alfred buried in Hyde abbey), **1214, 1232, 1246, 1276** : (Arthurian associations), **1100** : (bishops), **3834, 4038, 4073** : (bowl), **8550–51, 8612** : (cathedral organ), **7321** : (charters, 49 texts, 1032–1178), **338** : (Hyde abbey), **1214, 1232, 1246, 1274, 1276, 3741** : (mint), **9258, 9286, 9303** : (Missal), **5747** : (School of illumination), **7130, 11844, 11847, 11926** and *see also* Benedictionals of St. Æthelwold and of Robert of Jumièges
Wine [trade], **3149**
Winefride, *St.*, **5094, 5107, 5111, 5123–24**
Wing, Bucks., **10323**
Wingham, Kent, **7758, 8164, 8172, 8597**
Winnoc, Winnosa, *St.*, **5120**
Winster, Derbs., **8080, 8217**
Winston, Nhd., **10918**
Winterbourne Steepleton, Dorset, **11020, 11034**
Winterton, Lincs., **10263**
Winwædfield, *battle* (655), **1104, 1126, 1144, 1155, 1965, 6077**
Winwalloc, 1st *abbot of Landévennec*, **5199**
Winwick, Lancs., **1111, 1118, 1136, 1978, 4355, 6113, 10880, 10893**
Wirksworth, Derbs., **1910**
Wirral, Cheshire, **1332, 2848, 3523, 6511, 6521, 6666**
Wissey [river], Norfolk, **6475**

Wistan, *St.*, **4389**
Wists [food], **3099**
Witan, **2340** : (at Gloucester, 1048, etc.), **1364**
Witham (Withambury), Essex, **7892, 7918**
Witham [river], Lincs., **6445, 8580, 8712, 8732**
Witham, Somerset, **6758**
Withburge, *St.*, **4399**
Witley, Surrey, **10441, 10445, 11633**
Wittenham, Long, Berks., **8391–92, 8396, 8755, 8785**
Witton, Warw., **2975**
Wi-wara-wics, **6119**
Woden, **3473, 7534a** : (Woden's dyke), **7837**
Wodnesbeorh, *battles* (592 and 715), **6083, 6188**
Wolverhampton, Staffs., **10727, 10734** : (charter, 994), **289, 363, 410**
Womanby, Glam., **6950**
Women, **2615, 2629, 2677, 6325** : (monasticism and), **3588** : (names), **564, 605, 612** : (property), **2469, 2500, 6326** : (released from military service), *see* Cáin Adamnáin : (rights of, Celtic), **2528**
Wonford, Devon, **1686, 6066**
Wonstan, Hants., **2022, 2095**
Woodbourne, Isle of Man [treasure trove]. *See* Douglas
Woodchester, Glos. (charters), **284**
Wood Ditton, Cambs. (deed of exchange), **295**
Woodland. *See* Forest
Wool, **3144–45**
Woolsthorpe, Lincs., **8313**
Worcester, **1923, 10301** : (cathedral and monastery), **741, 3801, 3841, 10324, 10327** : (its charters), **298, 329, 360, 395** : (its library), **7126** : (manuscripts), **7216, 7245, 7294, 7301** : (mint), **9097** : (monastic writers), **52, 98** : (place-name), **6506**
Worcestershire (antiquities), **1813, 1824** : (cemeteries), **8286, 8298–99, 8301–02** : (charters), **352** : (conquest of), **886, 907** : (Domesday), *see* Domesday (Worcs.) : (economic history of), **2663** : (place-names), **6517, 6523** : (roads), **6189, 6195, 6203** : (sculpture), **10735** : (social history of), **2663**. *See also* Aston-on-Salwarpe, Birton, Blockley, Brickle-

Worcestershire (*continued*)
hampton, Clifton on-Teme, Ecking-
ton, Evesham, Feckenham, Hanley
Castle, Hartlebury, Malvern (Great),
Pershore, Rous Lench, Upton
Snodsbury, Worcester
Worfield, Staffs., 1871
Workington, Cumb., 8717, 10810, 10813,
10819, 10856
Worth, Kent, 8547
Worth, Sussex, 10385, 10388, 10392,
10407–08
Worthing, Sussex, 2004
-worthy, *suffix*, 942, 6371, 6764
Worthyvale, Cornwall, 9575
Wrangham [birthplace of St. Cuthbert],
(? near Doddington), 6082 : (?
near Melrose), 4307
Wraxall, Somerset, 11684
Wray (Moreton Hampstead), Devon,
6034, 6042
Writs, 2477–78
Wrottesley, Staffs. (grant of to Evesham
abbey, 1072), 332
Wuerzburg, 5265 : (Gospels), 5687 :
(scriptorium), 5399
Wulfgeat, of Donnington (will of, 1005),
1852, 2462
Wulfhere, *abp. of York* (coins), 9033
Wulfhilda, *St., abbess of Barking*, 4406
Wulfred, *abp. of Canterbury* (coins), 8902,
8958, 8980
Wulfric Spott (will of), 330, 2459, 2467
Wulfrun, *sister of Æthelred II* (charter to
Wolverhampton, 994), 289, 363, 410
Wulfstan I, *bp. of Worcester, and II abp.
of York, Saint and homilist (d.* 1023),
1381, 5655, 5768, 5801–12 : (as
writer), 52, 97, 5759–60 : (laws
attributed to), 2403, 2421, 2434,
2435 : (letter re ordination), 3543
Wulfstan, *St., II bp. of Worcester*, 4025a–
32, 4043
Wulfstan, *seaman temp. Alfred* (nationality
of : an Angle), 6151 : (voyage of),
6146–85
Wunebald, *brother of St. Willibald*, 5229
Wycombe, High, Bucks., 11473
Wye [river], 6446 : (territories of Vorti-
gern on), 961
Wye, Kent, 6119, 11558
Wye down, Kent, 11544
Wyhtel [? = quail], 7381
Wyke Regis, Dorset (charter, Æthelred
II, 988), 294

Wylye valley, Wilts., 2078
Wymondley, Herts., 7940 : (in Domes-
day), 2890
Wynfrith. *See* Boniface
Wyrd, 3334, 3351
Wyre Piddle, Worcs., 10317

Yarm, Yorks., 9489, 9506
Yarrow, Selkirkshire, 6904, 9871–72,
9877, 9891
Ycean-ho [= Iken, Suffolk], 6122
Yelford, Oxon., 8271
Yellow plague, 7440–43, 7447, 7504
Yeovil, Somerset, 2067
Yetminster, Dorset, 6752, 6760, 11021
Yevering, Northumberland, 1933, 7962
York, 1929, 1966, 1975b, 1988, 1994a,
7093, 8484–85, 8488, 8515, 8624,
8636, 10353, 10928, 10946, 11604,
11624, 11653 : (archbishops), 4045,
4061 : (their coins), 9017–80 *passim* :
(their jurisdiction in Glos.), 3349 :
(abp. Thomas I's rights in city),
373–74, 3816 : (canons, community
of secular), 3345 : (centre of learning), 6962 : (defences), 7955, 7958 :
(Eric Bloodaxe in), 1283 : (metrical
calendar), 4151 : (mint), 9217, 9232,
9266–67, 9283–84, 9287, 9312, 9314,
9325, 9333–34, 9340, 9351 : (place-
name), 6640, 6643, 6650 : (St.
Mary's abbey), 10141 : (St. Mary's
Bishophill, junior), 10358 : (St.
Mary's Castlegate), 9486 : (St.
Peter's school), 6975, 6986 : (Scandinavian kingdom of), 1971 : (Vir-
gin), 10934 : (York versus Canterbury), 3344, 3817
York Gospels, 3200, 7223 : (surveys in),
413
Yorkshire, 1944, 1964a, 1972a, 1982,
1985–86, 1996, 6027 : (archaeology),
7741, 8352, 8355, 8362–63, 8366,
8775 : (carucates), 3069 : (charters),
261 : (Domesday), *see* Domesday
(Yorks.) : (earthworks), 7834, 7949,
7951–53, 7956 : (ecclesiastical history), 3584, 3846 : (inscriptions),
9472–9513 *passim* : (mints), 9298 :
(Norman conquest of), 1526 :
(place-names), 6620–50, 6661 : (river
names), 6451 : (sanctuaries), 3460 :
(sculpture), 10925–75 : (sheriffs),
3165 : (surveys, in York Gospels),
413. *See also* Aldbrough, Almond-

Yorkshire (*continued*)

bury, Bardsey, Bedale, Bentham, Beverley, Bilton, Bingley, Birstall, Bradford, Bramham, Brompton, Catterick, Cave (South), Cleveland, Collingham, Conisborough, Crayke, Croft, Crofton, Dewsbury, Driffield (Little), Duggleby howe, Easby, Eastburn, Ecclesfield, Eccleshall, Edstone, Elloughton, Elmet, Elmswell, Ferrybridge, Filey, Flamborough, Frodingham (North), Gargrave, Gilling, Goldborough, Grimthorpe, Hackness, Halifax, Harrogate, Hatfield chase, Hawkswell, Hawnby, Hornsea, Hovingham, Howdenshire, Howe hill, Huddersfield, Hull, Ilkley, Ingetlingum, Jervaulx, Keighley, Kildwick-in-Craven, Kippax, Kirby hill (Boroughbridge), Kirkburn, Kirkdale, Kirkheaton, Kirklevington, Lamel hill, Lastingham, Laughton-en-le Morthen, Leathley, Leeds, Loidis, Lowthorpe, Malton, Manningham, Masham, Meaux abbey, Menston, Newbald (North), Nunburnholme, Occaney, Patrington, Ripon, Roos Carr, Rotherham, Rothwell, Sancton, Sandall, Sawdon, Scarborough, Seamer, Selby, Sheffield, Skelton, Sowerby (forest of), Stamford Bridge, Streoneshealh, Sutton-on-Derwent, Thornhill, Thorpe Salvin, Thrysbergh, Ulleskelf, Undeby, Ure (river), Wakefield, Walton, Washburn (river), Wensley, Wetwang, Wharram-le-Street, Whitby, Winwædfield, Yarm, York

Youghall, co. Cork, **9629**, **9631**

Ythancaester, Essex, **1770**, **10192**, **10201**

Yttingaford [? site], **6091**

Yule, **456**, **7554**, **7573**